CITY OF SCHOOLS

A History of Public Education
in Northfield, Minnesota

CITY OF SCHOOLS

A History of Public Education
in Northfield, Minnesota

Bruce William Colwell

LOOMIS HOUSE PRESS

© 2018 Northfield Public Schools
Design and production by Mark F. Heiman, Loomis House Press, Northfield, Minnesota
Printed in the United States of America

ISBN: 978-1-9352432-4-3 (paper), 978-1-935243-26-7 (cloth)

All photos courtesy of the Northfield Historical Society, Northfield Public Library, Northfield Public Schools, and the *Northfield News*.

This publication was made possible in part by the people of Minnesota through a grant funded by an appropriation to the Minnesota Historical Society from the Minnesota Historical & Cultural Heritage Fund. Any views, findings, opinions, conclusions or recommendations expressed in this book are those of the authors and do not necessarily represent those of the State of Minnesota, the Minnesota Historical Society, or the Minnesota Historic Resources Advisory Committee.

Contents

vii	Acknowledgments
ix	Preface

CHAPTER ONE

1   Public Education in the Frontier River Town: Becoming the "City of Schools" (1856–1900)

CHAPTER TWO

37   New Facilities and the Response to Progressive Education (1900–1930)

CHAPTER THREE

77   Public Education in Challenging Times: The Northfield Public Schools during the Great Depression and World War II (1930–1950)

CHAPTER FOUR

97   Postwar Growth and Expansion: The Emergence of the Modern Northfield Public Schools (1950–1970)

CHAPTER FIVE

131   The Modern Northfield Public Schools (1970–1990)

CHAPTER SIX

151   Strengthening the "High Performance/Low Cost" School System: Northfield Public Schools in the Twenty-first Century (1989–2018)

196	Northfield Education Timeline
206	Endnotes
213	Index

Acknowledgments

Educational institutions have been a defining feature in my life and in the history of my hometown, Northfield Minnesota. Consequently, when I embarked on a second career as a local historian, it was perhaps inevitable that I would write this history of the Northfield Public Schools.

For assistance and support with the creation of this book I am grateful and indebted to:
- Cathy Osterman and Stephanie Hess, Northfield Historical Society.
- Donita Delzer, Anita Aase, and Val Mertesdorf, Northfield Public Schools District Office
- Charles Kyte and Cris Richardson, former NPS Superintendents
- Matt Hillmann, Superintendent, Northfield Public Schools
- Melinda Hutchinson, Minnesota Historical Society
- Dr. Jeffery Snyder, Associate Professor of Educational Studies, Carleton College, and Susan Garwood, Executive Director, Rice County Historical Society for helpful and insightful critical reviews of the manuscript

A special thanks to:

- Earl Weinman, grant project director, teacher at the Northfield Middle School, and director of the Northfield Historical Society's Student Community Outreach Program Experience (SCOPE).
- Scott Richardson and Nancy Ashmore for their expert editing.
- Mark Heiman for editing, image selection, and design that enlivened the text and enhanced its readability; to the extent that this publication reads well and looks good, Mark deserves the credit.
- The Minnesota Clean Water Land and Legacy Amendment's Arts and Cultural Heritage Fund

Bruce William Colwell
Northfield Minnesota
November 2018

Preface

Public Schools in an Education Town

In 1914 Northfield adopted "Cows, Colleges, and Contentment" as the town's slogan, recognizing its award-winning dairy cattle, two colleges, and comfortable quality of life. Yet earlier the editors of the *Northfield News* had viewed their small southern Minnesota city as an education town. *News* editor Joel Heatwole's 1895 publication *Manual of the Public Schools* proclaimed Northfield "The City of Schools" that made their small town of fewer than 4,000 "a good city in which to locate." A 1900 *News* Supplement, "Northfield as an Educational Center: A Glimpse of What Our City Has Done and Is Doing in an Educational Way," claimed that "as an educational center few places excel or even equal our city.... Education here is 'the power behind the throne' and truly through its agencies is Northfield made what she is!" Although the town's two liberal arts colleges, Carleton and St. Olaf, would bring Northfield national acclaim later in the twentieth century, in 1900 local residents were most proud of the public schools of Rice County District #3.

Throughout the twentieth and into the twenty-first century, the *Northfield News* continued to define the town's identity around education. In 1920 the *News* called education "Northfield's Number One Business," noting that the public schools and the two colleges were Northfield's primary employers.

Early in the twenty-first century, district Superintendent Terry Tofte endeared the school district to Northfield citizens when he characterized their schools as "high performance/low cost" public institutions, a phrase that simultaneously honored two cherished community values — high quality education and fiscally conservative public spending.

In practice, however, the pursuit of high quality/low cost public education was challenging and difficult. It also set up a tension and contentiousness around school financing that has defined the history of the Northfield Public Schools. Although the desire to operate high quality schools at the lowest possible cost was arguably present in most school districts in the state and country, it was especially problematic in a small college town like Northfield, where the major industry — educational institutions — was tax-exempt. Consequently, the history of the town's financial support for public schools is replete with apparent contradictions: although the public school was the first city service established, in the early 1900s it took a decade of conversation, condemnation by the Minnesota Board of Health, overcrowding, and a fire before voters finally approved funding for a new high school; voters regularly approved maintenance levies at levels that supported a first-rate teaching staff and bond referendums for quality facilities, but often not without long contentious debate and by harrowingly narrow margins. Northfielders came to believe that they could indeed have high quality schools at low cost. This history chronicles how this was accomplished.

Public Education in America and Minnesota

Although American public education has historically been organized, financed, and administered locally, its shape and substance has been remarkably similar across the states and the nation. After 1900, the classroom curriculum (what was taught) was increasingly determined and shaped by the National Education Association (NEA), state departments of education, and university colleges of education. Similarly, teacher training (how teachers were taught) was directed by state education departments and colleges of education. Ironically, the decentralized American public education system nonetheless produced a notably uniform public school educational experience. Consequently, this history of Northfield's public schools will be examined in the context of national and state educational history.

The common school movement in the United States in the middle of the nineteenth century established local tax-supported free public education in every community. In the eastern half of the country it provided schooling for the poor and growing middle class and was an alternative to private schools. In Midwestern states like Minnesota, universal public education came with statehood and few private schools were established. By 1900 the vast majority of American children were enrolled in public elementary and secondary schools. Most of the elementary schools were neighborhood schools, and most of the secondary schools were comprehensive schools. It was significant, educational historian Lawrence Cremin observed, that in rural and small towns like Northfield that meant children of various class, ethno-religious, and racial backgrounds would attend the same public school buildings together.[1] With mandatory universal schooling, education moved to the core of the American experience, and Cremin argued,

> education not only became an ever more significant American undertaking in its own right, it was increasingly *perceived* as such and assigned an appropriate public value. Precisely for this reason, education became more political, as groups with conflicting ideas about the public interest sought to have their views prevail. One result was that many of the great twentieth-century battles over traditionalism and modernity in religion, politics, and culture were ultimately framed as educational issues and fought out in debates over education policy and practice... and established a continuing tug of war over what should be taught by whom and how in the nation's educating institutions.[2]

Particularly in younger states like Minnesota, public education was viewed as the foundation for the local economy, for civilizing the frontier culture, and for creating good citizens. Minnesotans developed a deep belief in both the practical utility of education for daily life as well as the immeasurable benefits that flowed to the community from learning. They looked to their public schools to teach basic literacy, to prepare children for work and citizenship, and to sort and select students for different economic and social roles. Minnesota historian Theodore Blegen believed education was a major force in the shaping of the nation and for Minnesota had even greater significance, when the state erected a system of public education, built on the belief in progress and democracy. A local historian sounded a similar theme, writing in the 1882 *History of Rice County* that the public schools were a distinctive institution that "Americanized" all "reared under its benign influence," prompting the pioneer settlers of Rice County to immediately establish common schools.

Northfield News editor Joel Heatwole expressed similar ideas with similar rhetoric when he extolled the virtues and benefits of education, calling his frontier river town a "City of Schools."

Image and Reality: Northfield as an Education Town

Heatwole expanded on the image and identity first promoted by founders John North and Charles Wheaton of Northfield as an education town, comprised of intelligent citizens committed to learning and literacy. In the 1889 annual promotional booklet, "All About Northfield, Minn.," Heatwole, sounding like a latter-day Chamber of Commerce director, extolled the virtues of his beloved town with convenient train service, conservative and safe merchants, eight churches, two colleges, and graded schools "second to none in their successful management and results…. As a result of the educational atmosphere of Northfield its people are intelligent and cultivated, and its society refined and hospitable."[3]

The image and identity of Northfield was being carefully crafted, and less than thirty-five years after the town's founding, it was already well established in the local press.

Yet how accurate and verifiable was Heatwole's 1889 Northfield's self-described "Education Town" identity and image? A century later historian Cliff Clark asked a similar question of Minnesota's popular image in the introductory essay "Minnesota: Image and Identity" in *Minnesota in a Century of Change: The State and Its People Since 1900*[4] and suggested that while a state's (or town's) image was

> derived to some extent from actual experience, it is also constructed out of Minnesotans' hopes for the future… Like the fish story about the one that got away, the image of the state has expanded beyond simple descriptions of reality to encompass the hopes and dreams of its people. Indeed, the mythology of what the state is and should be has even shaped the ways in which the state has developed. In short, the popular image of the state, as it has evolved since 1900, provides clues to what Minnesotans value, what they want, and — to some extent — what they have become."

The same may be true for Northfield. It is easy to imagine that Northfield's chosen image as an education center and education town was part reality — in 1900 the town did have two liberal arts colleges, two newspapers, a public library, an active Lyceum, and a high school with the largest per capita attendance rate in the state — and part aspiration and hopes for the future. However, the history of the Northfield Public Schools in the twentieth and twenty-first centuries suggests that Northfield has indeed been true to its values and realized its aspirations and been in reality an education town.

Primary Narrative Questions and Themes

Four major questions and themes are examined throughout this chronological narrative of the history of the Northfield Public Schools. Although this general comprehensive history is most clear and understandable as a chronology, the themes capture the importance and meaning of the Northfield Public Schools' history.

1. The public schools and Northfield's identity

How did the values and priorities of founder John North and other early community leaders, especially newspapermen Joel Heatwole, William Schilling, and Carl Weicht, shape the early history of the Northfield Public Schools? How was education and learning a part of the community ethos and identity of Northfield?

2. Distinctive qualities of the Northfield Public Schools

How was Northfield similar to and different from other small-town southern Minnesota school districts? What was distinctive about the Northfield schools?

3. The public schools and other Northfield educational institutions

How was the history of the Northfield Public Schools influenced and shaped by other Northfield educational institutions, the public library, the newspapers, churches (religious education), the Arts Guild, and especially the two colleges, Carleton and St. Olaf?

4. Financing the schools: the pursuit of high quality/low cost public education

How did the Northfield taxpayers support the public schools and balance simultaneously two cherished community values — high quality education and fiscally conservative public spending? What does the history of the annual maintenance tax levy and special capital bond issues tell us?

Context: Northfield History and Local Primary Sources

This is the essence of local history: this is not the history of just any American public school, but specifically the story of Northfield's public schools. As a consequence, the primary sources for this history are local: articles from area newspapers, especially the local Northfield newspaper, the *Northfield News*; minutes of the meetings of the Northfield district Board of Education and superintendents' annual reports; and interviews with recent district superintendents.

The newspapers were an especially important source in the early years, when local editors viewed their newspapers' mission and purpose as educational, like that of the public schools, the public library, and churches. In 1872, when businessman and editor of the *Rice County Journal* Charles Wheaton was carrying on town founder John North's commitment to education and culture, he promised his newspaper would "elevate rather than depress the moral tone of society, to invigorate and emphasize every effort made, or sentiment uttered in harmony with the grand idea of physical, intellectual, and moral advancement."[5] Although Wheaton had a remarkably lofty vision of the newspaper's role in the community, later local newspaper editors would play an advocate role throughout the entire history of Northfield and the Northfield Public Schools. Although journalists often professed to provide objective and critical coverage of local issues and stories, the public schools generally received positive, uncritical support from the local newspapers. Nevertheless, the newspaper was an excellent source of information providing community context for the history of the public schools. School board minutes and district publications were also useful primary sources of accurate information.

Northfield students traveling to school by horse cart

Chapter One

Public Education in the Frontier River Town: Becoming the "City of Schools" (1856–1900)

From the time of the town's founding in 1856, the citizens of Northfield, Minnesota, believed in the value of public education and were committed to local organizations and institutions that promoted learning and literacy. Founder John North, lawyer, businessman, abolitionist, temperance and women's suffrage advocate, educator, and "an emissary for Yankee culture,"[6] envisioned Northfield as an agricultural and educational center. Within a year of its founding, the infant village's first civic organization, the Northfield Lyceum, established a reading room, circulating library, and debating society. By the fall of 1856 a small one-room frame schoolhouse was constructed, and teacher Rollins Olin welcomed "twenty-five scholars to Northfield's first public school."[7]

By 1860 North had built two sawmills and a gristmill on the Cannon River, and with a general merchant, shoemaker, cabinetmaker, blacksmith, and carpenter among the first settlers, quickly constructed a small village of stores, businesses, and houses to serve as the commercial and cultural center for the area's farmers. Although North left the town he founded just four years later, selling his mills, stores, and hotel to Charles Wheaton to pay off extensive debt from a failed railroad enterprise, he left Northfield a legacy: a vision to become an educational and cultural center, populated by hard-working religious New Englanders and Norwegian immigrants, whom, an early newspaper editor claimed, were "among the most intelligent and enterprising in the country."[8] By 1861 the town could point with pride at its progress, with five churches, eighty houses, an active lyceum, a main street with merchants, artisans, and a public school. Ten years later the editor of the *Rice County Journal* wrote "the manufacturing and commercial interests of Northfield are not as extensive as they should be, but we expect that eventually our educational advantages will serve as the magnet to attract a good class of citizens to our little town."[9] Education was already central to the new town's identity.

Nationally, the American common school movement in the mid-nineteenth century established free public-supported schools throughout New England and the Midwest, and by the time of the Civil War organized systems of common schools had become commonplace throughout the northern and Midwestern states. The common schools emphasized reading, writing, arithmetic, and strict discipline. The schools were vital community institutions, reflecting the mores of parents and churches. Events at the local school were often important community events.[10]

Minnesota historian Theodore Blegen has argued that education was a major force in the shaping of the nation. For Minnesotans in the mid-1800s education was particularly significant, as the state erected a system of schooling at all levels to extend its influence to all the people. For frontier settlers like John North and his fellow Northfielders, Blegen contends, the "schools were ladders for their children to professional careers, to public service, and to cultural and social richness; they had an innate belief in the idea of progress and in a society of democratic ways. For their children they wanted opportunities that had been denied to them. Their faith and purpose were translated into self-sacrificing support of public education."[11] The public school system was often taken for granted because it was so widespread and visible, but it was an outstanding achievement of the early settlers in Minnesota.

Early Schools in the Village of Northfield (1856–1874)

The importance of the schools certainly was not taken for granted by the nineteenth-century settlers of Northfield. In the Rice County Schools section of the 1881 *History of Rice County*, the author proclaimed that it was the educational institutions that made Americans of all those who entered the frontier schoolhouse:

> No matter how much he may differ from his neighbor or the man more remote from him in religion, politics, or vocation, the American citizen is almost invariably a firm believer in the public school, which breathes a spirit of pure democracy, opening its doors alike to the poor, the rich, and the foreigner and offering to make of all intelligent, moral, and useful citizens in this land of the free.... The pioneer settlers of Rice County manifested the same eagerness to establish schools that they did in building themselves homes in this new land. As soon as there were a handful of children in each little farm or village community, steps were promptly taken to provide for them school facilities...[12]

In Northfield's first year, 1856, twenty settlers met at North's house and pledged almost $300 to construct the first public schoolhouse on the corner of Union and Third Street. On August 12, 1856, Northfield District #3 was established, with Ira S. Fields, Meril J. White, and John W. North serving as the first school board.[13] In November notice was sent to all residents for a special meeting "to rais [sic] a tax for summer school, winter school, stove, pipes, clock, out houses and all necessary fixtures."[14] In addition, the board decided that pupils (as students were then called) living outside of the village should pay three dollars tuition for five months and "those that had paid nothing for building the house should pay four dollars tuition." By the end of

John North, Northfield founder

the first year, seventy-three students had crowded into the modest-sized wood frame building.

A second larger building, "the envy of neighboring districts for a wide range," was added on the same site in 1861 at a cost of $6,000. The following year the district was reorganized, and the board levied a tax of two mills to maintain the two buildings and pay the salary of its two teachers, Miss Miller and Miss Cutlar, at eighteen and fifteen dollars per month, respectively. School was in session for five months in the winter and three in the summer.

In 1864 the State Legislature passed a seven-page special law, "An Act for the establishment and better regulation of the Common School of the village of Northfield,"[15] a charter which prescribed the processes for electing the school board and levying funds for the school district. The organization of Northfield's government paralleled that of the schools, evolving from a township (1858) to a village (1871) to a city (1875) when merchant Hiram Scriver was elected Northfield's first mayor. The first school board under the new charter was comprised of Myron Wheaton, Hiram Scriver, J. F. Wilcox, D. H. Frost, and S. P. Stewart. The staff of teachers grew with the increasing enrollment, from three in 1865 to four in 1867 to six in 1869. The first principal, a Mr. Bridges, was hired in 1868, and by 1871 the district's first superintendent, James McNaughton, was hired.

The Nineteenth-Century Schoolhouse Building: The Central School

In 1874 an independent school district was organized and a "large commodious building… of pressed brick, three stories high, and a liberal basement story"[16] was erected next to the public Central Park[17] at a cost of $30,000. The building dedication was called the most important civic event in the young town's history, and the *Rice County Journal* predicted, "Our citizens will not forget the exercises to come off at the Hall of the new school house tomorrow evening. We doubt not our citizens will find it an enjoyable treat, and it will furnish an opportunity for parents and guardians to learn from the exhibition how their children have been taught."

Two weeks later the *Journal* editor wrote a front-page article, "Public Schools: Our New Schoolhouse,"[18] addressing complaints from some residents that the new school was unnecessarily, even shamefully, large. The editor assured its readers that Northfield had "no cause for blushing with shame," and indeed "the only fault that occurs to us to mention is that it is not large enough," although it is nonetheless "superior to anything in the State, for the cost."

The schoolhouse, called "Central School" or the "Central Building," was Northfield's first substantial public building, and public reaction revealed a fiscal conservatism with public spending that would characterize Northfield throughout its history. No one questioned the necessity and importance of education, but some cautioned that public funds needed to be spent with great care.

To reassure readers that the new school was a good value and wise investment, the *Journal* described in detail each of the building's four floors. The basement had six "good well-lighted" rooms with ten-foot ceilings. The first story had six classrooms with thirteen-foot ceilings; the second story had four classrooms and two large recitation rooms with fourteen-foot ceilings, the High School rooms were nearly double the size of other classrooms; and the third story, "well-ventilated and easily warmed" by five Fuller and Warren Company's patented hot air furnaces with Short's Common Sense ventilation system,[19] contained the Great Hall and an auditorium with 715 chairs. The height of the main structure was over sixty feet, "surmounted with a splendid bell tower." "In short," the editors wrote, "it is a splendid building and an ornament to the town, and worth its cost in respect to the influence it will exert on public buildings hereafter."

The article also listed the town's "present teaching force" as "Professor W. S. Pattee, Principal; Miss M. M. Williams, Principal's ass't; Miss J. Latham, Senior Grammar Dept; Miss Davenport and Miss Emma Wheaton, Junior Grammar Dept; Miss Jennie Blake, 1st Intermediate; Miss Marion Wheeler and Mrs. Pelseye, 2nd Intermediate, and Miss M. S. Wheeler and Miss Adele Parks, 1st Primary." Professor Pattee reported that there was "such a rush of scholars last week" that he expected to add another teacher. But after years of overcrowding, there was welcome room to expand, as the new schoolhouse could accommodate five hundred pupils. The article concluded: "We have a first-class school-house, an excellent corps of teachers, and the District has furnished these at its own cost, and are freely entitled to its benefits." The local newspaper, with a vested interest in increasing the literacy rate (and thereby adding future readers), seemed satisfied that the public schools in the young school district were already an asset for a village not yet twenty years old.

When completed, the new four-story, mansard-roofed red brick Central School housed the entire Northfield school system, grades one through twelve. Elementary classes remained in the Central School into the twentieth century even as neighborhood elementary schools were added on the west side (Lincoln School in 1886, at the corner of Plum and west Second Street, razed and replaced by Longfellow School in 1899) and the near-south/east side (Washington School, in 1893). The high school, which initially occupied only the third floor of "Old Central," expanded to other floors as enrollment increased. However, before 1870 most Northfield children attended regularly through the primary grades and more sporadically at the intermediate level. Only a small number persisted into the high school years. Nationally the public high school did not yet exist; those who had the desire and money to continue beyond the eighth grade went to private academies, many actually lower divisions of private colleges. (Northfield College, renamed Carleton College in 1871, was founded in 1866 with a Preparatory Department that essentially functioned as a high school.) Not until 1871 was a "course of study" (curriculum) adopted for four years of high school. As late as 1895, Central School housed seven primary and intermediate classes (1 through 6, with two fifth-grade classes) and three high school classes for science, mathematics, and Latin and Greek.

Central School, c. 1880

Lincoln/Longfellow School (1886) and Washington School (1893)

The first through eighth grade classes quickly filled the space available on the first two floors of the new Central Building. After a decade of public discussion, the issue of over-crowding was finally addressed in 1886 with the construction of Lincoln School for west-side elementary children. The two-story brick colonial style building, adorned with two chimneys and a bell tower, cost $9,000 and housed four classrooms, grades one through four. Initially called the West Side or Lincoln School, by 1895 the building was renamed Longfellow and was served by a staff of six female teachers: Miss Martha Rogers, principal and fourth grade; Miss Anna Berke, third grade; Miss Grace Whiting, second grade; Miss Della Wittemore, first grade; Miss Elizabeth Anderson, music; and Mrs. E. G. Adams, librarian.

Despite the addition of a west side elementary school, the Central Building's primary classrooms continued to be overcrowded. And growing secondary level enrollment required more classroom space. The board's 1892 annual report called the high school enrollment growth (from 50 to 102 in two years) "rapid" and its present size "quite phenomenal."[20] Consequently, in 1893 an east side Washington Elementary School was constructed at Eighth and Washington at a cost of $11,157.

Washington School, c. 1895

The Northfield Public High School (1877–1900)

As noted earlier, in frontier Northfield and nationally the early public secondary schools were attended by only a small percentage of local teenagers. Most children, especially boys, dropped out and worked on the farm or in town by the age of fourteen. Many who did continue attended private "academies" like Carleton College's Preparatory Department, where the boundary lines between so-called secondary education and college education were extremely fluid.[21] Northfield Public High School graduated its first class of high school students, seven girls, in 1877.

A first, full, twelve-grade "course of study" (curriculum) was designed by Superintendent James McNaughton and approved by the school board in 1874. Coursework in the high school department for the first year included "Algebra, First Latin Book, Universal History, Descriptive Geography, and

Longfellow School, c. 1895

English Grammar."²² The high school course in toto required four years of Latin, two of Greek, two and one-third of mathematics, and two of universal history.

The early high school experience was defined as much by its attention to student morals, character, and pedagogy as by the content of the courses. Historian Dianne Ravitch noted that despite local control, the American public school experience was remarkably similar across regions, so that for Northfield, as elsewhere "the goals were few and simple: Children learned not only the basics of reading, 'riting, and 'rithmetic, but also the basics of good behavior. Principals considered character and intelligence to be of equal value, and neither was possible without 'disciplining the will,' which required prompt, unquestioning obedience to the teacher and the school rules."²³

In Northfield, good attendance and punctuality were expected; teachers could suspend pupils who had more than five consecutive days of unexcused absences. Overall, the late nineteenth-century Northfield public schools were similar to the common schools throughout Minnesota, the Midwest, and the nation, Ravitch wrote, in the "emphasis of reading, writing, speaking, spelling, penmanship, grammar, arithmetic, patriotism, a clear moral code, and strict discipline, enforced when necessary by corporal punishment. The values they sought to instill were honesty, industry, patriotism, responsibility, respect for adults, and courtesy."²⁴ The schools were vital community institutions, reflecting the mores of parents and churches, and school events were major community events.

The June 28, 1877, graduation exercise of the first Northfield High School class was indeed an important community event. The *Northfield Mail* estimated nearly one thousand people, "one of the largest audiences ever seen in Northfield," assembled to witness the ceremony.²⁵ After a "brief and appropriate" prayer from Reverend Gale, each of the seven graduates — Edith Hatton, Irene White, Kitty Bingham, Ida Clary, Alice Sayre, Cora Mosher, and Julia Riddell — delivered essays that the *Mail* claimed were "equal to the best productions of most collegiate." The state superintendent of public instruction, David Burt, made a few "appropriate and stirring remarks" and complimented the graduates on "the meritorious character of their essays." The size of the audience and the presence of the top state education official suggest the importance of Northfield's first high school commencement.

Nationally and locally high school attendance and graduation increased very slowly through the 1870s and 1880s. In 1880s' America it remained a rare thing to attend high school and an even rarer thing to graduate; in neighboring Wisconsin in 1884, only six percent of the enrolled high school students graduated. When the U.S. Commission of Education census for 1890 counted 202,963 high school students, it represented less than one percent of the population.[26] In Northfield in the 1880s, even though enrollment grew steadily, the number of graduates remained remarkably small. Even in Northfield, with two colleges and a relatively educated citizenry, graduation from high school, especially for boys, was very rare until the late 1890s. In the 1870s all but one of the 25 high school graduates were girls; in the 1880s. only three of the 46 graduates were boys. The Northfield graduation numbers were particularly low, with no graduates in 1886 and 1890, which may be partially explained by the presence of the Carleton Academy and the St. Olaf Academy, the preparatory departments at the colleges that served as local private three-year high schools.

Northfield high school graduating class, c. 1889

L–R: Louise Orr, Matie Drake-Larkin, Arthur Feiderman, Anna McKenzie-McChesney, Gertrude Ohm-Bunday, Anna Berk-Apitz, Joseph French, Gertrude Hall, Louise Hagen

Northfield High School Graduates 1877–1900

Graduation Year	Number and Gender of Graduates	Alumni Addresses in 1894
1877	7 girls (7)	Northfield; Minnesota (2); Montana; Africa; deceased (2)
1878	9 girls (9)	Northfield (2); Minnesota (3); California; deceased (2)
1879	8 girls; 1 boy (9)	Northfield (5); Minnesota (3); North Dakota
1880	3 girls	Minnesota; South Dakota (2)
1881	9 girls	Minnesota (3); Wisconsin; Kansas; Texas
1882	3 girls	Minnesota; Texas; deceased
1883	3 girls	Northfield (2); deceased
1884	3 girls	Northfield; Minnesota (2)
1885	2 girls	Northfield; South Dakota
1886	none	
1887	3 girls 1 boy (4)	Northfield; Minnesota (2); NY
1888	10 girls; 1 boy (11)	Northfield (7); Minnesota (3)
1889	7 girls; 1 boy (8)	Northfield (6); Minnesota (2)
1890	none	
1891	5 girls; 2 boys (7)	Northfield; Minnesota (5); Wisconsin
1892	1 boy	
1893	4 boys; 3 girls (7)	Northfield (5) Minnesota (2)
1894	6 girls; 4 boys (10)	Northfield (9); Minnesota (1)
1895	11 girls; 10 boys (21)	
1896	9 girls; 3 boys (12)	
1897	11 girls; 4 boys (15)	
1898	9 girls; 3 boys (12)	
1899	30	
1900	29	

Nationally, public high school enrollments more than doubled in the 1890s, spurred by compulsory education laws (though many only required attendance through age fourteen), urban migration (fewer farm children), and additional schooling needed for the technology of new jobs, which increasingly required literate workers. Educational historian Edward Klug noted that "although the intensive drive for industrial education lay nearly two decades in the future, there was a substantial demand among educators and other public leaders for manual training and business subjects."[27] Although manual training appeared in Minneapolis high schools as early as 1885, it was not added to the Northfield curriculum until 1911. Northfield's high school enrollments, already among the highest per capita rates in the state, continued to rise through the final decade of the nineteenth century; the front-page headline in the September 10, 1898, issue of the *Northfield News* proclaimed "High School has the Largest Attendance in Its History," enrollment rising to 189, twenty-seven more than the previous year.

The new American high school, searching for a role in the public educational system, came to be seen as the "missing rung" in the educational ladder, between the common school and college or employment. Consequently, public high school leaders developed a dual-purpose curriculum: academic courses that would provide the most talented with the skills and knowledge needed for college and more practical courses that developed the basic literacy, knowledge, and character traits (punctuality, following directions, teamwork) to function in the workplace. Yet the public schools were, historian Dianne Ravitch argued, taking on a singular importance for Americans:

> In the closing years of the nineteenth century, Americans prided themselves on their free public schools. Most children attended the public schools, and Americans felt a patriotic attachment to them. Unlike Europe... in America it was believed that the public school could enable any youngster to rise above the most humble origins and make good on the nation's promise of equal opportunity for all.
>
> The schools were expected to make social equality a reality by giving students an equal chance to develop their mental powers... What was most important was not learning a trade but learning intelligence and virtue... This was the American dream, the promise of the public schools to open wide the doors of opportunity to all who were willing to learn and study. The schools would work their democratic magic by disseminating knowledge to all who sought it.[28]

The tension between practical and the academic/cultural aims would persist through the twentieth century to the present and be regularly debated among educators, school boards, and the public. Edward Krug in his History of the American High School concurred that "there has been in American life a quest for culture running side-by-side with a demand for practical results.

As reflected in the Chautauqua movement, in the development of lyceums, in the growth of evening schools, in the popularity of public lectures, and in the development of public libraries, there was in the latter days of nineteenth-century America an appetite for knowledge, or at least information."[29] Ravitch agreed that by the end of the nineteenth century the nation's education leaders regularly debated "what high schools should teach and to whom... and whether they should educate students for college or for work: "...to one side was education for utility, to the other was knowledge for general intelligence."[30]

Northfield, with its educational ethos, two liberal arts colleges, and a declining farm population, would generally emphasize the academic/cultural purpose, which was reflected in growing numbers of college-bound students.

Northfield Public Schools in the 1890s

In February 1890, the *Northfield News* ran a four-page historical profile of the thirty-five-year-old city, headlined "Northfield Minnesota: A Historical, Biographical and Business Review of the Athens of Minnesota."[31] Author George W. Harrison credited the town's development from a wilderness to "one of the best cities of its size in the State" to "many natural advantages, aided by the strong arm of an enterprising people, the sure and legitimate results of an advanced state of civilization." Connected to St. Paul and Minneapolis by no fewer than three railroad lines, Northfield, the article claimed, was already "noted far and near for its beautiful location, its refined society, its colleges — Carleton and St. Olaf's — and its facilities as a business center."

After a brief sketch of Northfield's founding, Harrison summarized the town's public schools facility history: the one-room structure (1856), the large four-room $6,000 frame building (1861), the nine-room $20,000 brick Central schoolhouse (1874) that housed primary, intermediate, and high school classes, and the $9,000 four-room brick west-side building (1886). The classroom spaces, he wrote, were well equipped learning environments. The high school had a "small but growing" library, fifteen Harper's writing charts, a Shedler's relief globe, thirty large maps in Olmstead's patent spring roller cases, and a piano for music instruction. Furthermore, all of the school class rooms were "large, airy, well lighted and ventilated and abundantly supplied with blackboards." The furniture was "of modern and approved pattern," and the teachers were well supplied with maps, charts, reference books, apparatus, and "all necessary school room appliances." But most importantly, Harrison claimed, the Northfield public schools were effective and beneficial:

> The real, true, genuine work and influence of the public schools of Northfield cannot fully be measured and shown by tables of statistics. Yet statistics of school attendance, percentage of promotion, amount of money expended, and description of well lighted, well ventilated and convenient school houses, all indicate the successful working of the steady, progressive advancement of this most important arm of our municipal government… offering to all, the children alike of the rich and the poor, the opportunity and the inducement to become intelligent, prosperous and useful citizens.[32]

The Public School Curriculum and Pedagogy

By the 1890s, concluded educational historian Larry Cuban, American public schools had organizations and practices similar to those a century later: schools were graded kindergarten through twelve and in session nine months, teachers were expected to have some formal training, and each teacher autonomously ruled over his or her classroom. Rows of desks faced a teacher's desk

A typical nineteenth-century classroom (Library of Congress)

and blackboard, courses of study set the boundaries and expectations of what had to be taught and when, and report cards and homework had become standard features of the classroom.[33] Instruction in primary and secondary classrooms was group-taught and teacher-centered, with student movement allowed only with the teacher's permission, and the pedagogy consisted primarily of teachers asking questions and explaining, student recitation, and the class working on textbook assignments.

Cuban observed that teachers employed two primary approaches: as the intellectual overseer who assigned work, punished errors, and required memorization or as the drillmaster who "led students in unison requiring them to repeat content out loud." Occasionally, especially at the high school level, teachers served as the "interpreter of culture" and would clarify ideas and explain content. But in classrooms across America and Minnesota, teachers talked a great deal, and students recited passages from textbooks and worked at their desks on assignments or listened to the teachers and classmates during instruction time. Teachers assigned work and expected uniformity in behavior and class work.[34] Northfield teachers likely functioned both as overseers and drill masters, although with the influence of the two local colleges, more teachers may have taken a third, more liberal arts approach.

The philosophical foundation for the nineteenth-century public school curriculum was the doctrine of discipline, first articulated in the "Yale Report of 1828," which was "built on the theory that certain subjects had the power to strengthen faculties such as memory, reasoning, will and imagination" and that certain ways of teaching could invigorate the mind… "Just as muscles of the body could be strengthened through vigorous exercise, so the mental muscles, the faculties, could be trained through properly conceived mental gymnastics." The belief that the mind was like a muscle provided the rationale for the pedagogy of "monotonous drill, harsh discipline, and mindless verbatim recitation."[35]

Manual of the Public Schools (1895)

The organizational structure, rules and regulations, and curriculum for Northfield Public Schools in the late nineteenth century were well documented in the *Manual of the Public Schools: Containing Rules, Regulations, and Laws for the Board of Education and Public Schools*, written by District Superintendent E. G. Adams and published in 1895 by *Northfield News* Editor Joel Heatwole. Although the content of the publication suggested that it was written for teachers, parents, and students, it was distributed to the general public and apparently also used as a promotional publication, with an inside back cover that read:

> *The City of Schools*
>
> Northfield, Minnesota, has become known by the above name. It is picturesquely situated in the valley of the Cannon River, with two railroads, the C.M. & St. Paul and M. & St. L., the twin cities being reached by the former by an hour and a half's ride. Its population is 3,500 and its people are cultivated and enterprising. Waterworks, electric lights and three fine public school buildings, together with its parks, nicely kept streets and many beautiful homes attest to a spirit of thrift and appreciation.
>
> Its First Grade High School and good work done below it have called many here to secure these advantages. Carleton College and Academy and St. Olaf College are among the very best institutions of learning in the northwest. Northfield is a good city in which to locate.[36]

News *Editor Joel Heatwole*

Six years earlier, in the 1889 promotional booklet "All About Northfield, Minn." Heatwole sounded like a latter-day Chamber of Commerce director and extolled the virtues of his beloved town, with education the centerpiece: "Northfield has two colleges... The graded schools (twelve in number) are second to none in their successful management and results... Northfield, with the Cannon River running through its center, is at once one of the most

.. Manual ..

of the

Public Schools

Containing

Rules, Regulations and Laws

.. for the ..

Board of Education and Public Schools.

Courses of Study,

... Alumni ...

and Other Information.

PRESS OF ...
JOEL P. HEATWOLE,
... NORTHFIELD.

Title page of the 1895 Manual of the Public Schools

picturesque and healthful places to be found anywhere in the Northwest... As a result of the educational atmosphere of Northfield its people are intelligent and cultivated, and its society refined and hospitable."[37] People looking to live in a small town where education was highly valued, Heatwole fervently declared, could do no better than Northfield.

The Manual of the Public Schools was not intended primarily as a promotional publication. Rather it was Superintendent Adams' comprehensive description of the operation of the Northfield Public Schools, written for teachers, students, parents, and all Northfield residents. Except for full-page photographs of the three handsome school facilities, the Central Building, Lincoln/Longfellow, and Washington, the manual consisted of ninety-nine pages of dense narrative, opening with the roster of the seven-member Board of Education, which included one member at large and two each elected from the first, second, and third wards. The board officers were W. A. Hunt (president), S. Finkelson (clerk), and C. W. Blotgett (treasurer), and along with Charles Cooper, D. F. Kelley, T. J. Dougherty, and O. G. Felland they met monthly. Each board member served on two of the board's five standing committees — finance, supplies, school property, textbooks and courses of study, and teachers.

The Teachers Roster page listed all staff by building. In the Central School building the district's two administrators, Superintendent Adams and High School Principal Alma Stanford, supervised ten classroom teachers, high school teachers of science, mathematics, and Latin and Greek, and seven "Grade" teachers, first through sixth. Washington and Longfellow each had four classroom teachers, one also serving as building principal. The three schools shared a teacher of music and a librarian (Mrs. E. G. Adams), while each building had its own janitor.

The school calendar consisted of three terms: sixteen weeks in the fall, twelve in the winter, and eight weeks in the spring, with a two-week Christmas break and one-week spring vacation. There were seven school holidays — Labor Day, Thanksgiving Day, Christmas, New Year's, Washington's Birthday, Decoration Day, and General Election Day. Promotions to the next grade were made the last week in January and at the close of the year. State examinations were held the last week in January and May. The calendar page also announced that the 1895 tuition for non-residents was $15 per year.

The "General Rules and Regulations of the Board of Education" section indicated how directly and intimately board members, working through five standing committees, were involved in the operation of the school. The Committee on Finance attended to all the financial affairs of the district, including the approval of all bills, negotiation of loans, and bonds, and, with the board clerk, functioned as the district business manager. Even with a small administrative staff, a superintendent, and principals, the board administered the educational program. The Text Book and Course of Study Committee (with the superintendent as a member) selected for purchase "suitable text books" and prepared and printed a "systematic course of study" for all grades and classrooms. The Committee on Teachers, again with the superintendent, recruited, interviewed, and selected ("to satisfy themselves of the fitness of applicants") all teachers and in this process were expected to "ascertain the qualifications" and certify the "good moral character" of each "elected" teacher. The committee's responsibilities extended to regular supervision and assessment of the teachers, achieved by visiting the schools at least once each term to observe "the discipline, industry in preparation, and attention in the recitation of lessons, and the spirit and progress of the schools."[38]

The "General Rules of the Schools" section prescribed basic structure and the schedule:

> The public schools shall consist of the following departments: Primary, Intermediate, Grammar, and High School; and the course of instruction shall extend through twelve years. The Primary School shall consist of three years; Intermediate three years; Grammar School two years; High School shall consist of four years, B, A, [freshman and sophomore], Junior, and Senior classes… There shall be two daily sessions in all the schools, with a recess of fifteen minutes each, except the High School, which may have one session.[39]

The morning session ran from nine to noon, and the afternoon from one-thirty until four.

Classrooms were rewarded for good performance with early dismissal, as rooms with "no cases of tardiness" for the entire week were dismissed fifteen minutes earlier on Friday, and rooms which ranked first and second in punctuality, attendance, scholarship, and deportment for the month were granted a "half day holiday." General Rule #9 established the format for high school commencement exercises, requiring each member of the graduating class to "give a graduating exercise," an oration or musical performance.

The duties of the superintendent, the only district administrator in the 1890s, were delineated in an eleven-item list, the first of which summarized the scope of the position: the superintendent "shall have the general supervision of the schools, teachers, buildings, grounds, and apparatus." This was to be accomplished, the manual continued, by visiting each school, "observing and directing" the methods of instruction and discipline, evaluating teacher performance, and advising in the establishment of "judicious programs of study and recitation." The superintendent was also required to hold biweekly teachers' meetings to discuss the work and management of the school and the "best methods of imparting instruction."[40] The remaining responsibilities for Superintendent Adams included: assigning students to appropriate grades; conducting promotion examinations; suspending a pupil for "misconduct, disobedience, insubordination, indolence, persistent irregularity of attendance… or for contagious or infectious disease"; attending all sessions of the Board of Education; and writing annual reports for the board, the county superintendent, and the state superintendent. Even in it relative infancy, the superintendent's position was demanding and challenging.

The duties of the classroom teacher required a twenty-point list, the first item not surprisingly, being an expectation that they would "observe and enforce" the rules of the board and of the superintendent. Teachers were expected to monitor the physical environment of their classroom, giving "vigilant attention" to the room temperature (keeping it between sixty-five and seventy degrees) and to ensure that the room was "thoroughly aired." In the late 1890s parents and local physicians expressed considerable concern about classroom air quality, and along with overcrowding and fire safety, it was a prime motivator for razing the 1874 Central School building and constructing a new high school in 1910. At the end of each term, teachers were expected to return all books and apparatus belonging to the district to the superintendent and all keys to the building janitor. Teachers were also asked to exercise constant care to ensure that no school property be injured or defaced. Record-keeping duties included the "program of daily exercises" (lesson plans) and a monthly attendance summary for the superintendent, as well as a monthly report of scholarship and attendance sent to each pupil's parent or guardian.

The majority of the teachers' duties, however, involved teaching and classroom management, beginning with a broad expectation that they "shall exercise a kind and careful supervision" over their pupils in the classroom and at recess. Teachers were expected to "make the acquaintance" of parents in order to "better understand the temperaments, characteristics, and needs of their pupils and to endeavor to gain the influence and cooperation of the parents in securing a more perfect harmony between home and school government."

This language suggested that Adams and the board were moving away from the traditional pedagogy and adopting a more progressive, student-centered approach. Teachers were encouraged to attend to their professional development by visiting other Minnesota public schools to observe their methods of discipline and instruction and by being "progressive, to keep themselves posted on educational matters" by subscribing to at least one leading educational journal.

The duties regarding student discipline also indicated a more progressive approach. Although teachers had the power to suspend students, they were "especially urged to resort to no form of punishment that will make study repugnant to children." This suggested a softening of the strict, formal, almost grim taskmaster teaching to a warmer, more nurturing classroom environment. Teachers were cautioned to consult with the superintendent before "resorting" to severe punishment and that corporal punishment "shall be resorted to only when other means have failed, and not in anger."[41]

The General Rules and Regulations section concluded with twenty-two "Rules for the Government of Pupils." Many addressed basic operational concerns, including the stipulation that students should not leave school before the usual time but should leave the school premises immediately upon the closing of school (after-school programs were not yet part of the public school experience). Students needed to attend the school and class to which they were promoted or assigned; all pupils were required to take one of the regular courses of study prescribed by the board.

There were but two attendance rules: absent or tardy students needed a written excuse from a parent to return to school and four unexcused absences brought a suspension. The only excuses accepted were sickness, death in the family, leaving town with parental permission, and the religious observance of holy days. Four student behaviors were "forbidden" on school grounds — the use of tobacco, profane or indecent language, gross violation of any of the rules, and resistance to the authority of the teacher — and were liable to suspension or other punishment.

Alcohol use was not mentioned in the 1895 manual. But hygiene was, being addressed with a rule advising that "Any child that comes to school without proper attention to the cleanliness of person or dress, or whose clothes need repairing, may be sent home to be properly prepared for the school room." This early dress code seemed more focused on upholding the middle-class cleanliness value.

The last of the twenty-two rules prescribed the manner of movement around the building between classes and must have created an experience radically different from today's schools: "In passing up and down stairs and through the halls, pupils must, at all times, walk or march quietly and in line, and without communication, and no pupil will be allowed to enter another department without permission from his or her teacher."[42]

The remainder of the manual, nearly sixty pages, described the Course of Study (curriculum). In these course descriptions Superintendent Adams prescribed, for teachers and parents, the educational philosophy and pedagogy of the 1890s Northfield classroom.

One of the textbooks referenced in the 1895 manual

The language used and the recommendations offered indicated that the doctrine of mental discipline, while still intact, was being modified by the new progressive approach. The progressive education movement which began in late nineteenth century America challenged and sometimes reformed many aspects of the traditional classical American approach to schooling. Most progressive education programs had the following qualities: an emphasis on learning by doing — hands-on projects and experiential learning; an integrated curriculum focused on thematic units; strong emphasis on problem-solving and critical-thinking, group work, and the development of social skills; understanding and action, rather than rote knowledge, as the primary goals of learning; collaborative and cooperative learning projects; education for social responsibility and democracy; highly personalized education accounting for each individual's personal interests and goals; a de-emphasis on textbooks in favor of varied learning resources; an emphasis on lifelong learning and social skills; and assessment by evaluation of a child's projects and productions (a portfolio) rather than grades on exams and standardized tests. A few of these progressive notions appeared in the manual.

A set of "general suggestions" introduced the Course of Study section and revealed the progressive ideology teachers were using to modify the classic mental discipline pedagogy. After advising that "text books are not to be slavishly followed" and should be supplemented with oral instruction and good reference books, the manual nonetheless emphasized the importance of drill work: to learn a fact or idea "requires a thorough drill made up of repetition and frequent reviews." Promotions were processed twice rather than once a year, so that bright students were advanced regularly and "the slower ones are not so discouraged when kept back" as they do not lose a whole year.

Particular care was to be taken to introduce first grade pupils to school:

> Receive new students cordially and make their first impressions of school life pleasant. Give them something interesting to do at once... Remember impressions are quickly made and slowly lost... Be a student of child life and enter into this wonderful world. No exercise should give the children an exhausted feeling or a sense of weariness. That curiosity and imagination may be so developed to promote the work of this grade. That recitations should be the exception.[43]

The progressive student-centered precepts of joyful learning and harnessing children's natural curiosity and interest now comingled with the traditional emphasis on repetition, control, and order.

Before describing the specific curriculum for each grade level, the manual discussed subjects that were common to the learning environment of all classes and all levels: physical exercise, music, drawing, writing (penmanship), literature, room decoration, and moral teaching. Combined with the academic subjects — reading, math, physiology, spelling, language and grammar, geography, and history — this comprised the curriculum and the educational experience for grades one through eight in the 1890s Northfield classroom.

Physical exercise, though not yet formalized into physical education classes, was important and woven into the class day, recognition that physiology affected learning:

> Too much time is wasted because of lack of physical exercise. Let not the teacher scold when pupils are restless, look for the cause... The music teacher as well as the grade teacher will do well to have pupils stand erect and free from desks... It would almost seem that the ability to stand erect and gracefully is a lost art, so common is it to see slouching and leaning positions in the school room.

> Let the teacher aim to build up a sentiment on favor of manly bearing and the possession of a good physique.[44]

Teachers were to provide pupils exercises for breathing, control of the diaphragm, as well as "the usual marching and calisthenics." Habits of correct body positions (good posture) were to be included in the physiology lessons, and teachers were reminded that if they were genuinely interested in this "much needed reform, much can be done."

Music was important for all students at all levels, as "valuable mental training" as that derived from any other subject. Indeed, the manual claimed, singing was an underappreciated skill with physiological and social benefits: "Music is invigorating, it expands the lungs, strengthens the vocal cords, improves the quality of voice and last, but not least, raises the moral tone. The ability to sing is the best endowment parents can secure for their children; it is always the surest passage into the best society of town or city." Music was one of the important studies in the Course of Study and was to be taken seriously. Teachers were urged to give particular attention to "our national songs" and challenged to "never let a national holiday come and go without calling out the music so appropriate to the occasion."[45]

Superintendent Adams, the manual's author, lamented that "too little of the good in literature, art, and science is set upon our school tables" and advocated for increasing exposure to good literature in a section titled "Memory Gems, Food for Reverie, Thoughts for Idle Moments."[46] The basal reader and primer texts, he said, needed to be enriched with memorable quotations, powerful poems, and classic short stories and novels. Adams exhorted his teachers to "silence those who say the children of the present day can memorize with little power compared to those of the good old days of birch rod and homemade bench" and to motivate students through their love of literature. A three-page list of grade-appropriate selections followed and included works by Longfellow, Bryant, Whittier, Emerson, Browning, Franklin, Tennyson, Scott, Shakespeare, and Lincoln.

In "School Room Decorations" Adams made the case for a pleasant, visually stimulating, welcoming, home-like appearance and feel for the classroom. Perhaps remembering his past school days, he suggested schools were too slow to forgive teachers for the "chill of their school rooms, left plain and bare, with not so much as an autumn leaf to relieve their cheerlessness." The progressive classroom was a warmer, more stimulating learning environment than those of the past:

> There is too often left amid pleasant memories of school days, the recollections of irksome tasks, hard benches, cheerless walls, and even too often the teacher, whose life saw too much bitter instead of the ever seeable sweet. Let the teacher then make her school room a "homey place," as full of cheer as possible, for some will have lost nearly all unless found in the school room.[47]

The public school classroom, Adams suggested, should be a refuge from, in addition to preparation for, the cold harsh world.

The late nineteenth-century public school placed great importance on character development, values, and moral teaching. Quoting Matthew Arnold's maxim, "Conduct is three-fourths of life," Adams wrote that "of the agencies shaping conduct, none is more potent than the school." There were constant opportunities to teach moral lessons and engage students in ethical issues. Morning devotions were a "positive good," and the district's teachers, following the World Council of Churches' recommendation, had children in every Northfield classroom begin each school day by reciting the Lord's Prayer. Teachers were encouraged to promote the habits of "truthfulness, obedience, industry, order, neatness, and politeness." Teachers and parents were referred to White's School Management for its "masterly, helpful, and judicious treatment" of moral instruction and were reminded that through concrete examples and proverbs children would better understand the rules of conduct.

The 1895 high school curriculum in Northfield offered three "Courses of Study": the Latin Scientific, Classical, and English. While students could choose their curriculum, the four classes that they took each semester within it were prescribed. Some elective classes were available, but students could take only three electives in their four years.

The three curriculums were remarkably similar. The chart below, from the 1895 manual, summarized the entire high school curriculum. Everyone in B Class (freshman) took elementary algebra and physiology, though the English track substituted American literature and bookkeeping for Latin Grammar. Although the Latin Scientific and Classical were more rigorous and chosen by the few who contemplated college, the opportunity to take practical, less academic courses like manual training, agriculture, and domestic science was still more than fifteen years in the future.

Courses of Study for the Northfield High School 1895[48]

Grade Level	Latin Scientific	Classical	English
B Class (Freshman)	Elementary Algebra Latin Grammar Physical Geography Physiology	Elementary Algebra Latin Grammar Physical Geography Physiology	Elementary Algebra American Lit Book Keeping Physical Geography Physiology
A Class (Sophomore)	Plane Geometry Latin Comp. Greek/Roman Hist. Hg Algebra	Plane Geometry Latin Comp. Greek Grammar Hg Algebra	Plane Geometry Civic Government Greek/Roman Hist Astronomy Hg Algebra
Junior	Cicero Solid Geometry Chemistry English Comp.	Cicero Anabasis Solid Geometry Greek/Roman Hist.	German Chemistry General History Solid Geometry
Senior	Virgil Physics English Lit. Botaony	Virgil Physics Illiad 3 Books Botany	English Lit Physics Political Economy Botany Review Eng. Branches

Enrollment grew steadily through the 1890s. Even with the 1893 construction on the east side of Washington School (located in the Second Ward, east of the Cannon River and south of Fifth Street), Central School, and Longfellow School on the west side were overcrowded. By the fall of 1898 the front-page *News* article, "Public Schools Open: High School Has Largest Attendance in Its History," announced the new enrollment numbers, promising a busy and profitable year: "high school enrollment at opening was 189, an increase of twenty-seven over last year's enrollment, and Superintendent Adams expects the number will go to 200. The large attendance makes the assembly room terribly crowded at chapel time when the students are all together… The attendance in the other rooms in the Central building aggregates 247, the Washington building has 154, and the Longfellow building 115, making the grand total 705."[49]

By the summer of 1899 the Board of Education proposed a $35,000 bonding referendum to build a new high school and a new Third Ward (west-side) building. The *Northfield News* interviewed and quoted twenty-three citizens in a November 4 article titled "Expressions of Opinion from Representative

The Expansion Policy of Our High School.

1899 editorial cartoon in the Northfield News

Men on the School Question."[50] Most acknowledged that the city needed to expand its school facilities, but there was disagreement over when and how to build. Some, like J. S. Way, believed it was the wrong time: "I am bitterly opposed to bonding the city for $35,000 in face of the present indebtedness, and will certainly vote against it." C. S. Dougherty agreed, noting that the city faced major expenditures for new sewer and sidewalks. Others suggested reducing the size of the bonds by adding on to Longfellow rather than constructing a new west-side building. But physician William Greaves took the long view that passing the bond was a wise and appropriate investment in the city's future and would attract new residents:

> Northfield is an intellectual and educational city and is noted for its colleges more than for its banks or manufacturing enterprises. As a third more young people attend our high school, according to our population, than any town in the state, it behooves Northfield from a purely business standpoint to provide ample room and the best educational facilities for these young people. If she

does the next five years will see a growth in our population such as we have never seen before. People who have culture as well as money will come to our town and build good residences which will not only beautify our city but decrease our taxes. The Central school should be so enlarged as to accommodate the needs of our high school for years to come, and the children on the West side be provided for as the Board of Education, in whose judgment I have the utmost confidence, may see fit.

Unfortunately, the fiscally conservative Northfield voters rejected the referendum, and the district entered the twentieth century with a crowded, aging Central School.

The Northfield Public Schools in 1900

May 1900 was a busy time for the Northfield Public High School.

The *Northfield News* column titled "Public School Pointers"[51] previewed the last session of the High School Literary Society, a program featuring music, reading and recitations, and a debate — "Resolved that environment has more to do with the forming of character than hereditary traits."

The Class of 1900 presented the annual commencement play, this year Dickens' *The Cricket on the Hearth*.

A *News* front page article on May 26 announced that "the people of Northfield are always especially interested in the commencement exercises of the public schools" and that twenty-nine seniors and eighty-eight eighth graders would receive diplomas — larger graduating classes, the *News* claimed, than any town of its size in the state. The high school ceremony was held next door at the Congregational Church before a "large assembly of proud parents and admiring friends."

In July 1900 Dr. W. A. Hunt, former president of Northfield's Board of Education delivered a paper, "The Relation between Board and Teachers," at the National Education Association convention. The *Northfield News* printed a synopsis of the paper, in which Hunt summarized his beliefs about public education, school boards, and teachers: "The primary aim of the public school system is to train and educate the youth of the nation towards the highest morality and the best citizenship. The State has assumed the duty and claimed the right to educate its youth, to train them into useful and upright citizens."[52] The authority to supervise and execute "this most important task" was entrusted by citizens to elected school boards, whose primary task was "one of legislation with a corps of skilled laborers to execute and carry out its orders." The relationship of the school board and the "teaching force is of the greatest consequence to the welfare of the school." Hunt, who was board president when Northfield's *Manual of the Public Schools* was printed, stressed the importance of clearly defining the tasks and responsibilities of the board, the superintendent, and the teachers. Although the board should retain veto power over all its duties, Hunt believed that the selection and supervision of teachers and choice of textbooks should "devolve primarily" upon the superintendent, who was "best fitted by training and experience" to make these educational decisions. Ultimately, it was the quality and effectiveness of the superintendent and the teachers that mattered. To recruit and retain "capable and conscientious" teachers, Hunt advised, "salaries should be the highest possible consistent with a wise economy of public funds." This was an early expression of Northfielders' desire to have high quality schools at low cost to the taxpayers.

The *Northfield News* coverage of the fall 1900 school opening reflected the optimism that Northfielders felt for the new school year in the new century. Prefacing the enrollment numbers, the opening lines of the front-page article "Vacation Over: Public Schools Resume Work Once More" were positive and almost poetic:

> The ringing of the bell last Tuesday called together for study a large number of pupils. Those having previously gone to school and those entering upon the high school work, together with the cheerful little ones going for the first time, and those who shall this year finish a high school course, alike seem glad to answer the summons and take up the year's duties before them. The streets have been much enlivened by their going to and fro, and it is gratifying to "The City of Schools" to note the large and increased attendance over previous years.[53]

1900 enrollment statistics, by building, followed — Central, 442 (242 first–sixth; 200 high school); Washington (six–eighth), 137; and Longfellow (first–fourth), 118 — for a total of 697. Many classes were quite large, with three over forty (the Washington sixth grade class was the largest at forty-nine!) and seven over thirty, including both first grades with thirty-five and thirty-seven students. The article concluded with a listing of each teacher's residence. Nineteen of the twenty-one teachers were single women, of whom eight lived "at home" and eleven with other families, including high school teacher Miss Bishop, residing at the Dr. William Hunt residence.

Northfielders entered the twentieth century with a civic optimism and public spirit epitomized by its progressive city government and an active Rural Improvement Society (later called the Northfield Improvement Association). The city was paving streets, installing sidewalks, and expanding electric and telephone service. The improvement association planned the Bridge Square Park and encouraged homeowners to plant shade trees and grassy lawns and keep well-maintained homes. While beautifying the town's physical environment, community leaders also sought to elevate the social and cultural atmosphere. The public library was established in the YMCA building in 1898, and by 1910 the city of 3,500 residents would see the construction of three beautiful library facilities — the Carnegie Public Library on Division Street, St. Olaf's Steensland Library, and Scoville Library at Carleton. A. K. Ware's opera house and auditorium was opened in 1899.

Northfield's Carnegie Public Library

Northfield as an Educational Center (1900)

Its two liberal arts colleges and public schools brought nearly one hundred teachers into the Northfield community, a growing cadre of citizens committed to education and culture. Northfielders' self-identification as residents of an education center and the "City of Schools" had only strengthened since its founding by John North, thanks in part to the advocacy of early newspaper editors, especially Charles Wheaton (*Rice County Journal*) and Joel Heatwole (*Northfield News*), who had championed and promoted Northfield's educational institutions. Though partly motivated by self-interest, understanding that the public schools created new readers (customers), they also fervently believed that excellent schools created good citizens and attracted new businesses and residents to Northfield.

In December 1900, the *Northfield News* celebrated its twenty-fifth anniversary with a *Quarter Centennial Souvenir Supplement*[54] that paid tribute to the people, organizations, and institutions that had shaped Northfield's early history. *News* editor William F. Shilling and his staff wrote feature stories on

civic leaders like banker C. M. Phillips, theater owner A. K. Ware, and dairy industry leader C. H. Pierce. There were appreciative articles on "Religious Northfield," the Northfield Fire Department, and "Northfield's Military Organization," Company D of the 2nd Minnesota. "Northfield as a Fine Residence City" featured photographs of the town's grand homes and biographies of their prominent owners and included notable Northfielders D. M. Lord, L. W. Chaney, Professors W. W. Payne and H. C. Wilson, W. W. Pye, Drs. D. J. Whiting, H. L. Crittendon, E. G. Riddell, W. W. McGuire, and D. F. Richardson.

The *Souvenir Supplement*'s most prominent and extensive article, however, was "Northfield as an Educational Center: A Glimpse of What Our City Has Done and Is Doing in an Educational Way." It filled three full pages and honored Carleton, St. Olaf, and the Northfield public schools. There were large portrait photographs of each institution's leaders, Carleton's President James W. Strong, St. Olaf's President J. N. Kildahl, and Northfield Board of Education President A. W. Norton, as well as photographs of the Carleton and St. Olaf libraries and of Northfield's Central School Building.

That Shilling chose to give the schools top billing was not surprising. After all, it was his predecessor at the *News*, Joel Heatwole, who had dubbed Northfield "The City of Schools." What was remarkable was the almost hyperbolic rhetoric that Shilling used to describe the importance of the schools, learning, and education, for Northfield's identity, quality of life, and economic vitality. The essay opened with a description of those things that made Northfielders sincerely proud: "of her location, physical features, beautiful homes, churches, schools, and substantial business houses; with a population of thrifty, refined, and cultured people. As an educational center few places excel or even equal our city... Bearing the reputation of a city modern in every respect, progressive always, and made up of broad-minded people, Northfield stands at the head of American cities of her size."[55]

But schools and education were not merely one factor in Northfield's success. What, Shilling asked his readers, was the source of "these superior qualifications, this prestige, as a residence and business place?" His answer: "It is the result of education, the right kind of education... Study the majority of places termed school towns, and see if you will find many, if any, over which the moral and mental training has as great and valuable an influence." And why are we a superior people? Shilling asks. "We are as a whole educated, and

Northfield News editor William F. Schilling

carefully so." Editor Shilling proclaimed his belief that education's influence was the primary force shaping Northfield from its founding:

> Education here is the power behind the throne and truly through its agencies is Northfield made what she is! Even in its primitive state there was a design for the educational development of this little city. In selecting the location it was considered from an educational standpoint. Thus born, pre-ordained as it were, nourished and developed into a home of education is our beautiful Northfield.[56]

Shilling continued his unabashed glorification of the public schools, a "credit to our city," describing the town's three "splendidly constructed, modernly furnished and well equipped" two-story school buildings and asserting that Northfield was especially proud of her "proficient" teachers.

Not only did Northfield and its children benefit from the superior public schools, but the state and nation did, too. Shilling challenged Northfielders to "look over the record of our High School alumni" and asked "is there anywhere to be found a greater percent of ambitious, moral, and successful men and women in better fields of work than are they who have gone forth from the classes of learning in our schools?" It is doubtful that Shilling had any evidence for this claim but was rather simply stating the obvious: those superior schools would naturally prepare the children of Northfield's "refined and cultured" citizens for successful careers. Shilling further asserted that "in almost every instance" Northfield's high school graduates went to college, many choosing Carleton and St. Olaf. This too was likely exaggerated, although the small percentage of students at that time who actually completed high school were those with the ability and interest in college, so that graduates were likely to go to college. Many did indeed remain in Northfield for college: eleven members of the Class of 1899 matriculated at Carleton in the fall.

Even if editor Shilling was guilty of some exaggeration and hyperbole, his article did capture the passion for and commitment to education and schooling of many Northfielders, especially the educated and professional citizens. For them education and learning were essential in shaping the quality of community life and made Northfield a better place to work and live. The benefits of education, Shilling concluded in the final paragraph of "Northfield as an Educational Center," was evident everywhere:

> Northfield exists in a realm of education. It is the all prevailing and absorbing thought everywhere beautiful in its influence. It creates a desire to keep oneself directly in touch with the light and knowledge of broader subjects, the progress of art, music, literature, science, and current events. Instead of living an aimless,

listless, and uneventful life, Northfield is progressive, wide awake with "a shoulder to the wheel" continually reaching out through the power of education and broadening the minds and lives of her citizens, putting in her way advantages that are valuable, and a blessing to all in our own midst.[57]

Northfield's educational leaders entered the twentieth century supremely confident and proud of the town's educational environment and its public schools.

Northfield high school class of 1901 on the steps of Central School

Chapter Two

New Facilities and the Response to Progressive Education (1900–1930)

The Northfield public schools faced three major challenges in the first two decades of the twentieth century. First was a steadily growing enrollment, resulting from a growing population, new compulsory education laws, and the demands for a literate work force. More students were remaining in school longer; overcrowding was particularly acute in the high school. Second, the school facilities, especially the aging Central Building, were in dire need of expansion and improvement, though the voters were reluctant to fund it. Third, the board, superintendent, and teachers needed to respond to the progressive reform movement sweeping American education. Unfortunately, each issue only made the others more difficult to solve. In 1900 the enrollment growth and limited classrooms (both Longfellow and Washington had only four of them) resulted in third, fourth, and sixth grade classes with more than forty students, and this collided with "progressive" calls for more individualized learning and smaller class sizes.

At the high school, enrollment increased from eighty-nine in 1894 to 250 in 1903. Principal Alma Hall described how they responded to the seating challenge: to accommodate larger classes, seats were rearranged "two rows placed in contact, a new kind of old-fashioned double seat," increasing the room seating capacity. However,

> In time it became necessary for three pupils to sit in a double seat. Unfortunately, the seats were not all of equal height, so that one who sat on the "crack" had one side of his body elevated above the other. I never heard any complaints from the "inner man." If the inside one wished to march to classes, one outside mate had to rise to let him out.[58]

The overcrowding also meant that recitation classes were taught in the large assembly room alongside seventy-five-person study halls.

The Need for New Facilities

These factors presented daunting difficulties for the board, for teachers, but especially for superintendents. Perhaps it was their combined magnitude that prompted Superintendent Adams to tender his resignation in the spring of 1900. In June the board unanimously elected, at a salary of $1,500, Edgar George from St. Peter, whom the *Northfield News* noted came "highly recommended as an able executive" and whose daughter, Ethel, was a Carleton student.[59] Although the new superintendent was undoubtedly pleased to be leading one of the best small town school districts in the state, the inadequate facilities and the town's recent rejection of a bond referendum must have troubled George. The self-proclaimed

Superintendent Edgar George

"City of Schools" seemed surprisingly reluctant to meet its school building needs.

Failing in his first few years to convince the board and the fiscally conservative community that the facility needs were dire and urgent, George invited State Examiner of Schools George Alton for an inspection visit in February 1906. The resulting assessment, though clear and definitive, lacked the urgency and strength that George probably had hoped for. Alton told the *Northfield News* that the buildings were "deficient," but blunted his criticism by adding that "your beautiful college buildings make the comparison more noticeable than you realize" and noting that school "atmosphere" and the educational program was good.[60]

By the winter of 1908 the school board realized the facility issues needed attention, but with little apparent urgency it discussed only low-cost additions and improvements. It was the *Northfield News* that raised public alarm with its March 21 article, "A New High School: The Only Safeguard for Northfield Children Against Fire," reporting that word of a fire in the Central School building, though kept quiet by school officials, had reached parents who now felt anxious about sending their children to "the old fire trap." The *News* challenged citizens, asking "Will the people of Northfield let the cost of a new fire-proof building stand between them and the safety of the children in the central building?" Parents were urged to inspect the school building themselves, "call a mass meeting and decide on something." Editor Shilling chided and challenged Northfielders, looking to create urgency in the public mind:

> Nearly every town and city in the State have school buildings which puts the present Northfield high school building to blush. Yet Northfield is quoted far and near as a "city of excellent schools." Will the citizens let a pile of old bricks, rightly dubbed a fire trap, stand as a menace to the life of the children? Do something and do it quick.[61]

Although it was not presented as an editorial piece, this *News* article was a direct indictment of the inaction of the school board and City Council, reframing for the first time the building issue from a financial concern to a children's safety issue. It was yet another example of the town newspaper, rather than the board or council, serving as the school's strongest and most vocal advocate.

Two weeks later, State Inspector George Alton was at a special meeting of the Board of Education to discuss the construction of a new school building.

This time in his interview with the *Northfield News,* Alton "was not backward at all in his statements and began by remarking very vehemently,

> Take the old building down. It is very dangerous in its present condition. Without exception, it is the most dangerous school building in case of fire in Minnesota. The stairways are steep, crooked and worn and are of thin wooden construction. Why, even the outside steps are wooden. It would be impossible to construct a more perfect fire trap than the central school building of Northfield.
>
> As to the grade rooms, they are not two thirds large enough. You have six rooms on the first floor, where there is only room for four. The high school room is overcrowded and to say the least is inconvenient… If I were a citizen of Northfield I would not be in favor of putting one dollar for repairs on the old building. Instead I would suggest that the district borrow money for the construction of a modern and up-to-date building.[62]

With that damning public assessment ringing in their ears, the board and City Council, after nearly a decade of discussion, were finally ready to act.

Amazingly, less than a month later, the inevitable happened. The front-page, multi-headlined story in the May 2, 1908, *Northfield News* read: "Central High Burned: Fire Department Fight Stubborn Blaze in Old Fire Trap for 5 Hours." Two subheads followed, "Hope for New Building" and "Loss Fully Covered by Insurance and Salvage Might Be Used for Modern Building."[63] An investigation determined that the fire "started spontaneously" in the ventilation shafts, although rumors of arson arose from reports of a strong odor of gasoline earlier in the evening. The *News* reported that a large crowd witnessed the five-hour blaze, a strange scene in which many "expressed the hope that the building would be totally destroyed." The assembled cheered when the fire advanced and groaned when the firemen suppressed the flames.

The board, which had recently completed preliminary plans for a new building, told the *News* that a bonding proposal for construction would soon be put to the voters. The process of planning and funding new and expanded school buildings, which had started, halted, and floundered for nearly a decade, now appeared as if it could be completed in a matter of months.

A week after the fire the *News*, in another editorial-like article headlined "Erect New Building: Public Sentiment Strongly in Favor of New High School Building,"[64] argued that the "growing child should claim the first attention of the public-spirited citizen." Although there seemed to be no real opposition to a new building, the *News* devoted the article to refuting the case for the less expensive repair of the old building. The repair choice, it advised, would not meet the present, much less the future needs of the growing system, would not keep Northfield "abreast of the times" in educational matters, and would make the city less attractive to new residents and new businesses. It would suggest a rejection of Northfield's historical commitment to education. Equally important, the new construction was affordable and would be less of a financial sacrifice than the pioneer Northfielders had made to build old Central in 1874. Finally, editor Shilling cautioned, public school needs should not be forgotten as the new Carnegie public library building was being planned and constructed: "it would be very poor policy indeed, and would scarcely show a just sense of proportion were consideration for library needs allowed to obscure the greater needs of the schools of the city."

The following week the process seemed to be accelerating, with the May 16 *Northfield News* headline "A New School House: Board of Education Decides on Tuesday Evening to Build a New Central/Enlarge Ward Schools/The School Board Will Ask the Voters of Northfield for an Appropriation of $65,000." The article opened optimistically: "In a short time the voters of the city of Northfield will have an opportunity to vote upon the question of the issuance of bonds for the erection of a modern school building." The board proposed to construct a new building large enough to accommodate the high school and grades seven and eight and to add two classrooms each to Longfellow and Washington schools, at a cost of $65,000.

The *News* wrote that "the action of the board is very gratifying to the voters and the heartiest co-operation and support will be given it… and it is expected that shortly the proposition of issuing bonds will be placed before the voters."[65] But the momentum and the optimism were not sustained, and the new building advocates were again halted by the caution of fiscally conservative Northfielders. The board repaired the fire and smoke-damaged rooms with insurance money, postponed the referendum, and chose to have a series of architects again study the situation.

Nearly a year later, in February 1909, Carleton Professor Fred Hill gave a dramatic and critical address at a Methodist Men's Club meeting about the Central Building's deplorable condition. Hill remembered that "my blood fairly boiled at the criminal carelessness of the citizens of this town" when he recently toured the old Central School building. Every classroom had inadequate lighting and poor ventilation and was overcrowded, a poor learning environment indeed. Remodeling the old building to save money would simply not work: "Now gentlemen, that building could be remodeled from now until the crack of doom and it would still be an antiquated fossil... The only legitimate and decent thing for us to do is tear down that old shack and then put up a modern high school building."[66] The concern and outrage Hill expressed, however, was apparently not shared broadly enough to generate immediate support for a referendum.

Six months later, the *News* reported that the board had met with Minneapolis architect F. W. Kinney and approved a revised set of plans that would be "presented to the voters in a short time." In January 1910, the *Northfield News* printed elevation drawings and floor plans for the new high school building and the expanded and remodeled Longfellow. The plans addressed all of the critical needs of the rapidly expanding high school. The new building, to be located on the site of the old school, on the west side of Central Park at 306 Union Street, would be larger and contain more classrooms to accommodate two seventh- and two eighth-grade classes and a high school enrollment of 250. Fireproof corridors and a slate roof made for a "practically fire-proof

Perspective of Proposed New High School.
[For Floor Plans See Page 6.]

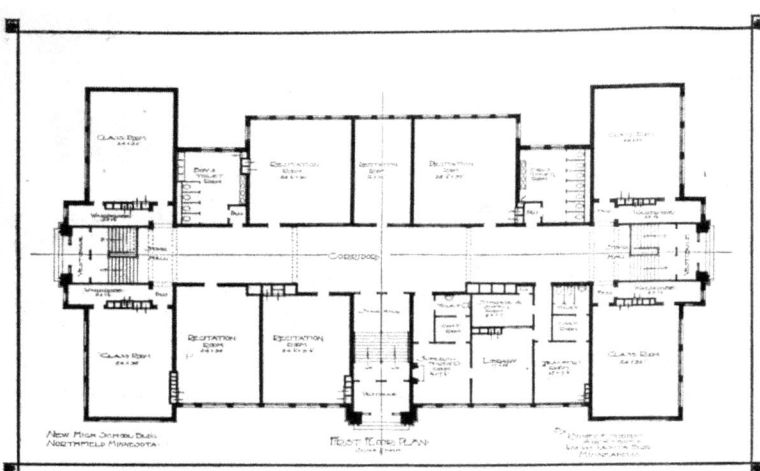

First Floor Plan of the Proposed New High School.

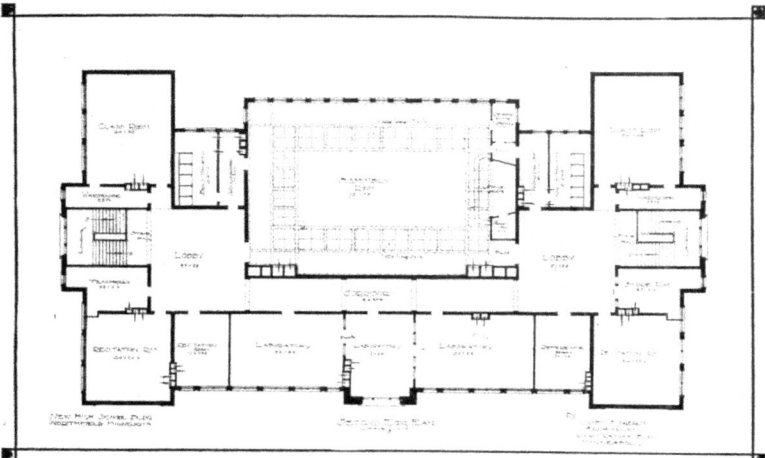

Second Floor Plan of the Proposed New High School.

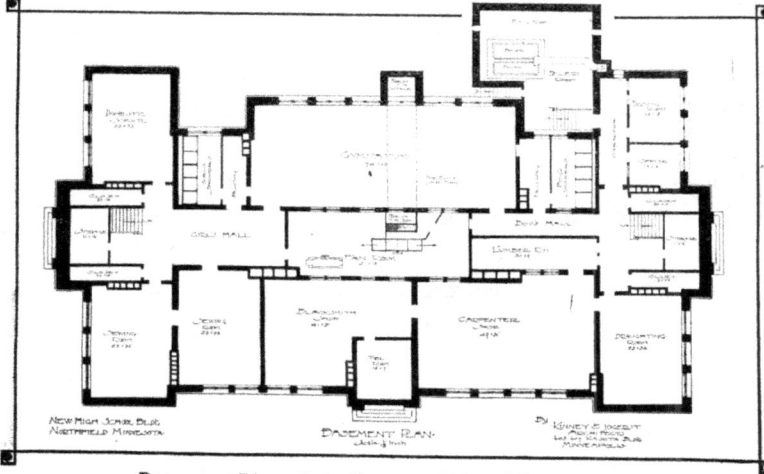

Basement Plan of the Proposed New High School.

building." Special attention was given to lighting, ventilation, and heating. The new learning environment would be safe, healthy, and attractive, with hardwood finish for the entire building.

The cost of making the school buildings "thoroughly safe and sanitary" would require a $100,000 bond issue, which could be achieved by raising the tax levy from twelve to seventeen mills — which meant that "the man who now pays $6 would pay $7." "This considerable addition to our taxes may seem a hardship to some," the *News* concluded, "but should not the health and general welfare of our children be given the highest consideration? With our two splendid colleges, these plans for new buildings would place our city without rival in the State as an educational center and desirable residence city. These conditions would certainly bring a most desirable class of citizens to us."[67]

On the eve of the bond referendum, the *Northfield News* printed a statement from Northfield School Board President John Street explaining the two-year process that led the board to conclude that the old Central Building needed to be replaced with a new, larger facility. Admitting that "at first most of the board believed that the old building should be retained," Street recounted the two assessments from State Inspector Alton and three separate architect reviews, which "all agreed there was no way the building could be rebuilt and be either economical or satisfactory." In the end, Street made a simple plea to his fellow taxpayers. Noting that "the enrollment in the high school is now 240, and there are but 129 single seats in the high school," he added a remarkably understated request: "It is hoped that every voter in Northfield will give the bond matter careful thought, as it certainly presents a matter of great importance to our city."[68]

On February 15, 1910, more than ten years after rejecting the last bonding proposal, Northfield voters returned to the polls. The results were far from certain. Weeks earlier the hopes of the bond advocates were at low ebb, but when the women of the city "became awakened" public opinion seemed to change. Minnesota law permitted women, not yet enfranchised for general elections, to vote in public school and public library bonding and board special elections, and the school bonding election was the topic of dinner conversations throughout town.

Many high school pupils were "unusually interested in the outcome"[69] as well. Indeed, on election day the high school students sang, "with the greatest of enthusiasm," a special song after each recitation period, appealing to the voters:

> Will you come with us, oh voters,
> To the old red school house there.
> We'll show you all the trouble
> And its grimy walls so bare.
> It's every weekday morning
> When we have left your side,
> We'll go up to the school house
> And half a seat we ride.
>
> CHORUS
> Vote for the school house,
> Vote for the school house,
> Vote for the school house,
> And we'll all graduate.
>
> Where the musty, leaky ceiling
> Is dropping to the floor,
> Where rats and mice hold meetings
> Behind each classroom door.
> Come listen to our story
> Our minds it will relax
> If you'll vote for bonds, oh voter
> And never mind the tax.[70]

Thirteen-year old Beulah Hulberg wrote in her diary "Feb. 15, Vote for the new School-house! It was a great day for High School. Between classes we sang this song of which every word is true."[71] Although the spirited vocal advocacy of the town's high school pupils probably had little influence on the vote, the election did produce the results they were after — and this headline in the *Northfield News* on February 19, 1910: "Wins By Eighty-Five: Voters Declare in Favor of Building and Improving Public School."[72]

Though the *News* called the affirmative vote (535, YES, 449, NO) an unexpected "large majority," the proposal lost in the Second and Third Wards. It was saved by a decisive 271–58 vote in the First Ward, which encompassed Carleton and the Central Building, among other east-side neighborhoods. This suggested a voting pattern that would be evident in future library and school bond elections: greater support from voters connected with the town's educational and professional organizations. Those with fewer financial resources and less of a commitment to education were considerably more conservative with funding public education. The *News* article concluded with an anecdote supporting proponents' contention that better schools would attract new residents to Northfield, writing that the vote was also joyful news to a recent home purchaser from Minneapolis who had several neighbors more likely to relocate to Northfield now that the city had the prospect of new, improved school facilities.

The new high school building's final cost was $90,000 and received statewide admiration. Former State School Inspector and University of Minnesota Education Professor A. W. Rankin told the *News* that the new facility "is one of the finest and best equipped school buildings in the state."[73] The building was nearly 200 feet long and 100 feet wide and contained a gymnasium, a 250-seat auditorium, manual training rooms, a fully equipped kitchen, new science laboratories, and a mechanical drawing room. The facility was designed to house four new departments and courses of study: normal (teachers), domestic science, agriculture, and manual training. Under a large photograph of the newly opened building, the *News* boasted that "of late Northfield has been receiving some very favorable advertising as an educational center" and noted that with over 275 students in the high school, 700 in the grades,

This Northfield postcard proudly cites the cost of the new high school

and more than 900 enrolled at Carleton and St. Olaf, Northfield could reassert its claim as "one of the leading educational centers of the Northwest."

The Northfield Board of Education

The Board of Education, led by lawyer William W. Pye, banker John Street, and physician William Hunt, was busy throughout 1910 and 1911 selling bonds and overseeing the design and construction of the buildings. One meeting approved lowering footings of all the walls for Central Building to the level of the old schoolhouse basement. At another the board "restored according to the original Plans and specifications the following items that had been cut out: the iron stairs, the slate roof and the cut stone fronts at an additional cost of $7,350."[74] Subsequent decisions were both large and small. On September 26, 1910, the board moved "to have our school appointed as one of the state agricultural schools," a significant designation. It also made a motion authorizing Superintendent George to buy some new dictionaries, globes, and maps.

John Street and William Hunt each served as board president before and after the new high school was built. Street, a banker from Iowa who moved his business and family to Northfield in 1901 when his eldest son, Claude, enrolled at Carleton College,[75] continued his banking interest and formed a loan and real estate business, Skinner and Street, with prominent local financier Miron Skinner. Local wags wryly suggested that "Street cornered them and Skinner skinned them," but actually the two men were highly respected and had a reputation for never losing their investors' money. After six years on the school board, Street served nine years on the City Council and one year (1919–1920) as mayor. Originally a Quaker, he was a member and the Sunday school superintendent at the Congregational Church. His professional financial conservatism fit well with Northfield's tradition of cautious use of public monies and may explain why the board moved so slowly to call for a referendum after the 1908 school fire.

William Hunt was a Northfield native (born in 1858) who attended the very new Northfield High School and graduated from Carleton in 1878. After obtaining a medical degree from Cornell, he returned to his hometown and practiced medicine for the remainder of his life. He also served the community and city as mayor from 1910 to 1914, when his effective and far-sighted administration of municipal affairs actually decreased taxes despite an annual

The Board of Education

Dr. Wm. A. Hunt, *President*
Member-at-Large

1—Prof. Fred B. Hill
First Ward

2—Dr. S. H. Stover
First Ward

3—Dr. Warren Wilson
Second Ward

4—Mr. Wm. H. Lee
Second Ward

5—Prof. Paul G. Schmidt
Third Ward

6—Mr. J. M. Walden
Third Ward

The 1916 Board of Education

$4,800 loss in city revenue. In the fifteen years he led or served on the school's Board of Education he put the schools on a sound financial basis, making them as efficient, the *Northfield News* claimed, as any in the state. Like John Street, he was deeply committed to excellent public schools, but also very careful with spending public funds. Ironically, Dr. Hunt had been called out of retirement to lead the board in a difficult period, and in February 1921, while headed to an evening board meeting, he slipped and fell on the ice on the school lawn and died.

Throughout the first three decades of the twentieth century, the Board of Education met monthly to oversee the operation of the school district. It was especially concerned with public financing, policy development, and the selection and supervision of the superintendent. The five-committee working board approved annually, upon recommendation of the superintendent and the Teachers Committee, the selection and contract renewal of each teacher. At a special meeting "for the election of teachers" in 1912, the board approved contracts for the twenty-three (twenty-one women and two men) district teachers, at monthly salaries ranging from $50 to $90. Superintendent George's annual salary was raised to $1,900.

Community relations were an important board role, and in June 1912 an attorney for the First National Bank claimed the board had acted illegally when it moved the district's banking business from First National to State Bank as the president of the board of education was also the president of State Bank. The board defended its right to use whatever bank it wished, but a few years later wisely decided to rotate its business among all of the local banks.[76]

The same year the board addressed an issue with the local Catholic church: "Motion carried that Catholic Children may upon request of their parents be excused from Chapel Exercises in High School, with the understanding that the Catholic Priests withdraw their objection to reading the Bible at the opening exercises of the High School."[77] Eight years later the board again considered a church/school issue, considering and approving a petition from the seven Northfield churches to "set aside the period from the afternoon recess until four o'clock on one afternoon each week, preferably Wednesday, wherein the public school scholars at the written request of their parents or guardians may for that length of time be under the religious instruction of the pastors of their choice."[78]

Community health emergencies also required board action. In October 1918, during the flu pandemic that is estimated to have killed 50 to 100 million people worldwide, including more than half a million in the United States, the board met with Dr. John Phillips, representing the city's Board of Health, and decided to close the schools for the week. The date of reopening them was left to Dr. Phillips and Superintendent Merton Fobes. In February of 1921 Fobes was authorized to "issue a circular letter to the patrons of the school advising them as to the status of small pox in the town and to suggest vaccination as a measure necessary to prevent future closing of the school."[79] Students were required to obtain written clearance from their doctor before returning from these serious illnesses.

The Twentieth-century Curriculum: Responding to the Progressive Movement

Although by 1911 the school board and Superintendent George had finally addressed the facility deficiencies, they continued to work to strengthen the school's educational program. Nationally, wrote educational historian Lawrence Cremin, schools were revising curriculums in response to new demands for highly specialized knowledge and skills for the workforce. Proponents of vocational education sought to "shift from apprenticeship to schooling as the basis for preparing new practitioners for their specialties — the thrust was at the heart of the movement that culminated in the Smith-Hughes legislation of 1917 which established programs of federal assistance for the teaching of agriculture, the trades and industry, and home economics in the high schools."[80] In addition, Cremin argued, American public education became more political, and as a result "many of the great twentieth-century battles over traditionalism and modernity in religion, politics, and culture were ultimately framed as educational issues and fought out in debates over education policy and practice... a continuing tug of war over what should be taught by whom and how in the nation's educating institutions."[81] Northfield educators chose to add the practical courses and equipped the new high school to do so, while continuing the traditional academic courses for the growing numbers of students preparing for college.

The increased enrollment capacity of the building expansion was also part of a national trend. By 1918 every state had enacted compulsory schooling legislation, and by 1920 more than 90 percent of American children between the ages of seven and thirteen were reported as enrolled in school.[82] While requiring students to attend school until they were fourteen was a step forward, it meant that high school was not yet compulsory. That led Superintendent George to "plead for the whole class of 1910's eighth-grade graduates to return next fall" to benefit from the new high school laboratory and gymnasium equipment. The following year (1911), Northfield added a Normal Training or teacher preparation curriculum and announced that "a large, well lighted, beautiful room in the new high school has been set aside for this special department."[83]

Nationally, and in Northfield, curriculums were changing. After 1900 the eighteenth-century advocates of mental discipline were replaced by four education groups that historian Herbert Kliebard claimed determined the course of the new American curriculum.[84] First were the humanists, the "guardians of an ancient tradition tied to the power of reason and the finest elements of the Western cultural heritage." Arrayed against this traditional group were three kinds of reformers: first the child-study group, which advocated harnessing the natural curiosity of the child; second was the social efficiency group, which applied the standardized techniques of industry to the business of schooling and "thereby made the curriculum more directly functional for the adult life-roles that America's future citizens would occupy"; and third were the social meliorists, the interest group that "saw the schools as a major, perhaps

1911–12 Report Card for a high school junior

the principal, force for social change and social justice." The early twentieth century became the arena where these four versions of the central function of schooling competed. While no single interest group gained absolute supremacy, in the end what became of the American curriculum was "a loose, largely unarticulated, and not very tidy compromise."

All four of these educational philosophies were at play in Northfield in the first three decades of the twentieth century. The humanists remained dominant, especially at the high school, but the child-centered reformers made inroads in the primary curriculum, while the practical social efficiency model reigned in the high school's new Manual Training, Domestic Science, Commercial, and Agriculture Departments.

High school dairy and soils lab, 1914

Meanwhile, the State of Minnesota increased its role in the operation of local school districts. In 1913 the Public Education Commission was created to study public education and recommend a plan for the organization and administration of public school systems. In 1919 the State Department of Education and State Board of Education were established, absorbed the former state High School Board and assumed responsibility for school building inspections and state graduation exams. In 1911 University of Minnesota President Cyrus Northrop, a member of the High School Board responsible for monitoring the state exams, visited Northfield's new high school and was impressed, telling the *News* that with its new facility, added apparatus, lengthened course of study, and present teaching force, he saw no reason why in two or three years Northfield High School might not rank number one.[85]

In the spring of 1913, the high school had a significant student dishonesty incident, when more than thirty students were involved with illegally obtaining, selling, and buying state examination questions. Four students admitted that they had driven to the Cannon Falls High School late one evening, entered the unlocked building, and, according to testimony from a board investigation and hearing, "entered the Superintendent's office through transom. Found envelopes containing questions, opened them with a match. I got Solid Geometry, German Grammar and German Literature questions."[86]

Two of the four also admitted to entering Northfield High School and stealing questions from Superintendent George's office and a wastebasket in Principal Bishop's room. The four junior and senior boys obtained all the exam questions, including botany, plane geometry, Latin grammar, civics, modern history, physics, chemistry, zoology, senior English, junior composition, and algebra. The boys then sold the exam questions to twenty-five students. The board took swift and firm action and expelled nine students, suspended two, and failed nine others in the courses for which they had purchased questions. As academic honesty was central to the school's moral education efforts, the board undoubtedly felt compelled to invoke significant penalties.

The Orange and Black.

A collage of photos from the 1916 Orange and Black

High School Yearbook: *The Orange and Black*

The first student yearbook, *The Orange and Black*,[87] was published in 1916. It described, from a student perspective, the high school's leadership, staff, curriculum and activities, and in the process provided a glimpse of high school education in Northfield just before World War I. Photographs of the seven-member Board of Education graced the first page. The president, Dr. William A. Hunt, a member at large, was in the center, surrounded by Carleton Professor Fred Hill, Dr. S. Stover, Dr. Warren Wilson, Professor Paul G. Schmidt, William H. Lee, and J. M. Walden. With three physicians and two college professors, the board was dominated by highly educated professionals.

A tribute to recently retired Superintendent Edgar George followed, announcing that he had moved with his family to California, where he was "now enjoying the busy leisure earned by long years of service in the schools of Minnesota." The student editors, perhaps with assistance of their faculty advisor, praised his fifteen-year tenure in Northfield, writing George had "won the respect and sincere regard, not only of the pupils and teachers, but of the citizens of Northfield." Furthermore, they said Superintendent George

> was a man of high ideals and always worked for the best. Mr. George had a remarkable memory for names and individuals, and took a personal interest in every pupil from the primary grades thru the high school. He settled their difficulties with rare tact and judgment. Every graduate feels that in Mr. George he had a wise counselor and a sympathetic friend.[88]

While George was undoubtedly spending most of his time working with the board on policy, financial, and facility matters and supervising the teaching staff, he was apparently visible and available to district pupils, especially the high school seniors. George was equally liked and respected by his board, who thanked George for his "long and faithful service to this district in particular and to the cause of education in this state generally."[89] Under his leadership the Northfield schools experienced steady growth and were ranked very high, and "much of this splendid progress must be accredited to the judicious and efficient management of Mr. George," the board agreed.

Next the yearbook introduced George's successor, M. P. Fobes, providing a brief biography. Born, raised, and educated in Potsdam, New York, Fobes graduated from Potsdam Normal in 1887, taught two years in New York and Iowa, and served fifteen years as superintendent in Sutherland, Iowa. In 1903 he continued his superintendent work for the Marshall, Minnesota, schools, serving twelve years there before succeeding George. The student editors wrote that in his first year in Northfield Fobes had immediately "won the deep regard and respect of not only teachers and pupils, but of the entire community as well, and had proved himself a thoroly [sic] efficient and excellent superintendent."

The core of the 1916 yearbook described Northfield's traditional high school curriculum with three courses of study, Literary, Scientific, and American that continued to grow, but was now supplemented by practical courses in four new departments: normal, domestic science, manual training, and agriculture. While students needed to fulfill the graduation requirements of one of the three courses of study, they could add practical vocational courses from the new departments.

The Normal Department introduced girls (boys could take Normal courses, but apparently none did) to teaching by adding civics and hygiene courses to regular talks on teaching methods and discipline. Afternoons provided classroom experience, as girls observed and assisted with district grade teachers, taught small groups, assisted teachers by "preparing busy-work," and served as substitutes for ill teachers. Students could receive a first grade certificate and a letter of recommendation upon successful completion of the Normal courses, something that apparently was sufficient for working in some, especially rural, school districts.

"We are very fortunate," the 1916 yearbook claimed, "to have Domestic Science in our high school, as it helps the girls to learn to sew and become good housekeepers." The ninety-minute sewing and cooking course was taught over two years. First-year classes were dedicated to learning how to sew stitches, seams, hems, and simple garments and how to prepare simple foods, pastry, and meats. In the advanced class, more complicated garments were sewn and more sophisticated meals were made. At the end of the year, students demonstrated their skills with luncheons, banquets, and garment exhibitions. In 1915 about eighty girls participated.

The Manual Training Department offered two classes: shop and mechanical drawing. Students designed and constructed furniture, which included chairs, writing desks, and tables. Like Domestic Science, it was open to all students, but in practice was selected exclusively by one gender, in this case, boys.

The student yearbook writers expressed pride in their "excellent" Agriculture Industrial Department, claiming it was one of the best in the state and that the soils laboratory was "the best among the secondary schools in the country." No supporting evidence was provided for that claim (it may have come from teachers or administrators), but the department and the educational outreach of the farmers' clubs was an important part of the economic and social cooperation between city and country. Ninety-six students (40 percent of the high school enrollment) participated in the four-year course of classes in agronomy, animal husbandry, soils and dairying, and farm engineering and management. The popularity of the agriculture course and the class focusing on dairying both indicate that many of the students were from one of the area's many nationally renowned dairy farms.

The pioneering work of Agriculture Professor Albert M. Field contributed greatly to Northfield's reputation as a town that "fully combined both agriculture and education."[90] He organized more than twenty farmers' clubs in the surrounding communities and received state-wide recognition (including a full-page article in the *Minneapolis Tribune*) for his lecture tour. His work served as the precursor of the county extension program. The High School Boys Glee Club accompanied Field on some of his trips, and apparently "their singing was very much appreciated by the farmers." Four years after founding and building both the high school agriculture program and the farmers' clubs, Field departed to spent thirty years on the faculty of the University of Minnesota's College of Agriculture. The *Minneapolis Tribune* was impressed with Northfield's town and country relationship as well:

> The little city of Northfield, Minn., has attained prominence for what has become known as the Northfield Community idea… Northfield is a rare example of a town and its surrounding country abiding in perfect business and social harmony… That is all there is to it. The people are of one mind. All are pushing in the same direction instead of pulling and hauling in all directions. Nothing could be simpler than the Northfield Community idea and there is no patent on it.[91]

A review of the Board Minutes from the 1920s also reveals the challenges and difficulties that confronted Northfield District 659. Much of the board's work was regular and predictable: monthly approval of bills, the annual March approval of teacher contracts, and the annual May approval of graduates and diplomas."[92] Much of the board work continued to be accomplished in the five committees, which in the 1920s were Finance, School Buildings and Grounds; Teachers and Salaries; Supplies; Organizations, Athletics and Hygiene.

The Annual Public Meeting of Electors

The state legislative act that established the school district and provided the process for Board of Education elections also required an annual "public meeting of the electors" to approve the maintenance tax levy and annual operational budget. As public participation was critical, a two-week meeting notification was required in the local newspaper and at polling places. The *Northfield News* article on the 1912 annual meeting announced the results with the multi-layered headline "School District Passes Budget: $23,000 in Taxes Levied for Support of the Schools During the Coming Year; Estimated Expenditure is $36,137; Twenty-six Voters, One More than Necessary Quorum, Were Present."[93] A special levy amount was required to supplement the state aid allocation and the existing mill tax to equal the expected expenditures. At the 1920 annual meeting a special levy of $58,700 (of a total budget of $79,800) was approved and a committee was established to "consider the advisability of changing the organization of the district to that of an independent district under the laws of Minnesota."[94]

In addition to the critical funding and financial business transacted, the annual meeting served as a forum for discussion of major community/school issues. The 1927 annual meeting had three discussion items on the agenda: overcrowded classes at all levels, during which it was noted that the opening of the Catholic Rosary School in the fall of 1927 would not significantly help; establishing public school kindergarten in Northfield; and "[d]iscussion… as to the reading of the bible in the schools, this practice having been held constitutional by the supreme court."[95]

Finances and Funding

Although it took nearly a decade to convince Northfielders to pass a bond referendum to build the new high school, approval of the budget and maintenance levy at the annual meeting was routine. As enrollment steadily grew, the voters were willing to raise the maintenance levy, exhibiting trust and confidence in their fiscally cautious Board of Education to be good stewards of their tax monies. Taxpayer support for the annual budgets also indicated resident endorsement of the work of the district teachers. The steady growth of the budget and the major income sources, the local levy and state aid, is summarized below for the second and third decades of the twentieth century.

Finances and Funding 1912–1930

Year/Population	Total Budget	Maintenance Levy	State Aid	Federal Aid	Salaries
1912 / 3,438	$36,137	$22,000	$6,000	—	$21,295
1920 / 4,023	$79,800	$58,700	$14,900	—	$56,120
1930 / 4,153	$85,775	$63,000	$11,300	$975	$64,000

Public education was a labor-intensive operation, with the largest expense being staff (mostly teacher) salaries.

Staff Salaries 1915–1930

Year	Total Salaries	Superintendent	High School Principal	High School Teacher (average)	Elementary Teacher (average)	Comments
1912	$21,295	$1,800	$1,100	$900	$500	Agriculture teachers: $1,500
1915	$24,000	$2,000	$700	$1,400	$550	Agriculture teachers: $1,800
1920	$56,120	$3,000	$2,100	$1,400	$1,200	
1925	$60,120	$3,300	$2,350	$1,485	$1,200	Agriculture teachers: $2,100 Football coach: $1,950
1930	$64,000	$3,500	$2,500	$1,485	$1,250	

All staff salaries rose from 1910 to 1930, though there were differences between position and grade level. The superintendent's pay almost doubled, reflecting the increasing professionalization of the position as well as the cost of attracting experienced leadership. The three male high school teachers were paid two hundred dollars more than their female colleagues, and the economics teacher/football coach received an additional two hundred dollars as well. The high school teachers made two to three hundred dollars more than the elementary staff.

Superintendents, Principals, and Teachers

Although the town and the board of education were satisfied with the district's "modern and well equipped" three school buildings, they believed the quality of the teaching staff was the real strength of the Northfield Public Schools. The early twentieth-century boards had two or three college faculty who understood that the public schools, like their colleges, needed to recruit and retain talented, well-educated, and dedicated teachers. Throughout the nation and the state before 1900, boards of education governed and directly administered the public schools, including designing the curriculum and hiring and supervising teachers. University of Minnesota Professor of Education Fred Engelhardt wrote about this in the 1927 *Minnesota Journal of Education*, noting, however, that in the new century "it had been clearly demonstrated that direct lay control of public schools was far from economical or efficient… and the progressive school districts were seeking professionally trained superintendents, principals, and supervisors in addition to trained classroom teachers."[96]

Northfield's early twentieth-century school district grew and strengthened under the leadership of three such professional schoolmen, Edgar George (1900–1915), Merton Fobes (1915–1924), and O. W. Herr (1924–1935).

Fobes succeeded the retiring George in 1915 after twelve years as superintendent in Marshall, Minnesota, and was credited with building one of the best small-town school districts in the state. While Northfield's population was growing slowly as a whole, during his ten-year tenure school enrollment almost doubled, requiring a budget that doubled as well. By the summer of 1924 Fobes was eagerly anticipating another year of growth and success. In July voters approved the largest budget in school history, to pay for the addition of three teachers, new equipment, and interest on new bonds for an

Superintendent Merton Fobes

addition to the Washington School building. When Fobes convinced highly respected high school principal, Anna Bernard, to withdraw her resignation, the *News* proclaimed that the entire community, but especially the high school students and parents, were delighted. Then an unexpected tragedy struck. On August 4, 1924, Fobes drowned while swimming in Carleton's Lyman Lakes.

The stunned community grieved. The *Northfield News* editorial, "The Community's Sorrow," said the whole town grieved together, with a "common sorrow that seems to weld the community into closer unity."[97] The tributes and accolades for Fobes the educator, the citizen, and the man filled columns of the *Northfield News*. Editor William Schilling wrote that "In the death of Superintendent Fobes Northfield loses a most valuable citizen, a far-sighted broad-minded educator, and the efficiency and standards of Northfield's schools today are a monument to his high ideals of service."[98] Fobes was a versatile administrator who "regarded the public school as the great foundation stone of American democracy… was just and fair to a fault, and never sacrificed principle for policy or popularity." School Board Member Julius Boraas called Fobes a "fine school man and public servant" who developed the Northfield schools "along constructive and wholesome lines." Board members and teachers all testified to his capability as an educator and administrator; pupils recounted his "sense of justice and fairness which made him the friend of all"; and his friends remembered his "true heart and noble character."

Board members remembered Fobes as reserved, humble, and a hard worker. Board member J. J. Sletten marveled at Fobes' ability to make board meetings enjoyable, by "spreading the sunshine" and accepting tasks large and small: "I can hear him say, 'All right, if you say so, I'll look after it.'" Fellow Lion's club member Reverend A. D. Stauffacher thought the "outstanding characteristic of his life was his deep interest in the individual boy and girl. He knew each boy, his home life, his interests, and he followed each boy as he left school... I never knew a man who was as genuinely interested in each boy and girl in the community as Mr. Fobes." Everywhere throughout the community, the article concluded, "have come expressions of sorrow at Mr. Fobes' death; everywhere there are tributes to his fine contributions to the life of Northfield."

Fobes received a final, belated tribute in the 1927 *Orange and Black* high school yearbook, with a large photo portrait and the caption: "To the memory of Mr. Fobes, who was Superintendent of the Northfield Public Schools from 1915 to 1924, the influence of his great work for the school and community, will remain always with those who knew him. His ideals, combined with ability to live successfully with others, made his a life of service."[99]

With less than a month left before the opening of the 1924 school year, the board searched for Fobes' successor, and from a pool of more than fifty applicants, found their man in the nearby river town of Red Wing. O. W. Herr, an Indiana native with education degrees from Valparaiso, the University of Indiana, and the University of Chicago, had served as superintendent in Oelwein, Iowa, and for the last nine years in Red Wing. There, the fifty-three-year-old administrator had established a junior-senior high system and led the campaign for the construction of a $250,000 high school building. Herr also strengthened the teaching corps and the reputation of the system. Northfield,

Superintendent O.W. Herr

with its crowded high school facility and outstanding teaching staff, seemed to be an excellent fit for the experienced administrator.

A second student publication, a student newspaper, was founded in 1922 and named, at the suggestion of freshman Lois Miller, *The Periscope*. The paper's staff explained the name choice in the second (February 17) issue: "In this advanced age when periscopes are being put to everyday uses, even appearing in crowds awaiting parades, our name should not be incongruous. We may use Periscope as the High School eye through which to watch and note the parade of school life as it passes by."[100] Like most American high school newspapers, *The Periscope* was entirely student-written and -run, with a faculty advisor. From the first year, the paper featured a regular "What Do You Think?" and "Alumni Notes" column, plus articles on student social events, clubs and literary societies, and athletic events.

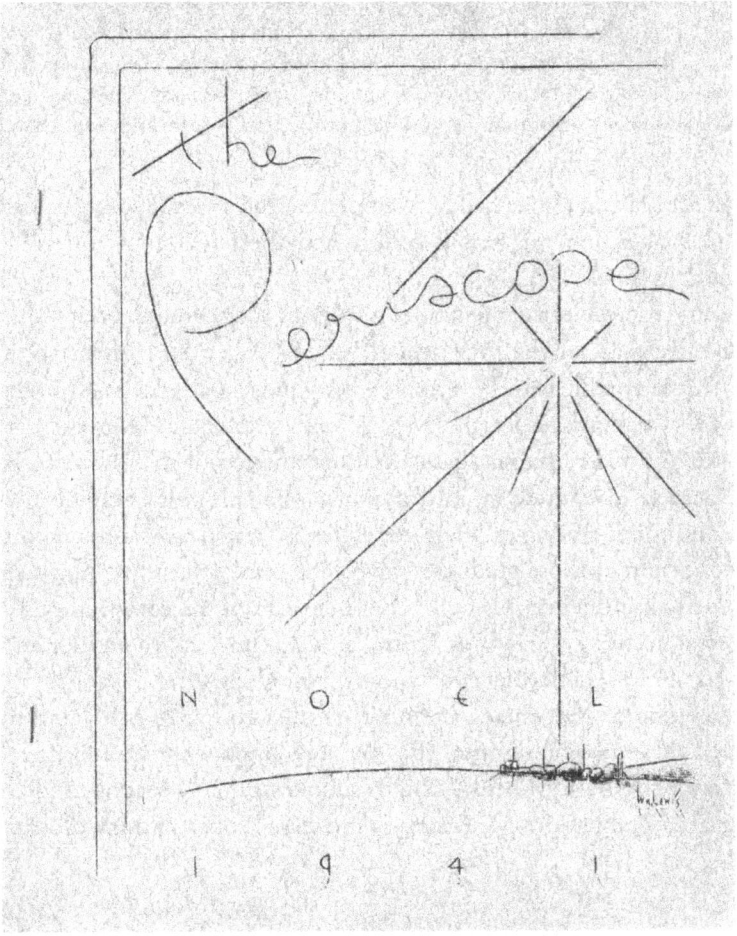

Cover of a 1941 issue of The Periscope

The 1927 *Orange and Black* Yearbook: Fiftieth Anniversary Issue

The 1927 *Orange and Black* yearbook, a special Fiftieth Anniversary issue commemorating the first Northfield High School graduation, provided a look at the high school in the 1920s and back over its first fifty years. Twenty pages of the annual yearbook were devoted to the high school's history in "The Golden Anniversary Department (1877–1927)."[101] Under the heading "What Northfield High School Means to Northfield," the yearbook editor's lamented that "too often today's student passes through today's high school and forgets that the institution has been a great force in developing men and women gone long before them" and expressed pride in the former graduates who were contributing to the "professional and civic live of their home town," including

> Lawyers, one of whom (Frank L. Clark '08) is president of the School Board, four regular physicians, two dentists, a judge, a bank president and several bank officers, the capable editor of a local newspaper, two councilmen, prosperous merchants, successful farmers of wide reputation, members of business and professional women's organizations, and last but not least, — the great numbers of good homemakers.[102]

The high school was also noted as a "feeder" to the two colleges that had sent students "conspicuous in various college activities — literary, forensic, dramatic, and athletic."

Superintendent Herr wrote a brief history of the school district's founding and the early years of the high school, titled "When Northfield High Was Young." Most notable was the emphasis on good attendance and punctuality and how few students, especially boys, actually graduated. From 1877 to 1894 there were but ninety-six graduates, and only fifteen of these were boys. But the graduation rates grew rapidly after 1895, and the high school now had fourteen hundred graduates. Herr concluded, "When it is considered that a large proportion of those graduates have gone onto college, we may begin to realize what an influence this high school has had in the community."[103]

The next section, "Greetings From The Alumni," contained letters from twenty-six alumni, including two from the first graduating class of 1877. Alice Sayre remembered that she experienced the first course of study and moved from the "old bare schoolhouse" into the new brick Central Building. Kitty Bingham taught in Northfield — high school, third, and second grade — for six years after graduation, got married, and raised four children, all of whom

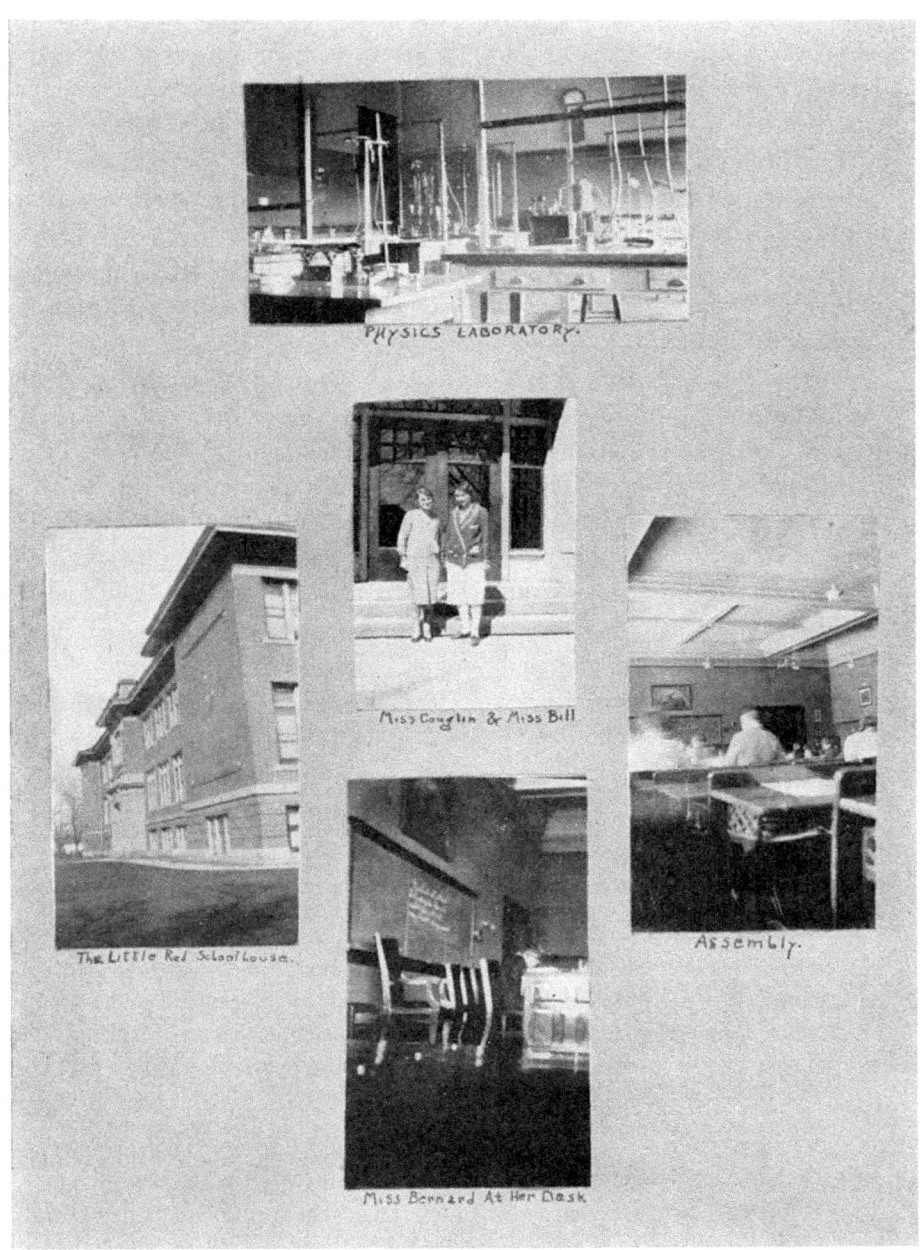

A collage of school scenes from the 1927 Orange and Black

went to college. She was now absorbed in "club work" and civic organizations in Minneapolis. A majority of alumni letters came from women educators or professional men who attributed their successful careers to an excellent high school experience. Their gratitude was reflected in a letter from Aimee Little McCandless '03, who wrote, "I should like to express my love and appreciation to those fine women in that faculty whose splendid influence we have felt through all these years."[104]

The Fiftieth Anniversary yearbook printed letters "From Teachers of Former Days," those "fine women" who recalled with fondness their Northfield teaching experience.

Former principal Alma Stanford noted the enrollment explosion, from eighty-nine to 250, during her nine-year tenure (1894–1903), and the challenge it presented to "keep a quiet room" conducting a recitation in algebra, German, or history alongside a seventy-five student study hall. Yet she marveled at the excellent work of the literary societies and their readings, orations, essays, impromptu speeches, debates, and music. Another former teacher recalled a special Beginning Latin class, marveling, "never have I been associated with so gracious, so studious, so brilliant a group of young people."

Most commented on the quality of the students and fellow teachers. A teacher at the beginning of the century acknowledged that a new building and additions to the curriculum and student activities gave the present students advantages and privileges unknown to older alumni, but most importantly "the high standard that was established at the beginning has been maintained, due mainly to the guidance and efficiency of a strong faculty."

One teacher's later experience in another place enhanced her appreciation for the high school:

> Northfield is a wonderful town from the standpoint of education, and the two colleges aid in inspiring the alumni of the Northfield High School to go on to college. The number of students who attend the high school is certainly large compared to the population... The place is wonderful for a cultural education and a high type of student should be the result — and I believe is the result — of the combination of a fine town, fine colleges, and an excellent faculty.[105]

This teacher, like earlier newspaper editors, superintendents, and community leaders, seemed to understand the educational synergy of two colleges and high quality public schools in one small town.

FROM TEACHERS OF FORMER DAYS

To former teachers, as well as alumni, this anniversary occasion brings a train of memories of Northfield High School. Events and characters of another day are recalled in the following letters:

From September, 1894, to October 23, 1903, I was principal of the Northfield High School, the latter part of that time being during the superintendency of Prof. Edgar George. After these many years, the high lights are the pleasant experiences, a few of which I will recall for the Annual. Any unpleasant experiences, of which there must have been many, I have forgotten.

The enrollment gradually grew from 89 the first year, to 250 the last year. At first, single seats with wide aisles accommodated the students. To accommodate the increasing numbers, all the seats were re-arranged, two rows of seats were placed in contact, with very narrow aisles at either side of this new kind of old-fashioned double seat. This increased the seating capacity so that each pupil could have a seat, but in time, it became necessary for three pupils to sit in a double seat. Unfortunately, the seats were not all of equal height, so that the one who sat on the "crack" had one side of his body elevated above the other. I never heard any complaints from the "inner man." If the inside one wished to march to classes, one outside seat mate had to rise to let him out.

I taught all my classes in the assembly room, where an average of seventy-five were having study-period, and it was no small job to keep a quiet room, and conduct a recitation in algebra, geometry, German, or history.

School began at 8:10 and closed its one session plan at 12:20 without intermission. There was a study session each afternoon for those who chose to come, and for those who had fallen below grade the previous month. The students clung to this one-session plan all the years I was there, in spite of some desire by teachers and parents for the two-session plan.

We held literary societies each Friday afternoon, the senior, junior, and sophomore societies in succession. The freshmen were placed in the three literaries to make the size of the societies as nearly equal as possible. Naturally, the largest number of freshmen belonged to the senior literary. Excellent work was done by these societies. Although each society had its officers and made its programs, the teachers had all the drilling to do. We had readings, orations, essays, impromptu speeches, debates, music and other features. Many visitors usually attended.

The students of those days will recall our great undertaking, in buying a Concert Grand piano. They made fancy and useful articles, and we had a sale and supper in a vacant store building, and cleared one-half the amount for the piano, and the Board of Education completed the amount. The piano was so large that the floor above the stairs had to be cut away in order to get the piano to the assembly room.

I intended to complete my tenth year at Northfield, but we found just the house we wanted, so I resigned, and left Northfield amid a shower of rice, Friday night, October 23, 1903, and was married four days later, at Lime Springs, Iowa, where I have since lived except for sixteen months spent on a Michigan fruit farm.

My life has been so busy, varied, and interesting, that I have had little time to think of teaching days. I entered at once into the social life of the town; became a charter member of a literary club, the week after our marriage, and still am an active member; a member of a large book club, member and officer of Eastern Star, secretary of several organizations, member of Presbyterian Aid society, church member; have studied landscape gardening and design grounds, and just now am reporter for our weekly paper. Incidentally, of course, I do all the housework. Mr. Hall was postmaster for ten years after we mar-

The High School Curriculum in 1927

The editors of the 1927 *Orange and Black* provided student versions of the high school curriculum with descriptions of each academic department. The language in the descriptions revealed the philosophical struggle of the humanists and social efficiency proponents. All of the traditional academic disciplines — English, mathematics, natural and physical sciences, social science, and languages — were careful to highlight their practical real-world benefits: how their subject would make you a better citizen, a better worker. The four newest departments — home economics, commercial, agriculture, and manual training — were most overtly practical, explicitly preparing students for adulthood. Some of the descriptions, such as English, were supplied by the department teacher, others were written by students identified with initialed bylines.

The four-year English sequence remained a foundational component of the curriculum, a full year required of every student every year. Through the study of grammar, composition, and literature, students learned to speak and write effectively, skills that would serve them in other disciplines, in advanced study, and in most vocations. Competency in the fundamentals of reading and writing satisfied new state standards of "minimum essentials." English IV (senior year) built on the foundation of the first three years and "broadened the pupil's view of English literature," with the hope that those that go on to college "find the transition to wider fields."[106]

Mathematics was a second traditional discipline that remained a foundation in the new curriculum. Math was "one of the most important and most useful subjects" taught in the high school; the "mental training" was of great value, developing the power of reason and analysis. Math was a prerequisite for advanced science study and for professions such as engineering and architecture. The course of mathematics at Northfield High School covered three years: first year, algebra; second year, plane geometry; third year, higher algebra and solid geometry. However, the department emphasized, in each course "some time is spent in the study of the relations between mathematics and real life,"[107] making it clear to all students and their parents why math was important and useful.

The natural (biology and geography) and physical (physics and chemistry) sciences claimed to be interesting and practical. The purpose of biology was "to know the relations between plants and animals, plants and animals to man and the understanding of the human body and its care. Biology helps make us better citizens." Geography included industrial geography, the study of commercial products and commodities, with field trips to area industrial plants. Physics, the oldest of the sciences at the high school, had been required until 1925, but now seniors could choose physics or chemistry. The object of physics was to "stimulate thought about the whys and hows of the physical world" but, the description continued, "Only very practical methods and illustrations are used, and on the whole it is a very practical subject, dealing only with the things of every-day life with which the student is familiar."[108] The practical and related-to-every-day-life themes were indeed a dominant and explicit part of the curriculum.

The social sciences — history, economics, civics, and sociology — were "designed to prepare the students for useful citizenship." The department recognized that an "unusually high percentage" of Northfield graduates went on to college and therefore "employed methods useful in advanced work." Sophomores studied world history, juniors United States history, and for seniors a social problems course combined economics, civics, and sociology. In all courses, the department aimed to present the fundamentals of the subjects and "their bearing on the problems of the day." The social sciences, the yearbook editors wrote, sought to make their courses relevant and practical, as well as to teach valuable skills: "the development of reasoning power, rather than dependence upon memory alone, is carefully fostered."[109]

The study of languages — French and Latin — and art completed the academic disciplines in the 1927 high school curriculum. Though neither was required, both made a case for their value. French, which replaced German in 1919 as the modern foreign language, gave students the knowledge of a second language and another culture. Latin, an original department organized in 1876, promoted the skills that students of Latin develop: memory, imagination, judgment and reasoning, and the "acquisition of right habits, such as accuracy and concentration."

Art, the high school's newest academic department, was added in 1924 "because the importance of art in daily life was realized." Art had applications in many fields in the commercial world and taught "appreciation, taste, discrimination, and a desire for civic betterment." The new department expected to be taken seriously: "Learning to draw is learning to see, and its value cannot be truthfully questioned by any up-to-date school."[110]

While each of the academic departments emphasized their practical benefits, the four new twentieth-century departments — home economics, commercial, agriculture, and manual training — all expanded the school's social efficiency role and were primarily vocational, practical preparation for the adult work world. All courses in these departments were electives, not required for graduation. The explicit purpose of home economics was to "train girls for homemaking" and enable them to "participate in the vocation of homemaking with interest, skill, and the appreciation of good standards for homemaking." Available to freshman and sophomore girls, its courses were devoted to "food study and cookery" and to the study of "textile and garment making." The department opened in the new high school building in 1911 with a kitchen, dining, and sewing room, but with continued enrollment growth, by 1924 the dining room was converted to a history classroom and the sewing room was shared with the new art program.

The yearbook student writer claimed that the high school was "noted for its fine commercial department" in which one-fourth of the students took one or more of its three courses, bookkeeping, shorthand, and typewriting. Each course was designed to be "as practical as possible": bookkeeping utilized actual books and papers of a modern business firm; the Gregg Writer company provided students a standardized test and a certificate for proficiency; and the typewriter companies gave awards for typing competency. The commercial courses offered students a "means for economic independence" and something that would be of "personal utility all through college and later in life whether it is used professionally or not."[111] The new high school curriculum was explicitly preparing students to be productive and effective citizens.

By 1927 the agriculture department had grown to ninety-three students, fifty-eight of whom were high school students. The department functioned much like a university extension program of later years and resembled an internship or apprenticeship for future farmers. The three-year program had evolved into first-year classes in agronomy, horticulture, soils, and animals, a second year of fields and animal husbandry, and a third year of farm management, dairying, agricultural economics, and rural sociology. But much of the program was out of the classroom and out in the countryside. It included demonstration teams, conducting farm surveys, and students assisting with culling poultry, grafting, pruning, budding, testing soils, diagnosing and advising treatments for diseases of farm animals and crops, supervising club work, testing seeds, and keeping production records of herds.[112] This was the most real world and practical component of the high school curriculum; the students were learning agriculture by doing agriculture.

The fourth of the new applied departments, manual or industrial training, had a two-fold purpose: the development of hand skill and knowledge of industrial work. The training was of a general nature for the purpose "of fitting the boys with a means of earning a living." The coursework progressed from elementary woodwork and mechanical drawing for junior high students to advanced manual training in woodwork, cabinet-making, electrical work, and auto mechanics. Each course contained both instruction and hands-on practice. Now that compulsory education had been extended to sixteen-year-olds, the high schools were providing training and apprentice work for the very students who were previously leaving school to work.

The yearbook descriptions of the high school academic departments confirmed that two of the major national educational philosophies, traditional classic humanism and the new social efficiency principles, formed the foundation of Northfield's curriculum in the first three decades of the twentieth century. The humanists strengthened the academic core courses with introductory and advanced work in the traditional humanities and the new emerging social and natural sciences, a course of study especially well-suited for the stronger students preparing for college and university. Northfield's academic core was unusually strong for a small town in rural Minnesota, uniquely shaped to fit Northfield's specific circumstances. The town's many college faculty and well-educated professionals and a dedicated talented high school teaching staff had established a community identity and environment committed to learning and education. Yet the academic courses were increasingly infused with the progressive social efficiency principles of practicality and usefulness, preparing students, whether college bound or not, to be better adults and better citizens. While the academic courses were designed to serve all students, the four new vocationally centered classes were added for those whose future vocation did not require post-high school education. For Northfield area boys, this meant preparing to work in agriculture or a skilled trade; for girls, it meant preparing for secretarial work or to be homemakers. Northfield prided itself on providing a first-rate education for all its students.

Music

ORCHESTRA

The Junior and Senior orchestras were organized under the leadership of Miss Walker of Carleton. They have progressed very rapidly during the year and now the Senior orchestra has practiced hard for the district musical contest. The Senior orchestra appeared once before the high school, taking part in an assembly program. Its members are:

Donald Warner, *violin*
Douglas Munroe, *violin*
DoLores Gilbertson, *violin*
Delmore Festler, *violin*
David Munroe, *'cello*
Kirk Roe, *drums*
Clair Davison, *violin*
Margaret Cowling, *violin*
Hans Linn, *piccolo*
Stanley Swenson, *clarinet*
Jerome Davison, *clarinet*
Ella Rolvaag, *violin*
Kenneth Lee, *violin*
Erling Nordberg, *violin*
Madison Hunt, *cornet*

Hazel Taylor, *cornet*
Catherine Fath, *violin*
Rolf Engstrom, *violin*
Marie Sletten, *violin*
Suzanne Cooke, *piano*
Mason Swarts, *trombone*
Lloyd Johnson, *saxophone*
Conradine Johnson, *clarinet*
Gertrude Ersland, *violin*
Dagny Mellby, *violin*
Elizabeth Watson, *piano*
Lucille Gunderson, *bells*
Anna Marie Klein, *saxophone*
Margaret Simpson, *saxophone*
Dorothy Strunk, *bells, kettle drums*

The orchestra page from the 1927 Orange and Black

The High School Co-curriculum

After devoting nearly two-thirds of its pages to the fiftieth anniversary and the academic curriculum, the 1927 yearbook described the activities and organizations that comprised the growing extracurricular or social component of the high school experience. Before 1900 the schools had few organized after-school activities; there were no athletic teams, clubs, organizations, or programs. Indeed, Rule #14 of the "Rules for the Governance of Pupils" in the 1895 *Manual of the Public Schools* was quite explicit: "Pupils shall leave the school premises immediately on the closing of school, unless special permission be given them to remain by the Superintendent or teacher." The message was remarkably different by the 1920s, when the introduction of the social activities section provided a progressive rationale for the importance of the expanding co-curriculum:

> We take legitimate pride in the work of our debating league, our dramatic clubs, our musical organizations, our study clubs, and our girls' social club for they give students opportunities to participate in activities that encourage initiative and give social experience.
>
> Dr. John Dewey says that growth is not something done to pupils; it is something they do. If this is true, real growth results from extra-curricular activities as well as from classroom work.[113]

Singing or glee clubs were among the earliest organizations, and by 1927 the co-curriculum included a boys and a girls glee club and two mixed choruses. The clubs practiced twice a week under the direction of a teacher and performed at regular assembly programs, the annual concert of the combined musical organizations, and for the community at the annual Christmas school program at Carleton. They also entered district and state competitions. In 1926, under the direction of music professor William Fletcher of Carleton, the girls and boys glee clubs won first place in the district contest, and the boys took second in the state. The band was newer, first organized in 1922 when the superintendent was urged by the town's businessmen to start an organization of this kind. The first group was directed by agricultural teacher Mr. Buckton (who had played in the Iowa State Teachers college band), but by 1927 the band was under the direction of St. Olaf's Oscar Overby.

Athletics at Northfield High School had, the yearbook claimed, "kept well apace" with other area schools. Although there were only a few boys' interscholastic teams — football, basketball, baseball, and track — many girls and boys were involved in intramural athletic activities. In the late 1920s, Coach Vincent Hunt established a very successful boys' football and basketball program. The football team went undefeated in 1925, 1926, and 1928, and the basketball team won a district championship three times. The athletic teams benefitted from the presence of the two colleges and played their football games at Carleton. Athletic teams played other schools in the district, including Faribault, Owatonna, Red Wing, and Farmington, but were not yet in an organized league. However, the January 1928 board minutes noted that "Supt. Herr spoke of the movement which was on foot in the southern part of the state listing as its purpose the forming of an athletic league to be known as the 'Big Eight.' The supt. was of the opinion that Northfield had no reason for entering such a league. The Board concurred in this judgment."[114]

Evolving Twentieth-century Education

In the April 1930 *Minnesota Journal of Education* article "Then and Now" 1905–1930, University of Minnesota's College of Education Professor W. E. Peik reviewed the major changes in Minnesota public education in the twentieth century. Peik suggested that significant changes in educational practice were the result of better educated and prepared teachers and the adoption of a "scientific attitude" toward teaching. Educational research at the nation's teachers colleges had created "standardized mental and achievement tests with grade and age norms, a refined curricular content, more definite diagnostic and remedial procedures, and a new emphasis upon the adjustment of the school to individual differences."[115] Out of this new scientific research came new practices in the classroom: an emphasis on silent reading, standardized drill material, new methods in spelling, a decreased emphasis on grammar, and better record-keeping and reporting. The research also supported the junior high and nursery school movements. Perhaps most importantly, teachers had adopted a new mindset toward teaching and learning, "more forward looking, open-minded… and less dogmatic." Northfield's teachers, well-educated and progressive, were undoubtedly utilizing these new approaches and practices in their classrooms.

Spending on Minnesota school buildings rose over 700 percent (while enrollment increased only 30 percent) between 1904 and 1928. These extensive facility expenditures dramatically improved the classroom learning environment. The list of facility improvements was long: movable, adjustable seats, better blackboards, maps, and globes, more attractive interior decoration, improved lighting, heating, and ventilation. New facilities were added to the schoolhouse: gymnasiums, auditoriums, libraries, and rooms equipped for home economics and shop work. The teacher's classroom, formerly barren and austere, now had cabinets, bookcases, work tables, bulletin boards, graphophones (an improved version of the phonograph), radios, projection lanterns, and pictures and displays. Northfield school buildings made this transformation in 1910 with the construction of the high school and expansion and renovation of Longfellow and Washington. By 1930, although the high school was again overcrowded, the Northfield school district had a first-rate school system, one with well-trained dedicated teachers and high performing students, working in modern and well-equipped school buildings.

Northfield high school class of 1933

Chapter Three

Public Education in Challenging Times: The Northfield Public Schools during the Great Depression and World War II (1930–1950)

The Great Depression of the 1930s slowed Northfield's economic growth and eroded the town's close connection with the hard-hit agricultural community. The shrinking tax base reduced the value of the maintenance levy and put enormous pressure on the school's annual budget. Yet the Depression, historian Cliff Clark wrote, "stimulated the town's sense of responsibility," and its many civic organizations rushed to assist the growing numbers of needy citizens. The Northfield Community Chest was founded to raise public awareness that "better health and less sickness, more self-dependence and less poverty, better citizenship and less crime"[116] should be community goals. The Izaak Walton League and Northfield Improvement Association recognized the growing pollution of the Cannon River and pushed for a sewage treatment plant. Fortunately, Northfielders also understood the increased importance of the educational needs of the community's children during difficult economic times.

In the early 1930s the Board of Education continued to oversee and guide the district with monthly business meetings, the work of five committees, and the public annual meeting. Each monthly meeting agenda included approving bills, a treasurer's report and a report from the superintendent. In March, all staff position contracts were reviewed and renewed, in May a list of graduates was approved, and in June a budget, including a maintenance tax levy request, was prepared for the July annual meeting.

In May 1930 the board completed the always positive task of approving diplomas for more than seventy seniors, along with the sad task of sending condolences to the family of long-time Central School janitor Albert Fremont who had died May 2 after falling from a ladder while trimming trees on the school grounds. Fremont's May salary was provided to the family. At the 1930 annual meeting voters approved a $85,775 budget and a tax levy of $63,000. In the discussion of the tuition for non-resident (rural) students, one resident argued that the district must always be open to "help any worthy boy or girl to obtain an education," though Superintendent Herr noted that with fewer than a dozen rural students in the high school, this was not a significant financial issue.[117]

Often the board was responding to parental or community requests. In 1931 the board, responding to a petition from forty-eight parents that dancing be permitted as part of the annual Junior-Senior Party, granted permission "with the understanding (1) that at least twelve parents be selected… to be responsible for supervising the dancing; (2) that the dancing be terminated at 11:45; (3) that the additional expenses for a janitor be charged to the party; and (4) that the participants be limited to present members of the NHS Junior and Senior class."[118] Minutes from the next meeting stated that a Mrs. Peterson appeared before the board and "made a protest against the method of corporal punishment which had been inflicted upon her granddaughter." After discussion, the board instructed the teacher that in the future "less severe measures would be used in matters of discipline." Other topics appeared on the 1931 annual meeting agenda: the reintroduction of German into the high school curriculum; more emphasis on penmanship; and acknowledgment of "the matter of mental arithmetic as an important subject for study."[119]

The board's primary challenge throughout the early years of the Great Depression was, unsurprisingly, financial: how to operate the school district with shrinking tax revenues. Northfield was a "special" district operating under a state charter granted before 1891, which required voter approval of the budget and maintenance levy at the public annual meeting. Voter approval had become routine; indeed, in some years attendance at the annual meeting failed to meet the quorum (twenty-five) and required staff to search Division

Street for additional participants. By February 1932, however, as the economic depression deepened, Superintendent Herr wrote an article in the *Northfield News* appealing to the voters for their continued understanding and support. Under the headline "Many Problems Confront Board: School Authorities Trying to Maintain Efficiency with Economy," Herr reminded voters that the maintenance levy had remained the same for the past four years, and that teachers' salaries comprised the largest budget item. "There are all kinds of teachers in the field, good, fair, and poor, but Northfield set the pace years ago by demanding the best that can be had,"[120] although "salaries paid now in Northfield are about average as compared to other schools our size and wealth."

Finances and Funding 1930–1940

Year/Population	Total Budget	Maintenance Levy	State Aid	Federal Aid	Total Salaries
1930 / 4,153	85,775	63,000	11,300	975	64,000
1940 / 4,573	94,500	49,000	1,200	1,125	70,500

Public education is a labor-intensive operation, with the largest expense being staff (mostly teacher) salaries.

Staff Salaries 1930–1940

Year	Total Salaries	Superintendent	High School Principal	High School Teacher	Elementary Teacher
1930	64,000	3700	2500	1485	1250
1935	61,000	3400	1800	1250	950
1940	70,000	3400	2500	1500	1000

Cuts in teacher salaries and program turned out to be unavoidable. In the 1933 budget the board proposed reducing teacher salaries and eliminating the kindergarten program and the art department. Two hundred voters filled the high school assembly room for the annual meeting. Two vocal groups of citizens, one led by Carleton Professor Leal Headley that was interested in restoring the art and kindergarten programs and another led by lawyer William Pye that was determined to cut school taxes, squared off for three hours of discussion and debate. The *Northfield News* reported, "out of a torrent of motions, amendments, withdrawals, and suggestions"[121] voters approved a budget of $85,000 (three thousand more than the board proposed) that "allowed for the continuation" of the kindergarten and art departments. However, by eliminating a $7,000 dollar levy to accelerate payment on the 1910 high school building debt, voters did "effect a drastic tax cut" of $20,000.

During the summer following the annual meeting, the board reworked the budget and concluded that with the reduced tax levy it was not possible to continue art and kindergarten. This brought a petition from voters to call a special meeting of the school district to "reconsider the question" of financing the kindergarten and art departments. On September 2, 450 persons gathered at the high school, and Headley again "urged the importance of art and kindergarten." He restated his understanding from the annual meeting that art and kindergarten could be continued "in spite of the tax levy reduction" by drawing on an existing surplus.[122] The board president explained that the $16,000 balance at the end of fiscal year 1932 was not a genuine surplus, but a fund to continue to pay down debt during periods of deficit spending. Pye made another "plea for economy and drastic reduction of school expenditures" and "cited distressing conditions in which many people are losing their homes to show the imperative necessity of cutting the tax burden." Finally, after three hours of discussion, voters approved the action of the Board of Education in eliminating art and kindergarten by a convincing margin, 322 to 98. Four years later, at the 1936 annual meeting, the art and kindergarten proponents again lost a vote to reestablish the departments. A majority of Northfield taxpayers, regardless of their commitment to quality public education, were unwilling to raise school taxes until the local economy had recovered.

Each year between 1930 and 1935, the board reduced the operating budget and the maintenance levy, primarily with reduction in staff salaries. But with enrollment high and class size large, no positions were eliminated, except in kindergarten and art. The year 1933 was typical. The *Northfield News* reported the board's action with the front-page headline "Drastic Cut in Local Teachers' Salaries Voted: Board of Education Re-elects Entire Staff, But Orders 15% Reduction."[123] The board explained that they were responding to public demands for "drastic cuts in taxation and for economy in the school operation" and pointed out that the salary cuts were reasonable and "in keeping with lessened living costs and current salary trends." Other actions were taken during the Depression years to reduce expenditures: sharing a nurse position with the city, allowing the city to use school facilities for a new adult education program, and establishing a required retirement age of sixty for staff.

Superintendent Herr completed his eleven-year tenure in 1935 and retired. The board "regretfully" accepted his resignation and issued a statement of gratitude for his service, noting how fortunate Northfield was after former Superintendent Fobes' sudden and tragic death

> to find another person as well qualified for this position as was Mr. Herr because of his extensive experience, his marked ability, and his exceptional temperament. During these eleven years, due to Mr. Herr's quick and yet controlling influence, the interests of the schools have been promoted with a minimum of display but with maximum of efficiency. The members of the Board of Education have taken great pleasure and satisfaction in the conviction that the affairs of the schools were being administered wisely, effectively, and justly.
>
> In a community such as this, the work of the schools constitutes an item of common interest and concern. The superintendent of schools, therefore, is one of the leaders in determining the course of this community life. In this respect, Mr. Herr has shown clear insight in regard to the opportunities and responsibilities of his position. Throughout the eleven years he has shown, in numerous ways, himself to be a most useful and exemplary citizen.
>
> With the record of his achievement in mind, we feel that we can without any reservations offer Mr. Herr the assurance that he is coming to the end of his period of valuable service to the Northfield Schools and community richly deserving the high respect in which he is held by his pupils and by his fellow citizens. His name is inseparably connected with this period of Northfield's history, and his influence is stamped indelibly upon the character of the hundreds of young people who have come under his care.[124]

The superintendent in a small-town school district was arguably a most visible and influential civic leader. This was especially true in Northfield, "city of schools," where "education was the number one industry." Both Fobes and Herr seemed to be appreciated and respected, especially by the town's newspaper editors, parents, and students.

Superintendent J. H. Wichman

March 1935 board minutes confirmed that two finalists had emerged from the state-wide search for Herr's successor, "Mr. Andrews of Lake City and Mr. Wichman of Redwood Falls."[125] After interviews Jess H. Wichman emerged as the consensus choice. After a committee visited Redwood Falls to confirm and "ascertain such facts there as might be pertinent," the offer was made. Like Herr, Wichman was an experienced administrator looking at Northfield as his crown jewel in a long career in public education. Wichman, the *Northfield News* wrote, "comes with a fine record of training and experience"[126] — a Hastings, Nebraska, native with a BA from Wayne State Teachers College and North Central College and a MA from the University of Chicago, who taught and coached in rural Ithaca, Nebraska, and then rose through the administrative ranks in Minnesota as a high school principal in Lake City (1916–1919), superintendent in Plainview (1919–1923), and superintendent in Redwood Falls (1926–1935). Wichman, the *News* added, was a member of the Congregational Church and had been "active in civic affairs" at Redwood Falls.

As the board announced the arrival of the new superintendent, they accepted the retirement of Lillian Stewart, the longest serving teacher in the district. She was completing her twenty-fifth year as the chemistry and physics instructor at the high school. The *News* credited her with developing the natural science program with a "lifetime of faithful and skillful teaching" and called her one of the outstanding teachers in the Northfield schools." Superintendent Herr praised Stewart as a "wonderfully fine worker... keenly interested in the welfare of the boys and girls... one of the school's real assets — an ideal teacher."[127]

The 1935–1936 High School Addition

The magnificent 1910 high school building, of which the town was justifiably proud, was overwhelmed by steadily growing enrollments. By 1920 the board was again facing acute overcrowding issues. Superintendent Fobes studied the facility issue and made a case for an expansion. When O. W. Herr arrived in 1924, high school expansion became his top priority, but even in the economic boom of the 1920s, Northfield's fiscally conservative board and citizens resisted calls for raising taxes for new construction. With the 1929 stock market crash and the Great Depression which followed, expansion fell off the agenda, and Herr struggled to minimize the needed reductions in programs and salaries. However, when in 1935 state and federal Works Progress Administration (WPA) funds were made available for local school construction, Herr and the board put together an expansion proposal financed by a federal WPA grant of $54,000 and a bond issue of $70,000 at the extraordinarily low interest rate of 2.5 percent.

The board did not, however, make the bond proposal public until after the July 26, 1935, annual meeting. The board's proposed budget requested a small increase for teachers' salaries (their first increase since 1929) and a new athletic field. Yet with lower indebtedness and a larger cash balance, the tax levy would not be raised. The *Northfield News* editor reminded readers of the special importance of the annual meeting in two extraordinary editorials. The first called meeting attendance a "healthy sign" when there is genuine interest in the schools as a center of community and neighborhood life and noted, using business language, that the annual meeting was the only time when the "stockholders or citizens of the district… receive directly an accounting from their board of directors, the board of education. In Northfield the meeting is of added significance because the district charter gives the voters, directly, the right to determine the tax levy."[128]

One week later the *News* editorial implored citizens to "attend the school meeting tonight" and launched into a four-paragraph civics lesson.[129] Acknowledging that the plethora of Roosevelt's federal programs had alarmed many as an abandonment of the principle of self-government, the annual school meeting, "borrowed from the New England town meeting idea," was an important and valuable "agency of local self-government." While some citizens were apparently "irked" that the authority to approve the annual budget and levy school taxes was delegated to the district voters, this practice of direct democracy had the "salutary effect" of keeping the voters informed and the school board accountable. The arrangement had worked well, as the taxpayers usually accepted the board's proposed budget and levy. Yet the annual meeting was not, the editorial concluded, merely a symbolic activity:

> The most successful school system is one where the board of education is responsive to the will of the whole people, while free to adopt and carry out truly efficient and economical policies for the schools. In this process, the annual meeting is of real importance and value. When it is well attended, its possible dangers are minimized, its advantages greatly enhanced."

In the eyes of the *News*, the case for the bond and the expansion was quite obvious. An August 1935 article headlined "600 Attend School Built for 350: Crowded Conditions Produce Problems"[130] described the educational cost of the overcrowding. Obviously, there were not enough classrooms and teachers. As a consequence, classes were too full, "not only for comfort, but for the best teaching efficiency." Educational "authorities" considered thirty pupils as the maximum class size; in 1935 seventeen high school classes had between thirty and forty students. The Commercial Department turned away students for lack of space, and the Chemistry Department "could easily have filled another section, had room and teacher been available." The crowded facility was clearly affecting the educational experience at the high school.

In September, the board approved addition plans from the architectural firm of Jacobson and Jacobson of Minneapolis. They provided for an "auditorium-gymnasium," six classrooms, and several basement rooms. The front-page *Northfield News* article, "School Addition Plans Provide for Wing at NW Corner of Central: Federal Grant and Low Interest Rate to Aid Funding," featured floor plans and drawings of the addition and seven "Facts." The addition would provide the much-needed classroom space, eliminate the overcrowded classes, and provide a classroom for each teacher. It would provide "suitable quarters" and allow the band and choruses to meet during school hours. The auditorium-gymnasium, with thirteen hundred seats, would allow the development of an intramural program and strengthen the physical education program and "make possible a community building for various events and sports." And finally, the addition would preserve the school's accreditation from the North Central Association and the Minnesota Department of Education.

The special bond referendum was held October 18, 1935, and the *News* headlined "Bond Issue Is Submitted for Addition: School District Will

Getting out the vote for the 1935 school bond

Decide the Question of Issuing $70,000 Bonds: All Voters Urged To Cast Ballots."[131] Given the importance of the question to the people of Northfield, "widespread participation" was urged. Various Northfield organizations had endorsed the proposal, including the West Side Parent-Teacher Association, Rotary Club, American Legion, the Junior Chamber of Commerce, and the East Side Parent-Teacher Association. No organized opposition to the bond issue, the *News* noted, had developed. The school board, school officials, the *News*, and other bond proponents were cautiously optimistic. Yet everyone was surprised by the margin of victory, as the voters overwhelmingly approved the bond issue, 986 to 119!

Northfield News editor Carl Weicht congratulated the town in an editorial "We Put Our Best Foot Forward," calling the "nearly unanimous" decision a "cause for real rejoicing."[132] The remarkable margin of victory, the *News* believed, indicated that the community not only appreciated the school's need, but possessed the "will and vision to accept those responsibilities" to address the problems. Furthermore, it was "not easy for any community in these times, even with federal aid, to vote added debt upon itself, but when it does so in such a decisive way, it means that a businesslike proposition was offered, the people understood it, and they were not afraid of the future."

The election results did more for Northfield than finance an expansion of its high school. More important for the community, the *News* noted, was the "spirit of goodwill and united community loyalty which marked the entire discussion. The support given the school proposal… came in practically equal measure from every section of the town and district, from every civic agency, and from people generally without regard to faction or group." This unified support was remarkable and unusual. In other funding elections support had varied by location or economic status or education level; the many smaller communities that made up Northfield were typically not unified in their vote. This, the editors concluded, was the transcending importance of the decisive vote for Northfield:

> All this speaks well for the community. The schools should be the unifying center of community life. The result of the election shows that in Northfield they occupy exactly that place. The attitude of the groups and individuals working for this favorable result likewise bespeaks civic energy and interest. And the election demonstrates the soundness of the ideal of local self-government, that, given the facts and confronted with an honest solution of a pressing problem, the people themselves can be counted upon eventually to give a sound decision.[133]

Editor Weicht also wrote in his "private column," *Across the Editor's Desk*, about the contributions of the two previous superintendents, Fobes and Herr, to the successful vote. It was a matter of "keen regret" to Mr. Herr, Weicht claimed, that he could not remain to see the building hopes become a reality, as it was he who studied the need, arranged the financing plan, and effectively made the case for expansion with the public. Herr's message to Weicht upon hearing about the vote was ecstatic:

> Words cannot express my joy at the outcome, and by so handsome a majority! When I first came to Northfield someone told me that the place was very slow to make up its mind, but when once they did they never failed to register a

News *editor Carl Weicht*

decided vote. Well, I still have to rub my eyes to see whether I'm dreaming! Now the boys and girls of the Northfield community will soon have the things for which they have been waiting so long, and it looks like they will have them soon."[134]

Weicht also credited Fobes, who put the Northfield School District on a "sound financial basis as well as a high scholastic plane," with laying the foundation for the vote. Together these men, over two decades, "pointed the way, and the community, when the time seemed most appropriate, followed their leadership, and that of Northfield's splendid new school head, Mr. Wichman, and the board of education with singularly united spirit and good will."

Northfield News Editor Carl Weicht was Northfield's most prominent civic leader in the 1930s, remarkably active in the town's community and social affairs. He was an organizer of the Community Chest, served as president of the Lions and master of the Masonic lodge, and director of the Community Club. His deep and passionate interest in the public schools led to his election to the Board of Education in 1938, and he served as board president until September 1942, when he resigned and entered the United States Army.

The front-page *News* article, headlined "Carl Weicht Expects Call to Serve Uncle Sam — Resigns as President of School Board, Other Civic Groups,"[135] listed his other resignations, which included president of the Rice County Historical Society, president of the Northfield Golf Club, chairman of the Nerstrand Woods Committee, secretary of the city charter commission, and district supervisor of the Masonic Grand Lodge of Minnesota.

After the official approval of the WPA grant, David Jacobson of Minneapolis was selected as architect and General Standard Construction of Minneapolis as the general contractor and construction commenced. By the fall of 1936 the high school finally had adequate classroom space and teaching staff, reasonable class size, and first-rate facilities for athletics, music, and theater activities. The community now had an events venue, and the board immediately established a community use policy for the new high school auditorium to "cultivate the ideal of making our schools a center of community life." So that the community organizations would fully benefit from the new facility, the use policy had few restrictions and was affordable: fifteen dollars rental for free public events, twenty-five dollars for fee events, and no charge for community-wide events like the Memorial Day program. The school board's desire to make the schools the center of community life was advanced with the 1937 establishment of a recreation board to "operate a program of public recreation and playgrounds as joint agent of the city and school district."[136] This marked the beginning of Northfield's community education and recreation program.

In the late 1930s, as the nation slowly emerged from the Depression, Northfield's public school fortunes improved along with those of schools across the country. However, the hard-hit farmers struggled much longer and the rural welfare relief rolls continued to rise until 1940.[137] Teachers received small salary increases and the kindergarten and art programs were restored. In September 1937, H. E. Flynn, state director of high schools, reported the positive results of his annual visit, writing that the Northfield school system "makes steady progress. The administrative policy is sound, the junior-senior organization is improving yearly, the high school building is adequate and well kept, teaching facilities are being steadily added... All in all, the school situation is commendable."[138] He did note problems with the ventilation system ("the so-called gravity system") in one of the grade school buildings. Two years later Flynn, after another visit, wrote the board that

1937 photo of the high school addition from the northwest

As usual I found, when I visited Northfield, a splendidly kept school plant, carefully selected and well-maintained teaching facilities, a noticeably fine pupil attitude, and with some exceptions purposeful class room instruction, and fine teacher pupil relationships. Your school is making steady improvement. However, I again bring to your attention the fact that you still have one ungraded school building (Longfellow) without forced ventilation.[139]

After the 1936 building addition, the board and Superintendent Wichman focused on the less visible internal issues of strengthening the teaching and educational programs. The board recognized Dr. Julius Boraas, who served as a board member and treasurer for more than twenty years, for his "distinguished educational leadership and understanding, together with his rich fund of knowledge of school problems and his analytical ability."[140] Apparently the public became quite comfortable with the board's management, as interest in annual meeting plunged; board minutes reported that at the July 1939 annual meeting only eighteen voters were present, though "after considerable effort, attendance of eight others was obtained to complete a quorum of at least twenty-five for official action by the voters on the financial statement and adoption of the tax levy."

The Northfield Public Schools in the 1940s

The opening of schools each September was front page news for most districts in the state, and Northfield was no exception. The *Northfield News* 1940 bold, banner headline stretching across all eight columns announced, "Northfield's Schools Ready for New Year." The sub-headline read "Vacation Days Close Tuesday for Thousands: Wheels of Major Industry of Northfield Community Turning Again."[141] But the *Northfield News* devoted far more than a front page article to coverage of the new school year, with an eight-page "Back to School Edition" supplement section, explaining under the banner headline that "No activity of the Northfield Community merits as keen and active an interest as the schools, and it is appropriate, therefore, that the merchants of Northfield in cooperation with *The News* should participate in a Back-to-School edition."

The special section contained messages from thirty-one "business houses" and articles and pictures of the community's schools that readers "will find worth reading and saving."[142] Superintendent Wichman described the registration process and "urged all pupils to be present the first day." The next page featured a large photo of the Central High School building under the title "Northfield Has Modern and Well-Equipped School Plant." An article listing all of the district teachers demonstrated the stability of the staff, noting there were only two new hires among the fifty-person staff. Another article, "Many Teachers Recruited Here: Northfield Furnishes Large Group of Persons in Educational Work," listed nearly one hundred and fifty Northfielders engaged in teaching, proudly proclaiming that "one of Northfield's outstanding claims to fame as an educational center is the large number of persons who go out each year as teachers in public schools, high schools, and colleges." The impressive list was certainly a reflection of both the high school's strong college prep program, as well as the high number of graduates with teachers for parents, and was yet another example of the profound effect of two colleges in a small community.

Another article profiled a new issue for the school district, transportation for rural students. In 1938, Northfield purchased its first bus, a 36-passenger Schurmeier bus mounted on a Dodge chassis. The next year a 42-passenger Wayne-Chevrolet was added. This year's new 48-passenger Superior-White school bus (cost: $2,846) brought the district fleet capacity to 125. Although the district owned and operated the busses, the transportation cost was paid by the rural districts and parents of the pupils served. Yet another large photograph displayed the "Northfield High School Excellent Fifty-Piece Uniformed Band," the caption explaining that under the direction of Paul Stoughton, director of music, the high school had developed an excellent band and that the uniforms were provided by the American Legion.

Students and bus drivers, c. 1940

The 1942 "Back to School" section contained the usual articles on registration, teachers, transportation, and school activities, but it featured a report from the National Institute on Education and War urging an "immediate adjustment of elementary and high school programs to co-ordinate their curriculum with the war program."[143] American schools were encouraged to make a special contribution to the war effort, the report stated, and adopt the slogan "fighting with learning" and a ten-point program to prepare students to meet the demands of the armed forces. The program included an emphasis on mathematics, with problems drawn from the fields of aviation and mechanized warfare, industrial arts courses related to war needs, more practical courses in cooking and sewing, social study courses "to impart knowledge of war aims and issues," units of study about the armed forces "to lessen the time required for induction," and instruction on the "global concept of war and post-war living." The report challenged local educators: "Never was there a time when educational workers faced heavier responsibility for adjusting the school program to a great national need." It is unclear to what extent the Northfield curriculum was "adjusted," though many local teachers undoubtedly looked for ways to involve their students in learning about the war effort.

The costly world war against totalitarian Germany and Japan certainly influenced America's thinking about education and democracy. The *News* wrote in the editorial welcome to its 1944 "Back-to-School" issue, "Our Schools Train Our Youth to Live the American Way," that "unlike the children in European nations, our boys and girls are taught how to live better, how to get along with their neighbors without resorting to force, to develop their minds as well as their bodies, and to become good citizens — in other words they are trained to live the 'American Way.'"[144] Although many educators of the time might not limit the purpose of public education to teaching the "American Way," this declaration did capture the all-consuming patriotism of the war years. The *News* concluded the welcome article with this praise:

> We are proud of our local schools. Teachers and students have so conducted themselves that the Northfield schools have attained an enviable position. With a fine record of scholarship, good citizenship, and high achievement in several departments, the faculty and students are entitled to, and do have, the confidence and respect of the Northfield community.

In the summer of 1945 Superintendent Wichman resigned to go into business in Los Angeles, California. He was succeeded by Erling O. Johnson who, unlike his three predecessors, was in an early stage of his administrative career. A native of South Dakota, Johnson had a BA from Luther College and a master's degree in educational administration from the University of Minnesota. After only two years of teaching, the twenty-four-year-old became superintendent at tiny Verdi and then Janesville and Mountain Lake. He arrived in Northfield at age thirty-five. After eight busy, productive, and successful years in Northfield, he would move to larger districts in Mankato and Anoka. As superintendent, Johnson oversaw the construction of a new Longfellow building and the consolidation of rural districts. Immensely popular with teachers and townspeople, Johnson was active with his church, the Boy Scouts and Girl Scouts, Rotary, and the Chamber of Commerce. With a reputation as a diplomatic, tireless worker, he was recognized by the Minnesota State Board of Education as among the best in the state.

The year 1945 also marked the beginning of the school lunch program. An ad ran in local papers for "a lady to prepare and serve a hot dish, bring it to school and take care of dishes at noon at the Longfellow school." By the following year the program had expanded, and the "School Lunch Report" in the board minutes stated that a hot lunch had been served every day in January at the high school and since January 9 at Washington and Longfellow, and that about 230 pupils were served. In 1950, the board approved a request for the Rosary School to participate in the school lunch program.

Superintendent Erling O. Johnson

In July 1946 the board approved on-the-job training for local farmers: "Be it resolved that the Northfield High School shall offer a special, intensive course in agriculture for out of school persons."[145] The Federal Veterans Training in Agriculture program subsidized the agriculture teacher's salary and the farmers' tuition.

An influx of new families after the war resulted in overcrowding, especially at the high school and Longfellow. The board proposed constructing a new larger west-side elementary building and adding athletic fields to the west of the high school in Central Park. With the growing post-war economy, voters were willing to invest in the schools. At a May 20, 1947, special election voters approved, by a 734 to 130 margin, a $298,000 bond "for the purpose of building a school building on the northwest corner of the Longfellow site." When bids came in far higher than expected, the board requested an additional $80,000 to cover the costs of completing, furnishing, and maintaining the new Longfellow school, and in June 1949 voters again approved the bonds by an impressive margin, 434 to 84.

Looking Forward With Our Schools

Artist's Sketch of Proposed Building

SPECIAL BOND ELECTION
TUESDAY, MAY 20, 1947
9:00 A. M. to 5:00 P.M. Regular Voting Places

What the best and wisest parent wants for his own child, that must the entire community want for its children.
—JOHN DEWEY.

Voter information booklet for the 1947 bond election

Adding the new athletic fields proved to be difficult, however, as Central Park neighbors opposed the cutting of trees necessary for the construction of the fields. The board put the question to the voters, and when their plan prevailed, the neighbors sought a court injunction to prevent the tree clearing. Central Park was preserved when the Northfield American Legion donated twelve acres of land between Fifth and Seventh Streets for a new Memorial Athletic Field. The July 1948 bond election to build the athletic field there for $38,000 passed easily, 528 to 54.

From Special District to Independent School District #3

In 1949 the Minnesota Legislature passed a law that would convert the remaining twenty-three "Special" districts into "Independent" districts unless the voters chose by election to retain their special status.[146] The special districts, which included Northfield, were operating with charters established before 1900. With this change the Northfield School District would operate under the same laws as the other 450 Minnesota districts.

The new status brought only two significant operational changes: school board members would be elected at large rather than by ward, and the Board of Education, not the annual meeting of voters, would approve the annual budget and tax levy. The district annual meeting would no longer be required by law. When Northfield voters failed to file a petition to vote on the question, its status was officially changed to Independent School District No. 3. There was no indication in the *Northfield News* that the town was abandoning the annual meeting that its editor, Carl Weicht, had so passionately defended thirteen years earlier. But the reality was that the mid-twentieth century school district had become so large and complex that it was best governed as a representative rather than a direct democracy.

Students at the Northfield high school, 195

Chapter Four

Postwar Growth and Expansion: The Emergence of the Modern Northfield Public Schools (1950–1970)

The postwar decades of the 1950s and 1960s were years of population and economic growth for Northfield and the nation. They were also the years during which the Baby Boomer generation flooded schools. Northfield's growth was relatively small in the 1940s — the town's population increased by only 177 — but the return of veterans and the families that followed was sufficient to cause an immediate modest housing shortage and put pressure on the public school system and its aging facilities.[147]

While they were not ignored, it would be years before these public school challenges were addressed fully. Meanwhile Northfield continued its tradition of attending to the town's quality of life in other ways. In 1948 its historic identity was strengthened with the establishment of the annual fall Defeat of Jesse James Days festival. A decade later cultural life was bolstered with the creation of the Northfield Arts Guild, an organization dedicated to providing "people in all walks of life an opportunity to learn, participate in, and enjoy the various creative and performing arts." Throughout these years Northfielders also continued to build and strengthen the quality of community life by expanding social services, preserving the historical downtown area, restoring the riverfront, expanding the park system, and raising the level of social services for those on the margins.

The National Educational Context: The 1950s

Nationally, the postwar era was also defined by expansion: the population exploded with the Baby Boom generation, and the nation's school enrollment, physical plant, and programs all expanded in response. American society saw a return to normalcy and political conservatism and a slowly rising middle-class affluence.

Educationally, the progressive movement lost its energy and suddenly collapsed.[148] Many of its reforms having been adopted, the pendulum swung back as critics argued that the social- and child-centered progressives had weakened the academic core of the American public school curriculum and maintained that "intellectual training" needed to again be the primary objective of the nation's schools. Some critics also suggested that teacher training was more effectively delivered by liberal arts colleges and universities rather than by teacher's colleges and university schools of education. It can be presumed that educational leaders in Northfield, home to two liberal arts colleges, fully embraced these calls to strengthen the academic core of the curriculum.

Historian Lawrence Cremin wrote that "John Dewey observed in 1952 that progressivism had altered the 'life conditions in the classroom'" and little else in elementary schools, with hardly any change appearing in high school classrooms. Cremin noted how much more talk there was about change than actual alterations in classroom conditions. Dewey also observed that the "fundamental authoritarianism" of the old education persisted in various modified forms. Cremin argued that "whereas the central thrust of progressivism had been expansionist, it revolted against formalism and sought to extend the functions of the school to address social problems, the central effort of the 1950s was rather to define more precisely the school's responsibilities."[149]

In 1957 the weakened progressive educational movement was buried by the national crisis sparked by the launching of the Soviet satellite, Sputnik. It led to an interest in educational reform to strengthen schools' science and math curriculum and the passage of the National Defense Education Act. Federal education policy now called for a return to a more traditional, academic-centered curriculum.

The Northfield Area Public Schools in the 1950s

On June 1, 1950, Principal William F. Carlson and Superintendent Erling O. Johnson presented diplomas to 110 seniors at the high school's 73rd commencement. Carl Swanson, dean of men at St. Olaf College and father of a member of the senior class, delivered the address, titled "Prescription for Success." Swanson stated that what the postwar world needed most was graduates of character and principle: "We cannot have peace without loyalty — wholehearted devotion to something bigger than self... Are the things to which you consider yourself loyal, stronger, finer, and better because of you?... We read too much about democracy, but live too little of it."[150] Swanson's comments reflected the hope of progressive educators that American public education could produce more compassionate and responsible citizens.

The student speakers echoed Swanson's idealism. Sheila Fick suggested that the Second World War had caused her generation to be more keenly aware of societal problems and their responsibility to their homes, nation, and freedom and challenged her classmates to think for themselves. "There is a need for educated persons, not only in the professions but in the basic work of the world," she said. Barry Schuler expressed a similar sentiment: "We are on civilization's race track, running toward a goal which has never yet been attained — harmony, brotherly love and everlasting peace... The school, family and the church have prepared us in mind and body and now pass on to us the baton of responsibility... Now at the mid-point of the century, we must utilize all their advice, add our courage and ambition toward the great goal of unity

The 1950 Northfield board of education. L to R: P. B. Hinds, Erling Johnson, H. H. Mader, Paul Symes, Kenneth Wegner, A. J. Lashbrook, Peter E. Fossum, J. Oliver Sletten

that lies beyond the end." This kind of idealism was not embraced by many in their age cohort nationwide — those who would go on to form the 1950s "silent generation," one that focused more on economic security and living a normal life than on independent and altruistic thinking.

In the 1950 student yearbook (*The Norhian*) Superintendent Johnson and Principal Carlson both suggested that preparation for citizenship was a primary purpose of public secondary education. Johnson wrote to the seniors that "Our greatest problem as a nation is to make our democracy strong and dynamic. Your school aims through all activities, curricular and co-curricular, to give you the knowledge, the appreciations, and the attitudes that are essential to good citizenship… May the years following graduation be interesting and enjoyable, and may your activities as a citizen contribute toward making and keeping our country strong."[151] Carlson shared a similar message, claiming that the activities and experiences from the high school years "should have helped prepare you as citizens for a society greatly in need of men and women who can bring understanding and meaning into the lives of all people." Northfield's two top administrators were again expressing the idealism of American progressive education. As they saw it, the public school's primary purpose was to turn out good citizens and good people.

That same summer Dr. Julius Boraas retired from the Minnesota State Board of Education after thirty years as a member and president. *Northfield News* editor Herman Roe extended an "admiring salute" to Boraas, a "great educator," for his career as a teacher in rural schools in Goodhue County, a faculty member at the Red Wing Seminary and for thirty years at St. Olaf College, and volunteer service on the Northfield and Minnesota boards of education: "It would be difficult to measure the contribution that he has made in a lifetime devoted to service in the world of education… To a distinguished educator, inspiring teacher, and unselfish public servant, *The News* joins a host of friends in a grateful salute and tribute of appreciation."[152] Boraas was typical of a long line of St. Olaf and Carleton faculty who served on their local school board and whose presence in the community made the public school district one of the strongest in the state.

The annual "Back-To-School Edition" of the *Northfield News* presented parents with a comprehensive guide to the people, programs, and facilities of the 1950 Northfield Public Schools.[153] The front page alone contained opening day information, biographical sketches (with photos) of Superintendent Johnson and Miss Ann Oversea, the first elementary principal and coordinator, introductions (with photos) of the district's eight new teachers, and articles on the health, social studies, and occupational training programs. The biggest school news: the new Longfellow building had opened, with eight classrooms, library, offices, and a cafeteria. To give all Northfield elementary school children an opportunity to experience the new facility, all fourth, fifth, and sixth grades were assigned there; the first, second, and third grades attended their neighborhood school, east-siders going to Washington and west-siders to the old Longfellow building. The new school building was absolutely necessary: from 1944 to 1949 the number of children in Northfield under nine years of age had increased by 46 percent; the number of ten- to twenty-year-olds grew by 23 percent. The postwar growth and expansion had begun.

Under the front-page photograph of the superintendent, the *News* wrote that "Erling O. Johnson, the genial and capable superintendent of Northfield's public schools for the past five years, has demonstrated his capacity as a successful school administrator."[154] As it had done with previous superintendents, the *News* was publically supportive and complimentary of the town's top school administrator.

The front-page article "Health Programs In Northfield Public Schools" described the extensive role the public schools had assumed for the health of the community's children. The health program had two distinct phases: to provide specific health services and to ensure a "healthful" school environment. While acknowledging that student health was a joint responsibility of the individual and the community, the school system nonetheless provided a remarkable array of services: health examinations of pre-school children, dental examinations, annual Tuberculin tests (and chest x-rays for positive reactors), vaccination and immunization clinics conducted by local physicians in the schools, hearing exams, and vision testing with height and weight checks by each classroom teacher. School nurses believed that providing these health services directly and in the schools was the most effective means for creating a healthy school learning environment.

The front-page of the Back-To-School Edition also featured the courses that addressed another of the mid-twentieth century public school's primary objectives, to "build good citizens." Social studies courses promoted effective living by providing students the information and experiences necessary for the "formulation of the values, attitudes, habits, and skills basic to good citizenship."[155] Social studies courses were offered for each grade, 7 through 12:

Geography and History and Community Life in Minnesota (7)

American History (8)

Community Civics and Vocations (9)

Modern World, Ancient, and Medieval History (10)

United States History (11)

Government, Economics, and Social Problems ("with emphasis on the latter") (12)

The influence of progressive education ideals was evident in the stated objectives of the social studies courses. The primary objective was to understand the social environment and thereby effectively address the problems of home, school, and community. Students would develop "attitudes of cooperation and responsibility... acquire knowledge essential to intelligent citizenship... become fitted for effective participation in the activities of their community, state, nation, and the world... and develop a greater appreciation of our heritage." This was a curriculum clearly designed to strengthen and sustain the democratic way of life that had been so severely challenged by the Second World War.

On the athletic front, the "Back-To-School" edition congratulated the 1950 boys' high school track team for winning its eleventh consecutive District Four track title the previous spring. The newspaper noted that ever since "Pop" Karnes had first initiated a balanced track program the "boys have achieved honors in nearly every major meet in the state." Northfield High School athletics would retain a tradition of excellence, especially for its relatively modest size, into the twenty-first century. Many of the local high school athletes were likely influenced and inspired by watching the student-athletes at Carleton and St. Olaf Colleges, something which thereby indirectly strengthened the small town's high school boys' athletic program. This was yet another way the Northfield Public Schools benefited from the local presence of two colleges.

A separate article celebrated the opening of the new Longfellow Elementary School building. In April of 1947 Northfield voters had addressed the population explosion of elementary age children by overwhelmingly approving a $298,000 bond levy by a vote of 784 to 130. But high bids from rising construction costs required a second $80,000 levy, which was approved in June 1949. Although initially joined to the old obsolete west-side school, the new building was an entire school plant with eight classrooms, a library, a two-story "physical education room with stage," a kitchen and lunch room, a music room with stage, bathrooms, a teacher's lounge, and administrative offices. The old Longfellow building was used for non-school purposes, and not demolished until 1963.

The new Longfellow Elementary School

Postwar Growth: Expansion of Student Population, Enrollment, and School Facilities

The addition of eight elementary classrooms in the new Longfellow building met immediate postwar facility needs, but the school-age population continued to grow. The district's K–6 enrollment had increased from 441 in 1944–1945 to 747 in 1952–1953. The Northfield Independent School District (ISD) #3 and the many small common school districts in the surrounding area all faced the daunting financial and administrative challenges of expanding programs and facilities to accommodate the rapid growth. The school board sought assistance in assessing the situation and addressing it. In 1952 it commissioned the Bureau of Field Studies and Surveys of the University of Minnesota College of Education to survey the forty-four school districts in the Northfield High School Area, which included three independent districts, Rice County #3 (Northfield) and #4 (Dundas) and Dakota County #51 (Castle Rock), and forty-one common school (elementary) districts in Rice (twenty-eight), Dakota (nine), and Goodhue (two) Counties. The survey summary report, "School Building Needs of the Northfield High School Area,"[156] issued in July 1952, evaluated the educational program and school facilities in the forty-four area districts, analyzed population and school enrollment trends, and estimated future school enrollments and school plant needs.

The Northfield High School Area covered a wide territory that contained more than 200 square miles, with a population of almost 10,000, and a total assessed valuation of more than $5 million to serve nearly 2,000 school-age children. The forty-four districts of the Northfield High School Area had been set up in 1938 by the superintendents of the high schools in Rice and adjoining parts of Dakota and Goodhue Counties. The common school districts were rural and sparsely populated, with school age enrollment ranging from three to fifty-seven, less than twenty students in seventeen of the districts. During the 1951–1952 school year thirteen districts operated one-room schools, while fifteen districts closed buildings and nine districts no longer owned a schoolhouse. Many rural elementary school districts were simply not financially viable. The result, the survey reported, was a national and state trend toward school district consolidation. The consolidation movement was so prevalent and inevitable, that even though there was at that time no formal reorganization proposal before the Northfield High School Area residents, the survey report calculated the financial and administrative benefits of consolidation and recommended reorganizing the many area districts into one administrative unit.

The survey report assessed the condition of all of the Northfield area school buildings, and found the facilities of the Northfield District #3's three buildings, the junior/senior high school and two elementary schools, Longfellow, and Washington, adequate but crowded. The high school contained eighteen general classrooms, thirteen special classrooms (including rooms for commercial, art, and agricultural classes, a music room, laboratories, and shops), a library-study hall, two gymnasiums (one combined with an auditorium), locker rooms and showers, offices, a lunchroom, service and storage rooms; it contained no uncorrectable fire hazards and appeared to be "life-safe." The new Longfellow Elementary School was a "fine, modern, fire-resistant" facility, but it lacked space for a kindergarten.

However, of the thirty-one school buildings located in the rural common school districts outside Northfield only six were deemed satisfactory. The twenty-five inadequate buildings were all one-story, one-room, wood-frame structures in fair to poor condition, many without indoor toilets or pressurized water systems. Only three one-room rural buildings were even judged adequate. The other three satisfactory rural facilities were multi-room elementary schools in Castle Rock, Dundas, and Dennison. The Castle Rock school, built in 1925 after a tornado had leveled an existing wood structure, was a masonry-and-stucco, one-story building containing four classrooms, a library (doubling as a stage), a gymnasium, an office, and modern toilet and heating facilities. Located on a level five-acre site, it was deemed "life-safe" as each classroom had a direct exit to the outside. The Castle Rock building operated in the consolidated Northfield district until 1970, sat vacant for thirteen years, and then in 1983 became the schoolhouse for a private progressive elementary school, Prairie Creek Community School.

The educational program, the bureau report concluded, was also "hampered by too few classrooms" and classrooms that did not meet two basic standards: an effective learning environment required no more than two grade levels in a classroom and fewer than thirty students in a class. None of the rural one-room schools met the first standard, and the crowded Northfield city schools averaged more than thirty-two students per classroom in 1951–1952. The Northfield High School building had a capacity of 600 students, but had a 1951 enrollment of 713, which grew to 740 by the end of the year.

The analysis was clear: the high school and elementary school facilities were already "overtaxed," and if all of the undesirable or unsafe classrooms in the rural schools were eliminated, there would be insufficient capacity to accommodate the area's public school pupils. The survey predicted that this classroom space shortage would worsen dramatically and "create acute problems" as the public school enrollment growth was projected to continue for the next fifteen years., with elementary (K–6) enrollment rising from 977 to 1,160, and secondary (7–12) increasing from 740 to 1,110.

Building improvement and expansion was badly needed, the report continued, and would need to be financed by a bond issue, as present maintenance and operating budgets were already "cut to the bone." The bureau estimated that the Northfield district's bonding capacity was half a million dollars, enough to meet all of the building needs for the elementary schools, but not for the area high school. The report concluded that only through unification (consolidation) of Northfield with the surrounding rural districts could each child in the Northfield High School Area be "guaranteed" both an elementary and high school education. The report recommended that Northfield meet its acute need for an additional elementary school by constructing an eight-classroom facility on a ten acre-site between 8th and 9th Streets in the southeast part of the city at a cost of $465,000. In doing so, the bureau was essentially endorsing early plans for what would become Northfield's third elementary school, Sibley. The report recommended that the new consolidated Northfield district modernize and enlarge the high school and maintain and improve as many of the rural schools as possible.

The Bureau of Field Studies' report made a compelling case for unification. Indeed, it seemed the most economical way to meet the building needs of both Northfield and the rural common school districts. But the report reminded the citizens of the area that the primary purpose of unification was not to save money but to provide "at the least possible cost equal educational opportunities and acceptable school facilities for all the pupils of the area."[157] No district acting on its own could provide all of the facilities needed. The report concluded with a stirring explanation and justification for consolidation. It was an argument for the financial and educational benefits of unification that was made in the 1950s across Minnesota and the nation: 1) all the needed elementary classrooms and high school facilities could be provided; 2) the problems of the area were best solved by collective action of the districts; 3) operational economies could be effected and duplication avoided, improving services to children in transportation, hot-lunch programs, and health care; 4) the cost of education and school plant could be spread equitably across the area; and 5) special classes could be provided for exceptional children and handicapped pupils.

Unification would further democratize the local public schools, as parents in the rural elementary districts could participate in the governance of the high school. Furthermore, the formation of a single large school district would encourage community spirit and create "bonds of common interest" as the "school plant itself" would be used extensively by the larger district community as a center of education, culture, and recreation for youth and adults. Given all of the benefits and advantages of unification, the bureau strongly recommended that the citizens of all the Northfield High School Area districts "unite and create a new district which can better meet the educational and social needs of the area: Individually, none of the present districts can support the kind of educational program which their children need. Together, as one district, the people of the area can create and support an educational system of which every citizen will be proud."[158]

With compelling analysis and recommendations from the University of Minnesota Bureau 1952 Survey Report, the Northfield School District was poised to execute its postwar growth plans. First, in November of 1952 voters approved the merger of Northfield Independent School District (ISD) #3 with thirty-two rural common school districts to form Independent Consolidated School District #42. As the new board prepared for a building expansion and facility improvement bond referendum for the new district's school plant, Superintendent Erling Johnson surprised the community with his resignation, announcing in January that he would leave in July to become superintendent of the larger Mankato Public Schools district (home to one of the state teacher's colleges). Johnson resigned with "the greatest reluctance," but he could not resist the lure of professional advancement. He genuinely enjoyed and appreciated Northfield, he noted, writing the board that it was "difficult to imagine a situation in which cooperation of school board, faculty, pupils, parents, and community could be as complete as here"[159] and that he "especially disliked" leaving so soon after the recent consolidation and in the midst of facility planning and a challenging bond election.

Despite Johnson's pending departure, by May of 1953 the new district school board had scheduled a special bond election asking voters to approve $1.6 million for additions to the high school and Washington Elementary and improvements in the rural schoolhouses. Johnson, the board, and a special citizens' advisory board made the case with the voters in a twelve-page publication, "Going Forward With Our Schools," mailed to every voter in the district. The cover featured an artist's sketch of the proposed high school

Voter information guide for the 1953 bond election

addition and a quote from progressive educator John Dewey: "What the best and wisest parents want for his own child, that must the entire community want for its children."[160] The publication opened with group photographs of Northfield's 135 kindergarten students, with the caption "Here are 135 Reasons Why We Must Build." A bar graph comparing district enrollment from 1944 and 1953 and projections for 1964 made the need graphic and clear. Floor plans of the high school and Washington additions portrayed what the bond funds would build.

Two pages of Q and A explained the funding numbers, soothed voter sticker shock, and assured citizens that every dollar being requested was needed. The $1.6 million would build the additions to the high school ($1.4 million) and Washington ($376,000) and pay for rural school improvements ($84,000). No further reductions were possible: a million in cuts had already been made by choosing to build on existing sites and removing an indoor swimming pool.

The bond request was less than half the new district's legal limit. While many other districts were bonding for the maximum allowed by law, Northfield was taking a fiscally conservative approach. Finally, the publication noted, the request was $90,000 less than the estimate from the Bureau of Field Study report. It concluded by moving beyond the financial numbers and appealing again to Northfielders' deep belief that public education is a responsibility of the entire community:

The Golden Rule

An elderly person said: "My children have all grown up, married, and gone away, but I want to do something for other children. When my children were small, others were paying taxes to help them. I will help them now."

One man said: "I have no children, but someone helped educate me, and I am going to do my share now."

A middle-aged son said: "My father gave me better opportunities and a better education than he had. I am going to give my children a better education than I had, and I will give them (and all children) all within my power and judgment that is possible."

This is progress.[161]

The voters in the newly consolidated school district, even those from rural communities, were fully on board, and on May 19, 1953, the $1.6 million bond referendum was approved by a four to one margin, 1,337 to 378. Equally remarkable was the fact that the two open board positions were filled by rural residents, A. D. Strachan of Castle Rock and Herman Johnson of Millersburg. The new consolidated school district had received a resounding vote of confidence from area residents, though the incumbent board chair, P. B. Hinds, did not. The only candidate from the city, he was soundly defeated, receiving fewer votes than any of the five candidates.

The Northfield School Board had clearly found a way to galvanize support for the funding needs of the school district, especially for facility bonds and capital campaigns. They appealed to the nearly universal belief that public education was the foundation of a healthy community and that strong public schools benefit everyone — young and old, wealthy and poor, those with children and those without children — and therefore is a community responsibility. They reassured voters that requests were reasonable, had been carefully studied (the University of Minnesota College of Education Bureau of Field Studies would conduct extensive survey studies before each of the next two Northfield capital bonding elections), and were necessary. And because public funds were being spent carefully, the community would have excellent schools at minimum cost.

Superintendent John Longstreet

The surprisingly positive election delighted John H. Longstreet, superintendent of the Windom Public Schools in southwestern Minnesota, who had been appointed in February to succeed the departing Johnson. At forty-four, Longstreet was a seasoned administrator with thirteen years of superintendent experience in Windom, LeSueur, and Caledonia, Minnesota, and nine years as a principal and superintendent for numerous North Dakota schools. The Iowa native held a BA and MA from North Dakota University. He was also an active professional schoolman, on the board of the Minnesota High School League, and a leader in Minnesota and national educational associations as well as state and national associations for school administrators. Longstreet was also a civic leader in Windom. He was a director of the Chamber of Commerce, an active Mason and Kiwanis member, leader of a Boy Scout troop, chair of the Windom Recreation Committee and the Windom March of Dimes drive, and a Sunday school teacher at the Windom Methodist Church. Longstreet had honed his skills and competencies over a twenty-year period leading a succession of small, Midwestern public school districts. In Northfield, he had found a prized small-town superintendent position. The match proved to be a good one. He served Northfield for twenty years until his retirement in 1973.

With the bond referendum approved, work began on the Washington elementary and high school additions. The Washington addition — seven classrooms and a general purpose room, a "more economical" combination gymnasium, auditorium, and lunchroom with tables that folded into the wall to allow for play space during the day — mirrored the Longfellow elementary addition and gave Northfield a new modern school plant for all its elementary students. The high school addition at the Central School building more than doubled the junior-senior facility, adding a large two-story gymnasium

Artist's rendering of the Washington school addition

WASHINGTON ELEMENTARY SCHOOL ADDITION

NORTHFIELD JUNIOR-SENIOR HIGH SCHOOL ADDITION

Dedication Exercises

Northfield Junior-Senior High School Addition

Washington Elementary School Addition

HIGH SCHOOL GYMNASIUM
SUNDAY AFTERNOON, NOVEMBER 6, 1955
2:00 O'Clock

1955 Dedication program for the new school additions

and smaller girls' gym, a dining room and kitchen, five modern science classrooms, an updated metal and woodworking shop and art wing, and twenty-one general classrooms. Northfield would be ready when the burgeoning elementary-aged classes reached the middle and high school.

This construction modernized and significantly expanded the Northfield school infrastructure. The importance of this investment in the town's schools was reflected in the dedication exercises[162] held in the new high school gymnasium on November 6, 1955. Superintendent John Longstreet presided over a program that included music from the high school orchestra and choir, welcomes from School Board President Peter Fossum and Northfield High School Principal William Carlson, and a dedication address, "You and Your Schools" from Carleton President Laurence Gould. The new buildings were presented by architect Donald Setter and accepted for the community by Fossum and students Helen Berg (high school student council president) and Martha Grout. The buildings were dedicated by F. E. Heinemann, director of teacher personnel at the Minnesota State Department of Education.

Despite the substantial additions to west-side Longfellow (1950) and east-side Washington (1955) elementary schools, continued enrollment growth required the funding and planning for a third Northfield elementary school. A November 1958 board resolution formalized the process:

> This Board has investigated the facts necessary to ascertain and does hereby find, determine, and declare that it is necessary and expedient... to borrow money by the issuance of its negotiable coupon general obligation bonds in an amount not exceeding $1,100,000, for the purpose of providing funds to build and equip a new elementary school building and remodel, add to and equip existing school buildings.[163]

Northfield voters twice, in December 1958 and again in March 1959, defeated the bond referendum, and the board again contracted with the Bureau of Field Studies to survey the district building needs. Its November 1960 summary report, "Northfield Facing The Future,"[164] again analyzed enrollment trends, assessed the condition of each school building and the district's bonding capacity, and recommended new building construction.

Enrollment growth was not the primary problem (the 1960 K–12 total of 2,400 was projected to rise slowly to 2,600 by 1970); the condition of the existing school plant was. There were five major problems with the elementary buildings: additional classrooms were needed, most of the elementary classrooms were too small (on average, 750 square feet, well below the recommended 900), the old portions of Longfellow and Washington were obsolete, the school sites were "dreadfully" small, and the older buildings were unsafe. The high school had three major issues: more classrooms were needed, opportunities to expand the building were limited, and the site was "miserably" small.

The most positive news was that the Northfield community could afford to increase its investment in school buildings, as the assessed valuation of both agricultural and non-agricultural land in the district had increased steadily since the district consolidation. The report reminded Northfield citizens that while school operational costs were supported almost equally by local taxes and state/federal funds, buildings were primarily the responsibility of local taxpayers. But the estimated bonding capacity assessment showed clearly that the Northfield School District had "ample" capacity for the future school building needs, and therefore the matter "evolves into one of deciding what level of physical facilities the district is willing to finance."[165]

The bureau recommended that the district construct a new building on another site for the junior or the senior high school (since the existing combined facility could not be expanded again), construct a new elementary school on the southeast side of the city, and expand the new Longfellow to twelve classrooms and two kindergartens, allowing the Old Washington and Old Longfellow buildings to be razed immediately. The cost of a separate junior high was estimated at $1 million. The report concluded that every dollar invested in a school expenditure was a stimulant to the local economy, and furthermore the educational benefits of an increased investment in education in Northfield "will pay dividends for generations yet unborn." That is, taxpayers' funding of public school facilities was a wise investment in the future of its children and in the health of the community. This was an argument that resonated with most Northfielders who, while cautious with the expenditure of public funds, believed in the value of excellent public schools.

Elementary School Building Projects in 1960s

Superintendent Longstreet and the school board immediately addressed the Bureau of Field Studies' recommendations that the district construct a new elementary school and a new junior or senior high building. Sibley Elementary School was constructed in 1963 on ten acres on the southeast edge of town and added two kindergarten and twelve primary (1–5) classrooms. The next University of Minnesota Bureau of Field Studies Survey (1968) was impressed with the new elementary building: "The Sibley Elementary School is an excellent facility. The ten-acre site, away from heavily-traveled areas, provides an atmosphere conducive to learning. The general classrooms, library, special classrooms, gymnasium, and special facilities all conform to present standards. The design and construction will require little or no modification of existing areas."[166] In 1964 two more classrooms were added to the 1950 Longfellow building, bringing the total number of classrooms in the near west side school to fourteen.

Northfield's Catholic School

Enrollment growth and the need for expanded facilities also faced Northfield's Catholic elementary institution, the Rosary School. Though the first parish church, St. Dominic, was dedicated in 1869, it was not until 1925 that a site was chosen for a parish school.[167] The Rosary School, run by the School Sisters of Notre Dame from Mankato, opened with an enrollment of nearly 200 students. In addition to elementary grades one through eight, the curriculum also provided, until 1942, for the first two years of high school. From its beginning, Rosary School featured a rigorous traditional program of academic and religious education and an excellent course of instruction in vocal and instrumental training, specializing in violin and piano. A diocesan boarding school that provided rooms in the convent and school for local boys and girls operated from 1928 to 1947.

By 1959 enrollment had grown to nearly 300 students, requiring a $248,000 expansion of four classrooms, office space, a teachers' lounge, library, cafeteria, and gymnasium. The addition designed by local architect William E. Broderson featured new concepts in school architecture to prevent the usual "institutional rigid look,"[168] and included a new prism-shaped design in structure and ornamentation, curved hallways, skylights, and wooded coat stalls rather than metal lockers. Although the addition modernized the private school's physical plant, the Rosary School lacked the special facilities and programs — especially shop, home economics, and science labs — that had been included in the 1954 junior-senior high school addition. Consequently, in 1978 an agreement was signed providing for shared-time classes at the Northfield Middle School for seventh and eighth grade St. Dominic School students to take these courses and integrate slowly into a public school setting they would eventually join full-time as ninth graders in the high school.

Northfield High School 1960

Life at the Northfield Junior-Senior High School in 1960 was documented in the pages of the *Raiders' Guide* and the high school yearbook, The *Norhian*. The *Raiders' Guide*,[169] though published by the student council, was clearly written by school administrators and teachers. Although High School Principal William F. Carlson writes in his "Welcome" that the information in the *Guide* was "prepared" by the student council, the content — a philosophy of education statement, faculty/staff rosters, everyday rules and procedures, descriptions of the curriculum and courses, the student council constitutions, and the school songs and yells — all read as formal official documents written, edited, and approved by administrators and advisors for the students. In this sense, it was similar to the descriptions of the high school in Heatwole's 1890 "All About Northfield" and in the *Black and Orange* student yearbooks of the 1920s. That is, it was more a description of how school administrators designed and organized the school than an expression of the actual student experience.

Principal Carlson's brief "Welcome," appearing opposite a photograph of the new 1954 west addition, was friendly yet stiffly formal: a "friendly and cordial welcome to all... We hope that you will like it here. We're very pleased to have you." The publication's purpose was to help students "become acquainted" with their school and to lift up some of the privileges and responsibilities of a "good school citizen." Carlson concluded that he was confident that all students would help continue the "traditionally good name" of the school and extended his "very best wishes for a successful and happy school life." There was little mention of learning or academic or personal growth; it was all about how to behave. That indeed described what followed in the seventy-page booklet.

The school district's "Philosophy of Education" statement revealed the extent to which the Northfield Public Schools had adopted the language (though perhaps less of the practice) of the progressive education movement, beginning with the social and civic purposes of education: "We believe that public education came into being to perpetuate the fundamental principles of democratic government." The curriculum was adapted to pupils' individual differences in interests, needs, abilities, and backgrounds. The program of education had eight objectives:[170]

> the understanding and appreciation of the rights and responsibilities of citizens in a democratic society
>
> command of the fundamentals of oral and written communication and mathematical processes
>
> skill in finding and applying facts to the solution of problems
>
> understanding and sharing of family privileges and responsibilities
>
> development of moral and spiritual values
>
> physical and mental health to meet the needs of everyday living
>
> familiarity with the resources for cultural and recreational enrichment and
>
> acquisition and development of vocational skills.

The final three paragraphs stated four more foundational beliefs of public education:

> that "sympathetic, alert, and well-trained" faculty used varied techniques to help individual students learn and develop
>
> that curricular and cocurricular work must be integrated
>
> that the "rapidly changing" society and world required continuous reexamination of the educational objectives and
>
> that the public school must work in "fullest cooperation" with the community's other educative agencies, the family, churches, and youth organizations.

The rosters of the Board of Education, the administration, and the teachers (called faculty at the high school) were dominated by men, despite education being a predominately woman's profession in twentieth-century America. Northfield's seven-person school board was chaired by businessman Orval Perman and included but one woman. Superintendent John Longstreet and High School Principal William Carlson sustained the tradition of male administrative leadership that has continued unbroken to the present. Thirty of the forty-nine junior-senior high school teachers were men, and only seven of the nineteen women were married. However, nearly all of the elementary teachers and principals were women.

The "Everyday Rules and Procedures" section opened with a description of the school day, which began at 8:30 a.m. with a five-minute home room and concluded at 3:30 p.m. with a half-hour activity or study period and was organized into seven fifty-five-minute class periods. Five ninth-year credits were required for entrance to the senior high school, and twelve credits (a full-year course was awarded one credit) were required for graduation. The "Attendance Information" section ran five pages, the *Guide* emphasizing that regular school attendance was a "very necessary and important factor in earning a good school record. Students should take the same attitude towards tardiness or absence from school as will be expected of them later in employment."[171] After quoting from Section 319 of the Minnesota School Laws that required every child between eight and sixteen years to attend school, the *Guide* detailed in twenty-seven steps the attendance policies and procedures, defined excused and unexcused absences and tardiness, and shared expectations for the movement of students. An excuse-admit-makeup report form, filled out and signed by a parent, was required for every absence. Arriving late for class was discouraged: "Tardiness is seldom excusable. Promptness is a very desirable habit to develop." Skipping was, of course, a most serious violation, for which the penalty was "as severe as we feel necessary" and might include expulsion by the Board of Education.

The 1960 Board of Education: Ralph Dilley, John Longstreet, Robert Scott, Oliver Sletten, Orval Perman, Harlan Foss, Mrs. Myron Sommers, Alvin Albers

There were rules and regulations for most school activities and locations, all designed to make school life safe and orderly and to allow students to learn and prepare to be good citizens as adults. Students were assigned a "definite seat" at assemblies, where attendance was checked and all were urged to be attentive and courteous during presentations as "we have a very good reputation for assembly conduct and we mean to keep it." Lockers were to be kept neat at all times. Movement through the corridors between classes was still regulated, though the silent passage of the late nineteenth century was no longer expected: "A good school citizen does not loiter nor run through the halls — he may engage in quiet conversation and is responsible for orderly and quiet halls. Running, loud talking, laughing or 'horse-play' is not typical of good school citizenship," the *Raiders' Guide* cautioned. Discouraging laughter seemed an odd admonition, but the restriction on running and horse-play made sense. Both shame and praise were enlisted to shape student behavior. Good citizens, students were told, did not congregate in nor vandalize their lavatories, which was "typical only of maladjusted individuals." Students were "complimented on their fine record in this respect. Let's keep it up!"

Appropriate dress and good grooming were also expected, because appearance was "so important in making friends, getting a job, and in all human relationships involved in daily living." Girls were not to wear slacks, jeans, or pedal pushers, though slacks were permitted when the temperature fell below five degrees. Boys were expected to wear a belt at all times. It was important to develop habits of cleanliness and good grooming at an early age. Clothing need not be expensive to be neat and in good taste, though conformity to accepted standards defined good taste: "unusual haircuts and clothing were not typical of good appearance." Although the school in the 1950s had promised to adapt the curriculum to pupils' individual differences in interests, needs, abilities, and backgrounds, it continued to discourage individual expression in personal appearance and dress.

Other behaviors were strictly forbidden. Racing one's car around town and the school grounds not only endangered the student and classmates, but was very poor public relations. Smoking cigarettes and drinking alcohol were not permitted and only required a single sentence in the *Guide*: "Any student found smoking or drinking an alcohol beverage while under the supervision of the school will be subject to suspension." Drug and alcohol education was more than a decade in the future; for now, these common adult behaviors were simply forbidden and taboo for students, not even topics for discussion.

Throughout the *Guide* students were encouraged and expected to be "good school citizens." The many rules and procedures were in place to help students learn and develop and to allow the school to operate effectively and safely. It was also important for each student to behave appropriately to protect his or her reputation and the reputation of the school. The rules and regulations section concluded with this Henry Van Dyke poem:

> *The Record You Leave –*
> *Our Record of You*
> Four things a man must learn to do
> If he would make his record true:
> To think without confusion clearly;
> To love his fellow man sincerely;
> To act from honest motives purely;
> To trust in God and Heaven securely.

The statement of philosophy and extensive rules section revealed the extent to which the mid-twentieth-century public school addressed the social, personal, and spiritual learning and development of its students and the emphasis given to preparing children to become good citizens and productive workers as adults. Yet the academic curriculum, which taught students how to think and provided them an understanding of themselves and their world, was the core and heart of public school education. The *Guide* claimed that the courses, or "Program of Studies," had been designed to offer each student the opportunity to "make the best of his interests and abilities," whether his postsecondary plans were for college, further vocational training, or employment. Consequently, only three English and three social studies courses (and two hours a week of physical education) were required for graduation. The remainder of the required 12 credits could be obtained through electives that suited the student's career path.

A majority of Northfield graduates were seeking further education, and the high school provided college prep courses in the academic areas of English, foreign language (four levels of French and German, three levels of Latin and Spanish), social studies, mathematics, and science (general science, biology, chemistry, physics, and aviation). Music and art courses were also available. Most academic departments offered advanced level classes for the gifted and college-bound, especially special accelerated courses in geometry, algebra, and trigonometry.

Those seeking vocational training or employment could choose courses from any of the academic areas, but especially from business education, which offered general math, typing, bookkeeping, consumer education, clerical practicum, occupational relations, and the cooperative work program, industrial arts, which offered drawing, woodworking, metals, and electronics, and home economics. The strong program in agriculture education continued as well.

The remainder of the *Guide* gave brief descriptions of the twenty-five clubs and organizations and the interscholastic sports for boys.[172] Included were organizations/clubs for art, audio-visual, camera, cheerleading, chess, French, Future Farmers, Homemakers, and Teachers of America, German, classics, junior Red Cross, annual yearbook (*Norhian*), pep, science, Spanish, thespian, and ushers. Girls could get involved in intramural sports with the Girls' Athletic Association or volunteer service activities with Kappa Gamma. Northfield was a "proud" member of the Big Nine Conference of Schools, nine public high schools in southeast Minnesota (Albert Lea, Austin, Red Wing, Faribault, Mankato, Northfield, Owatonna, Rochester, and Winona) that engaged in boys' athletic events in football, cross-country, basketball, swimming, wrestling, baseball, and track and sponsored events such as the Big Nine Student Council Convention, Music Festival, Speech Festival, Yearbook Clinic, and Play Day. The conference also sponsored idea and program exchanges which kept its member schools "among the most educationally progressive and sound in the area."

The student council was the "central" organization of students and student activities and was part of a national student council movement that provided students with "sound citizenship training" and a voice for student opinion. It also promoted good student-faculty relationships and coordinated projects and activities. Its activities included welcoming new students, the Little Brother-Sister program, fundraising drives for Community Chest, March of Dimes, Heart Fund, and Christmas Seals, the lost and found service, cafeteria supervision, National Honor Society, Maroon and Gold Day, Snow Week, and Homecoming.

The National Educational Context: 1960s

In the mid-1960s the federal government became a major player in school reform as part of President Lyndon Johnson's War on Poverty and the sweeping social programs designed to create his "Great Society." Johnson, himself a former school teacher in rural Texas, believed that education was the key to improved economic opportunity, famously noting, "Poverty has many roots, but the tap root is ignorance." Improved schooling was therefore the central weapon for fighting the War on Poverty, and with the passage of the Elementary and Secondary Education Act of 1965, Johnson declared a national goal of full educational opportunity: "Every child must be encouraged to get as much education as he has the ability to take."[173] This action was the beginning of increased federal involvement (and financial support) in state and local operation of the nation's public schools.

Within a decade, two other federal acts required local schools to guarantee civil rights and to provide equal opportunity for all of its students. Title IX of the 1972 Elementary and Secondary Education Act expanded opportunities for women and girls in schools by requiring all schools receiving federal money (which included Northfield and nearly all of the nation's schools) to provide equal resources and opportunities for women. It resulted in the establishment of high school interscholastic sports for girls. In 1972 Public Law 94-142, the Education For All Handicapped Children Act, required all schools to provide equal opportunity for students with disabilities. Handicapped children were to receive a "free appropriate public education which emphasizes special education and related services designed to meet their unique needs, to assure that the rights of handicapped children... are protected, to assist States and localities to provide for the education of all handicapped children, and to assess and assure the effectiveness of efforts to educate handicapped children." Each local district was thereby mandated to establish special education programs with only encouragement, professional guidance, and limited start-up funds from the federal government. This was the first of the unfunded or underfunded federal mandates that challenged and stretched the budgets of the states and the local school districts.

The New Northfield Senior High School

When Northfield opened its new "modern" high school in 1910, it was widely viewed as one of the finest and best-equipped school buildings in the state. Yet a steadily growing enrollment and changes in both school construction and educational programming required major additions in 1936 and 1954. But in 1960 the board expected and welcomed the recommendation of the Bureau of Field Studies' "Facing The Future" report that a new junior or senior high building was needed, noting that the existing combined facility simply could not be expanded again.

1965 architect's sketch for the new senior high school

In September 1966 the new Northfield Senior High School opened its doors to 682 ten- to twelfth-graders, on a 35-acre campus on Division Street on the south edge of town. The 174,588-square foot. facility, built at a total project cost of $2.75 million, was designed by the local architectural firm of Sovik, Mathre, and Madson.[174] The sprawling one-story building was comprised of four units: Vocational (heating plant and agricultural and industrial arts), Science (science, business education, mathematics, art, and home economics), Humanities (English, social studies, foreign languages, reading and publications), and Core Area (library, speech, AV aids, administrative offices, kitchen and cafeteria, physical education — including a gymnasium and swimming pool — and music rooms). The structure was large enough

Open house brochure for the new high school

to meet the expanding enrollment of the future — the core area was built to accommodate fifteen hundred students, and the capacity of the science, humanities, and vocational units was one thousand students, and designed to a) provide facilities that would allow flexibility in scheduling and accommodate new teaching trends and b) provide additional vocational training space.

The materials, selected on the basis of reasonable cost and minimum maintenance, created a durable fire-safe brick, concrete, and steel structure that carried minimum insurance rates, which undoubtedly pleased the frugal, value-focused Northfield taxpayers. The building also enhanced the learning environment. Each classroom was equipped with darkening shades, adjustable green chalkboards, and ample book storage. The library and AV area was centrally located to function efficiently as the instructional materials center. Folding walls between classrooms and laboratory centers allowed for flexible scheduling and team-teaching. Closed-circuit television and a public address communication system connected all classrooms. The high school was poised to utilize the new technologies in teaching and learning. Indeed, the

planning, construction, lighting, heating, ventilation, and sanitary facilities had "all been conceived in a manner which provided a physical plant conducive to good teaching."[175]

Northfield was justifiably proud of its new high school building. Though it would expand in future decades, with an M (math) wing, small auditorium, and the district offices, the basic 1966 building would serve Northfield High School students long into the twenty-first century.

Continually Looking to the Future

By the late 1960s, Superintendent Longstreet and the Board of Education had carefully and incrementally built the school plant and educational program needed to create a modern school system, Northfield Independent School District #659. Three new buildings were constructed and the other four facilities received additions or renovations. The educational program and teaching staff were expanded and strengthened.

Yet the school board, determined to provide the district's children the "finest educational opportunity possible," realized this lofty goal required impartial study, continuous assessment, and careful planning. Once again, Northfield contracted with the University of Minnesota Bureau of Field Studies to evaluate the school district and "formulate recommendations as to future growth and development." In December 1968 the bureau's subsequent summary report, "Planning Quality Education for the Northfield Public Schools"[176] was provided to the school board and residents of Northfield ISD #659. The report, like its two predecessors, included evaluations of the district's school plant and educational program, population/enrollment trends, financial status, and recommendations concerning future needs.

The district had responded to the postwar enrollment growth of the Baby Boomer generation by constructing new and renovating old buildings. Much had been accomplished with the district's seven school buildings. Elementary students from the former rural districts and the city of Northfield gathered in classrooms in five buildings: the updated and improved schools in Dundas (four classrooms and three other instructional areas) and Castle Rock (three and three), the new Longfellow School and addition (fourteen and three), the new Sibley School (twelve and four), and the new addition to the Washington School (fifteen and five). The new senior high school had fourteen classrooms and forty other instructional areas. The junior high now used the thirty-one classrooms and twenty-one other instructional areas of the 1910 (with additions in 1936 and 1954) junior-senior high school building.

The facilities in the five elementary schools ranged from outstanding in the newer buildings to marginal in the older sections of the Longfellow and Washington buildings and the village schools in Dundas and Castle Rock. All of the five kindergarten classrooms were of recent construction and thereby "excellent in terms of size, equipment and furnishings." However, classrooms in the older original section of Washington were smaller than desirable and with the wood construction "extremely susceptible to fire." Also, the special classrooms and offices in the basements of the older sections of Washington and Longfellow were small and evidence of the "congestion existing in the elementary schools." The schools at Castle Rock and Dundas were too small for efficient operation and were dangerously combustible.

The junior high facility was crowded, especially the small general classrooms located in the old 1910 section. But the new high school building received generous praise as an "outstanding" building, most notably for the movable walls, large general classrooms, and the excellent space for special departments like agriculture, industrial arts, art, music, physical education, and science. The library was spacious and audio-visual education well equipped. Indeed, the entire building, its location, and the adequacy of the site were a "credit" to the Northfield School District.

The board requested advice regarding four educational program issues under consideration: an innovative non-graded organization for elementary school instruction; a middle school organization concept in place of a junior high; flexible scheduling for the high school; and an expansion of the size of the professional staff. The bureau encouraged schools to continuously evaluate and update its facilities and educational program, noting that educational change was required in the rapidly changing world. The knowledge explosion, advances in the study of human development and the psychology of learning, and the increased impact of media demanded new approaches to the education of American children.

However, the bureau cautioned against moving to the non-graded organization,[177] in which a student could advance to the next "grade" level on the basis of performance rather than age and a set period of time. It pointed to research that indicated activities and the quality of instruction had a greater effect on learning than a particular scheme of organization. This approach may have been suggested by more progressive teachers who resisted the tendency to "teach to the middle," easy to do in large public school classrooms. The idea seems to have ended there, though it was later revived for experiments with multiple grade classes at Greenvale in the 1980s. Similarly, the bureau did not recommend immediately adopting the middle school concept of grades six, seven, and eight, as it would require an expansion of the secondary school building, though the change was made in the 1970s.

The bureau was more positive about flexible scheduling,[178] a growing trend in American high schools in the 1960s that allowed students more choice with how they allocated class time. Flexible schedule practices utilized modules of time, team teaching, varying sized instructional groups, and independent study. Northfield was encouraged to develop its own program ("don't purchase a packaged schedule program") of flexible scheduling, though not without a substantial amount of study and discussion, general faculty acceptance, and extensive preparation with students and parents. Northfield followed the advice and slowly developed more flexible schedule options for high school students.

Northfield's staffing levels, when compared to a national study, showed a below average pupil-to-administrator ratio, but an above average pupil-teacher ratio. Within the Big Nine Conference, Northfield had the lowest pupil-teacher and pupil-administrator ratios. Compared to schools in the Educational Research Council of the Twin Cities Metro Area, Northfield was at or above the ninetieth percentile in terms of classroom teachers per one thousand pupil units.[179] These numbers must have pleased Northfield citizens, who sought educational excellence and value from their school tax dollars and were more willing to pay for classroom teachers than administrators.

Analysis of the district's population and enrollment trends revealed a steady though modest growth in the city of Northfield, but a decline in the rural townships, due in part to the continued mechanization of agriculture and the growing size of local farms. Socio-economic trends indicated opposing forces at work: while the number of live-births in the area was declining, enrollments were steadily increasing due to increased in-migration; the Northfield School District appeared to be "changing from an agricultural and college-town economy to a more non-agricultural and commuter community on the outer fringe of the Twin Cities metropolitan area."[180] This was a trend that would continue for the next fifty years. The projected enrollment data suggested to the bureau that additional plant facilities were needed, and it concluded that the "most economical plan" for the district would be to construct eighteen additional elementary school classrooms, utilize the present junior high school for grades seven through nine, and use the present senior high for grades ten through twelve. Construction of additional elementary facilities would enable the district to provide more effective and efficient educational opportunities for pupils currently attending the small older Castle Rock and Dundas elementary schools.

These findings led the bureau to offer eight recommendations that would "improve educational opportunity and provide facilities adequate to house the projected enrollment" all within the financial capacity of the district.[181] The recommendations included:

- construct as soon as possible a new thirteen-classroom elementary school on a fifteen-acre site in the northwestern portion of the city;
- add six classrooms to Sibley Elementary School;
- discontinue the use of the elementary schools in Dundas and Castle Rock;
- raze the older portion of Washington Elementary School;
- proceed with a change to the non-grade organization of the elementary schools only if convinced it advances teaching approaches and learning outcomes;
- and move to a in-house, tailor-made flexible modular schedule at the high school only after extensive study.

The district would act on each of these recommendations over the next decade. The new elementary school, Greenvale Park, would offer a modified open-classroom design and curriculum to students beginning in the fall of 1971. After the addition of the nineteen elementary classrooms at Greenvale and Sibley, the Dundas and Castle Rock Schools were closed. The innovative non-grade organization scheme was discarded, though later implemented in part at Greenvale. And a flexible modular schedule evolved at the high school in the 1970s and 1980s.

Greenvale Park Elementary School under construction, 1970

Chapter Five

The Modern Northfield Public Schools (1970–1990)

In the decades of the 1970s and 1980s Northfield continued to build and strengthen the community with new economic development, preservation of the historic downtown, restoration of the riverfront, and expansion of social services. New industries, including Northfield Freezing Systems (1970), Fairway Foods (1975), and Cardinal IG (1986) bolstered the tax base, while the growth of the two colleges stabilized the local economy and added to its prosperity. An environmental women's group, Households Alert, purchased and deeded five acres of marshland adjacent to Sibley Elementary School for use as a nature study area. Northfield's historic commitment to its residents' quality of life was manifest in expanded facilities for both the Northfield Arts Guild, moving in 1979 into the former YMCA and City Hall Building on Division, and the Northfield Public Library, which tripled the size of the 1910 Carnegie building with a 1985 expansion and renovation. The Northfield Public School's physical plant expanded with the construction of Greenvale Elementary School in 1970.

Yet the overall economic prosperity and growth in the 1970s and 1980s, unlike the 1960s, was uneven, with periods of significant recession and inflation, which would produce dramatic fluctuations in state educational aid and throw the school district finances onto a funding roller coaster.

National Educational Context 1970–1990

With the federal Title IX gender equity (1972) and Students with Disability (1975) acts the Northfield district needed to add costly programs at the same time that growing enrollments required expanding facilities and the teaching staff. Fortunately, as long as enrollments grew and the local economy was strong, the growing tax base was sufficient to support a balanced school budget.

For most of the nation's schools, including Northfield, the thirty-year postwar period of sustained population and enrollment growth provided adequate funding for the new and expanded facilities, additional staff, and the new federally-mandated programs. But by the late 1970s the Baby Boomer generation had graduated and the public schools were faced with falling enrollments, reduced state support (which was based on enrollment), and a shrinking tax base. The challenge for the public schools in the '70s and '80s was to maintain the quality of education for all students, while devoting increased resources to disabled, poor, and immigrant children. When financial support diminished, schools were in the difficult, sometimes untenable position, of being expected to do more with less.

The national economic recession in the early 1980s took a toll on the nation's schools and led the National Commission on Excellence in Education to conclude that the United States had become a "nation at risk," meaning the "educational foundations of our society are presently being eroded by a rising tide of mediocrity that threatens our very future as a Nation and a people."[182] Citing evidence that American student achievement was declining, the commission drew the sobering conclusion that for the first time in the history of the country the "educational skills of one generation will not surpass, will not equal, will not even approach, those of their parents." The report called for the nation to commit itself to the "twin goals of equity and high-quality schooling," and to becoming a Learning Society, "where formal schooling in youth is the essential foundation for learning throughout one's life."[183]

The commission's' primary recommendations set the national educational agenda for the decade of the 1980s and included:

> strengthening state and high school graduation requirements;
>
> adopting more rigorous, measurable standards, and higher expectations for academic performance and student conduct;

1970 Board of Education; L–R: Dr. R. Geistfeld, B. Reese, G. Ness, Pres. G. Paulson, L. Stadstad, Dr. D. Dodson, Mrs. Stanley Miller

devoting significantly more time "to learning the New Basics
... requiring more effective use of the existing school day,
a longer school day, or a lengthened school year";

and improving teacher preparation and making teaching a
"more rewarding and respected profession."[184]

Northfield in the 1970s

Throughout the twentieth century the seven-member school board usually had one or two women representing the perspective of the community's mothers. The majority of the board, however, continued to be comprised of businessmen and male professionals, often doctors or faculty from one of the colleges. In May of 1970 the *Northfield News* reported that only two candidates had filed for the two openings on the board of education, though each represented a key constituency. George Paulson, a progressive Forest Township farmer, had served the board for six years, the last four as chair. Paulson, the *News* article[185] noted, was a "native of the community who had married a Northfield girl" and sent three children through the district's schools. He represented the many surrounding rural farming townships that had joined the district after the 1948 consolidation. Louise Wright, mother of seven children, six currently attending Northfield Public Schools, had not previously held public office, but she had extensive community service experience with the Girl Scouts, the Congregational Church, and the schools — as president of the PTA and Parents Council and a volunteer teacher's aide.

The 1970 *Northfield News* "Back to School and College" supplement[186] announced the beginning of another academic year in a town where education had long been the "major industry," noting that nearly four thousand young people were coming to Carleton and St. Olaf and a "high percentage of the permanent population enrolled in schools here." It was the familiar annual community ritual in which Northfield families, educators, business and professional people all geared up for that "sudden burst of activity, the opening of schools." There was one difference this year — for the first time the public schools and St. Dominic's opened *before* Labor Day. Until 1970, despite perennial calls for lengthening the school year, Minnesota's powerful agriculture and vacation/resort lobby had delayed school opening until after Labor Day.

Articles in the supplement provided the usual logistical information — bus schedules and routes, class schedules, and registration — and advice to parents. One titled "Students Want, Parents Provide Quiet Study Corner: Homework Center Requires Right Light, Work, Storage Space" suggested that providing a study area was the "best contribution" parents could make toward their student's successful school work. Another cautioned: "Don't Drive Child to School — Teach Him to Walk." Although driving their children to school had become, for many parents, as traditional as teaching proper tooth brushing, the American Automobile Association, sponsor of school safety patrols nationwide, recommended that parents teach and expect their students to walk. Not only was walking better for their health, but it reduced potentially dangerous traffic congestion around school buildings. It is unlikely, however, that the AAA's admonition had much effect on student transportation to school. Most Northfield children continued to ride the bus to school, though some parents, as demonstrated by the long drop-off and pick-up lines at the schools, continued to drive their children to school.

By 1970 new learning technologies were appearing in the nation's schools, and the *News* presented photos and text from an *NEA Journal* article, "See How We Learn" that "held up a mirror to modern schooling" showing how modern technologies — projectors, earphones, teaching machines, and TV cameras — "reshaped the substance and meaning of reality" and brought new strategies into the curriculum and the classroom. While these new technologies were now a "part of life and learning," the NEA cautioned that learning remained an individual human activity involving the excitement of discovery, and the "machine can only be interpreted in terms of human purpose and human consequence, a tool for the teacher to enhance learning," the article said. These new technologies, while a significant departure from a century of books and chalk boards, brought only modest change to the classroom; it would take the personal computer and the Internet of the 1990s and 2000s to genuinely transform learning and the classroom.

The most important article in the newspaper supplement described the innovative building design and curriculum for the new Greenvale Park Elementary School. The school district had decided to use the new elementary school to experiment with the late '60s "open classroom" movement, a return to the less formal, child-centered approach of the progressive classroom earlier in the century. The open classroom created a learning environment that responded to the needs and interests of individual students, subjects were merged into interdisciplinary student-directed projects, flexible schedules replaced structured class periods, and student groupings were based more on the needs and interests of the children than age, I.Q., or reading level. Teachers served in a supportive rather than a didactic role, guiding the children as a sensitive observer and active participant in the life of the classroom.[187] Students were allowed relatively free movement in the class space, and tables and desks were clustered for varied group instruction.

To support the open classroom concept, the new Greenvale facility was designed with large "pods" with movable folding dividers to create flexible learning areas. Within each pod was a teacher station for two to four teachers, allowing team teaching. This was a radical departure from the traditional one-teacher/twenty-five student classroom. The pods were clustered around a media center with a multi-level reading nook, separated by five-foot walls. The carpeted corridors surrounding the pods contained cloak areas, and pods were entered through portals without doors. While the *News* article called the new building a "cozy type of place," it also had parents asking, "Will my children be guinea pigs in this educational experiment?"

To support the increased individualized instruction, the district established "differentiated staffing" for Greenvale, assigning paraprofessional (unlicensed) teacher's aides to each pod. While this proved to be quite effective, it became a point of contention with the teachers' union, which feared that "differentiated staffing" might be used to eliminate teacher positions during budget crunches. Indeed, the teachers argued that the best individualized instruction came from certified teachers.

The postwar period of steady growth and expansion of population, enrollment, facilities, and staffing ended in the mid-1970s. The effects of nearly thirty years of a growing economy and tax base and school district consolidation were clear: Northfield's historically strong schools had expanded and strengthened and sustained its reputation as one of the best school districts in outstate Minnesota. The elementary facilities were modern and first-rate, with the construction of two new buildings, Sibley (1952) and Greenvale (1970), the new additions and renovations to Washington and Longfellow, and the closing of the inadequate small rural schoolhouses in Dundas and Castle Rock. The secondary-level buildings were equally impressive, with the new sprawling high school facility that opened south of the downtown in 1966 and the old 1910 junior/senior high facility that was expanded (1954) and renovated numerous times.

Yet by 1975 the last of the Baby Boomer generation had completed its school years, and the nation's population growth was slowing down. Enrollments for the Northfield district, and throughout the state and nation, were predicted to decline for the next decade. In the spring of 1977 the Minnesota State Legislature, concerned about an impending crisis in public school financing, seriously considered mandating further school consolidation along county lines before passing the School Planning Law, which required each district to develop a plan for "efficient and effective delivery of educational programs and services through 1983."[188] The Northfield Educational Planning Task Force, comprised of faculty, students, administrators, and community members as required by the new law, assessed and reviewed the district's organization, educational goals and programs, services and staffing, facilities, and transportation. Their summary report provided a snapshot of the district's schools in 1978.

The task force report proposed an educational philosophy for the district schools, a statement of purpose and mission that would provide the foundation for goals and objectives. The district schools were committed to meeting the educational needs of the community, assisting individual students to "develop the learning skills needed for a responsible and meaningful life," and facilitating self-development so that each person "may experience success." American reverence for the individual and his or her learning and development was the primary purpose of its public schools. Yet equally important were the social and civic purposes of public education. The school was a community where all members learned and lived together, and where students, parents, staff, and members of the board of education must "learn to treat one another with dignity" so that students would develop physically, emotionally, intellectually, socially, and morally. All members of this educational community "must realize and practice their rights and responsibilities in order to become contributing members in a democratic society."[189]

This Statement of Philosophy, reflecting Northfielders' belief in progressive liberal education principles, continued: "Learning is a lifelong process. Knowledge is essential. Equally important is the development of skills, values, and attitudes." The statement concluded with the acknowledgment that in our "continuously changing, interdependent, global society" schools, along with the family and other educational institutions, must "work together to prepare the individual for life."

To put that educational philosophy into action, the board adopted twelve School District Goals for 1977–1978.[190] Students, it said, must develop academic skills in mathematics and computation and develop communication skills in listening, observation and perception (nonverbal), reading, speaking, and writing. Students must appreciate and experience the arts through dance, drama, music, and the visual arts. More broadly, students needed to develop the "desire and skills necessary for continued learning," as well as creativity, initiative, and imagination. In the area of personal development, students needed to develop an awareness of personal values and skills in moral reasoning, wise and enjoyable leisure time activities, and practice the skills necessary for successful and responsible family living. They must participate in cocurricular elective activities (music, interest clubs, speech/debate/drama) for self-fulfillment and enrichment. From all of their educational experiences, students should practice positive personal coping behavior to solve problems and make decisions and develop a sense of self-worth and pride in their accomplishments. Finally, students should practice citizenship in a democracy.

Though the existing educational program had evolved without the benefits of much assessment or long-range planning, it was seemingly effective. All schools were meeting or exceeding the state Minimum School Standards in the required subjects of art, health, language arts, math, music, physical education, reading, science, social studies, home economics, and industrial arts. Staffing levels also met state standards. The district had 217 full-time licensed teaching staff; the student/staff ratio was 20:1 in the elementary grades, 17:5 in the junior high and 18:1 in the senior high. The present program, the report concluded, "though not perfect is highly effective in educating the children of our district." Yet if forecast budget deficits were to be addressed and eliminated, it would undoubtedly have a negative effect on the quality of programs. In that case, adjustments should be made in areas having the least impact.

The finances section addressed the financial ramifications of the predicted decline in enrollment. Historically the financial status of the Northfield School District, unlike many other Minnesota districts, had been healthy, able to afford excellent facilities and operate annually with balanced budgets. But declining enrollment had forced major operating cuts in the 1977–1978 budget, which included closing Washington School and reducing staff and programs. The study's assessment of the district's financial future was sobering. If current declining enrollments and inflation continued, the general operating fund would incur significantly larger annual budget deficits to maintain present staff and program levels. Deficits were estimated at $185,000 for 1979–80, rising to $379,000, $608,000 and $825,000 over the following three years. The conclusion seemed obvious: some reduction in staffing and program would be required, but effort should be made to make cuts and find savings that would least impact the quality of the educational program. Over the next five years the district administration and board went through the difficult process of reducing or eliminating staff positions and reducing program budgets.

Northfield in the 1980s

By the winter of 1980, after two years of painful budget cuts, Superintendent Jack Geckler and the school board were again facing falling enrollment, rising inflation, and the specter of more staff and program cuts. Attempts to increase revenue, including raising fees for driver's education courses, admission to athletic events, and the summer music program, helped, but more was needed. In May an extra "discretionary" levy referendum asked the voters to approve a 5.5 mill, four-year increase in property taxes levied for the school district. The Citizens Committee on the Referendum placed a series of articles in the *Northfield News*[191] explaining that the

Superintendent Jack Geckler

extra levy was needed to maintain the quality of the school program during this period of falling enrollment and rising inflation. Despite making large cuts in spending, including closing one elementary school, reducing clerical and custodial staff, cutting supply budgets, and eliminating thirteen teaching positions, the district still faced "major financial difficulties." All the members of the School Board and the Citizen Committee agreed that the levy referendum was needed to preserve the "quality of education" in Northfield for the next four years. The extra funds would be used to "maintain the quality of education at all levels" by limiting budget reductions and improving district programs in writing, mathematics, and staff evaluation and development.

There was deep skepticism and resistance, especially from area farmers and merchants who were struggling in the high-inflation economic recession. Rural voters had historically opposed referendums that would increase school taxes, most notably in 1958 when 77.5 percent of the rural voters negated a $1.1 million bond issue for new and expanded schools. The Citizens Committee addressed the skeptical voters' most basic questions. If enrollment was declining, why were costs rising? The answer: sustained double digit inflation; some costs (like utilities) are fixed and could not be reduced; state support, though based on enrollment, declined more rapidly than enrollment; and recent staff cuts had eliminated the least senior (and lower salaried) positions, so savings were always less than lost revenue. Are teachers' salaries too high? Absolutely not. Northfield teachers' salaries were in the bottom quartile statewide, and "near the bottom" among schools in the Missota Conference. But most importantly, if the referendum failed, the Citizen's Committee argued, there would be substantial reductions in basic educational programs, and class size would increase, reducing teachers' ability to assist all pupils, whether educationally handicapped, average, or gifted. In addition, at the elementary level, programs in music, art, physical education, and library services would be reduced or eliminated, while at the secondary level athletic and other extracurricular programs would face reductions.

The *Northfield News* editorial headlined "Without levy, mortal cuts" was unequivocal in its support for the levy, writing that although an increase in taxation was never popular, there were times when increases were "very necessary, and we think this is one of them."[192] Witnessing two years of budget cuts and watching bits of programs "snipped" and whole programs "slashed" left the editors "greatly saddened" by what was happening to education in Northfield: "Sometimes we feel the very heart is gone out of the Northfield program — that everything that has lifted it above the mediocre is threatened. Is this what we want for our young people?" But the editors shifted from this emotional appeal to a modest rational argument that would be better received by fiscally cautious Northfielders. The increased levy was not a "bonanza," but merely a way to stop the "chipping away" at the basic essentials in a public school education. Furthermore, the amount of tax increase for each taxpayer was "not really large." Indeed, "There are few of us that would not manage to save that amount of money for a very good cause." Although school leaders and referendum advocates were cautiously confident that support from the two city precincts would be sufficient for passage, they worried that rural resistance might bring defeat.

That worry proved unnecessary. Northfield voters overwhelmingly approved the $5.5 million district levy increase by an almost two to one margin, 1,344 to 729. District officials interpreted the decisive margin as a vote of confidence, and Board Chairman Cliff Clark told the *News* that the levy vote represented a "continuing citizen commitment to quality education in Northfield."[193]

Board Chair Cliff Clark

As expected, most rural precincts voted against the levy increase, but by smaller margins than some levy supporters feared. Support was overwhelming in the two city precincts. Board member Jane McWilliams in "Readers Forum" thanked the *News* for their excellent coverage of the levy referendum, attributing the success of the referendum in large part to the background information and excellent reporting provided by the *News*. The dedicated and hard-working Citizens Referendum Committee was congratulated for helping educate the community with telephone surveys, public meetings, and informational brochures. But McWilliams gave special praise and credit for the referendum success to the voters, citing the large turnout and margin of passage as a "vote of confidence in our school system, and assures those who work with and for our children that Northfielders believe what they are doing is worth digging deeper into their pockets to support... Approval of the tax levy increase will allow us to maintain our present quality, strengthen programs, and improve the quality of teaching."[194] This process of informing and enlisting the support of voters was repeated regularly in Northfield (see chart of levy and bond referendums, 1950–2010) throughout the twentieth century and confirmed the confidence that its frugal citizens had in the city's public schools.

Jane McWilliams

At the May 20, 1980, special election, voters also selected two school board directors in a closely contested horse race among Control Data manager Noel Stratmoen and rural farmers Harold Paulson and Phil Parsons. Paulson and Parsons, as expected, swept the five rural precincts, but Stratmoen won both city precincts to win a seat along with Paulson in the remarkably close finish: Stratmoen, 1,319; Paulson, 1,318; and Parsons, 1,254. Stratmoen's victory marked the beginning of the longest tenure in board history. Stratmoen has served, uninterrupted, from 1980 to the present.

Elation over the successful levy referendum was short-lived, however: an unexpected state budget deficit led to a $314,000 cut in state aid (more than half of the district's income), which left the district with a $320,000 deficit for the 1980–1981 year. After three years of budget-cutting and salaries (the district's largest expense) fixed by contracts, there were few places to find additional savings, and the board reluctantly agreed to live with the deficit. The additional $330,000 for the next year generated by the successful levy helped, but further reductions in programs and personnel were necessary for the following three years until the enrollment decline finally bottomed out. A new financial reality now faced local school districts: sudden drops in state aid could quickly throw the local budget into the red. The only short-term remedy was to build general fund surpluses to absorb last-minute state cuts. The exercise of designating reductions in programs and positions was a necessary response to inflation and fluctuating state aid support throughout the 1980s and 1990s.

In 1982 Northfield area voters again overwhelmingly (three-fourths voting yes) passed an excess levy referendum extending the additional $8.5 million levy for four more years, 1985–1989, providing more than $600,000 additional income each year. A week earlier a *Northfield News* editorial, "Continuing school levies is essential," had urged Northfielders to support the levy: "A community's public schools surely mirror the interests of the community. Therefore, one would expect Northfield's schools to be strong and adequately supported." The editors reminded its readers of Northfield's historical educational heritage: "If you think we say this simply because two of the nation's best small colleges are located here, you would be wrong. Certainly, those schools and the erudite faculties and staffs they bring to our city should and do have an effect on the type of education available in our public schools. But the rest of the Northfield district is peopled with solid citizens who do care what happens to their young people. The Northfield community has always placed a high priority on good education."[195] The fiscally conservative citizens of Northfield, once again, demonstrated their commitment to excellent education for their children.

Although school finances were the primary issue in 1980, other changes were happening in the district. The board, to improve communication, added an advisory student representative position, but then disbanded the Educational Planning Task Force, a group of citizens who had provided recommendations for budget cuts. The board revised the district policy on student discipline by banning corporal punishment, though allowing teachers and administrators to use "physical means to restrain a pupil from harming himself or others." At the high school, Principal Bill Gasho recommended scrapping the ten-year-old flexible modular schedule for the more rigid traditional eight-period, fifty-minute class, claiming that it would provide more student accountability and reduce the opportunity for truancy, vandalism, and class disruption. Despite strong resistance from students, the change was made.

1980 also marked the beginning of a program for gifted and talented students, a recognition that American public education (unlike Europe's) tended to teach to the middle as it educated the masses. A group of more than forty parents and teachers urged the Northfield School Board to adopt a resolution to "recognize the plight" of gifted students in the district, and a *Northfield News* editorial agreed: "It is high time that something be done for those who excel as well as those who fall behind."[196] Other parents cautioned that accelerating or tracking gifted students could stigmatize those left behind and preferred that efforts were directed at raising standards and challenging all students. But in November the board formally made developing guidelines for a gifted and talented program and strengthening teacher development as the district's top priorities. Over the next decade the junior and senior high school added accelerated and advanced courses, and in the 1990s Advanced Placement (AP) classes were established. It is not surprising that the Northfield schools, with a history of high college attendance rates, would develop programs for its gifted students.

The State Legislature had responded to the 1983 federal *A Nation at Risk* report with an Omnibus Education Act, which required each school district to create an annual Planning, Evaluating, Reporting (PER) report that summarized district administrative and curricular goals and student performance. The district educational philosophy had changed little from the 1977 statement: the public schools existed to ensure all students developed the learning skills "needed for a responsible and meaningful life."[197] The report was compiled by district teachers, administrators, and community representatives working with district committees in mathematics, science, computer literacy, language arts, testing (evaluation), and staff development. It listed the management priorities in each curricular area. The general administrative goals were five-fold: to conduct a comprehensive facilities and grade organization study; complete the study and determine the functions and structure of the administrative staff; develop a long-range comprehensive plan; establish a district supervision program; and seek external funding in high priority areas, including development of partnerships, foundations, and entrepreneurships. Northfield had discovered, along with districts throughout the state and nation, that the public schools needed to expand financial support beyond annual tax levies.

The centerpiece of the supervision program was the creation of a structured comprehensive teacher evaluation and development process designed to improve classroom instruction. Rather than depend on outside assistance, the district created an internal staff development program[198] centered on a network of effective leaders — teachers, principals, and central office staff. The network established a staff decision-making and communication system, criteria and procedures for staff evaluation, a team of evaluators, and procedures to develop and implement growth targets based on the criteria and assessed performance. It also enhanced teachers' skills to facilitate learning and improve instruction and added a "teacher advisor" position in each district building. The model used a five-step staff development cycle — preview, assessment, growth target development, growth target implementation, and evaluation and follow-up — to help teachers improve their teaching and their students' learning. Talented, dedicated, effective teachers were essential for a strong school system; the board and district administration recognized that their teachers were their most important resource.

The evaluation program consisted of the required Comprehensive Test of Basic Skills (CTBS), a series of norm-referenced, objectives-based tests designed to measure individual student achievement in academic basic skills (reading, spelling, language, mathematics, reference, science, and social studies). It was administered across the nation to all students in grades four and eight, along with voluntary aptitude college entrance exams (ACT and SAT) for seniors. The results of the CTBS standardized tests showed that Northfield students ranked above the national average in every subject. The Northfield scores on the ACT and SAT for the previous five years were "consistently higher" than the national average and compared "favorably" with Minnesota and Midwestern mean scores.

The reporting section of the PER report summarized the extensive communication and public relations efforts of the district, so critical in sustaining the confidence and support from local tax-paying residents. "Insights," a district newsletter, was published and distributed to community members through the local newspaper, and "Ask Your Superintendent," a ten-minute radio spot on KYMN, aired twice a month. Each building principal sent regular newsletters to students' families and held at least one open house annually. Parent-teacher conferences for each student were scheduled twice a year. Northfield Board of Education meetings, held on the second and fourth Mondays of each month, were open to the public, and a meeting summary was published in the *Northfield News*. The local media — the newspaper and radio station — were the primary vehicles for communicating with the public, with announcements and articles in virtually every issue. With the annual PER report and the extensive media coverage, the Northfield School Public Schools operated with considerable transparency and accountability.

After 1985 the state-mandated PER process and report shaped the way local districts implemented and assessed the public school curriculum. A ten-point checklist[199] from the Minnesota Department of Education summarized the requirements of the PER legislation. Each local board adopted a PER policy which included district goals, learner outcomes, including the "essential" learner outcomes developed by the state, a process of student and program evaluation, and a description of the curriculum review cycle. A PER Committee, two-thirds parents and citizens, was appointed to represent the community in the PER process. Each district was required to have a curriculum review cycle. For Northfield and many Minnesota districts this meant adapting the North Central Accreditation curriculum review cycle used in their accreditation process. Each local board was required to adopt a set of district curricular goals. With these four structures — a PER policy, a PER Committee, a curriculum review cycle, and curriculum goals — each district was mandated to document in their PER Report learner outcomes, testing results, district improvement plans, an assurance of mastery plan, and an evaluation of the district testing program.

In 1985 the board adopted a set of long range goals[200] to be realized by the end of the decade. Responding to the *A Nation at Risk* recommendations and the rapidly changing digital world, the future curriculum would teach higher order thinking skills to enable students to move "beyond memorization" to problem solving and comprehension. Northfield Public Schools promised to create a "diverse instructional delivery system" to meet the learning needs of individual students and to offer an expanded curriculum "appropriate to an information-oriented and global society" through foreign languages, technology, and the arts. By 1989 the Northfield Public Schools would have adequate, efficient, accessible, well-maintained facilities. To strengthen the district teaching program (the logo on the PER brochure read "Effective Teaching Promotes Learning), an individualized staff assessment and development program was established. The district was committed to providing "maximum opportunities for parents to become directly involved in the education of their children." Other long-range goals addressed other community stakeholders: finding opportunities for "persons in the educational community to acquire a vision and understanding" of their responsibility for student learning; a plan to increase community participation and support in budget decisions; and an expansion of Northfield Community Education and Recreation programs.

Some of the long-range goals were a response to the 1983 opening of the Prairie Creek Community School. The parent founders were dismayed at the large class size (many over the recommended twenty-five pupil limit) in the public school primary grades and believed that true individualized learning required classes of no more than fifteen. The new progressive school also emphasized foreign language, the arts, and interdisciplinary studies in an open informal classroom. Superintendent Dwight Lindbloom understood and appreciated the motivations of the Prairie Creek founding parents, acknowledging that when parents establish their own schools they are not only looking for more control and influence over the school, but looking for "a different instructional pattern, a different relationship between teachers and children than that found in the public school." Alternative schools were also formed around "a particular set of values" and "because of this control and reflection of personal values, parents have a greater commitment to assisting the growth of the institution... They are

Superintendent Dwight Lindbloom

committed to it because they put their efforts into it." Lindbloom appeared to genuinely welcome the new school, recognized possible benefits for the public schools, and concluded, "What I look at in a new school in Northfield is, 'What can we learn here?'"

When Lindbloom resigned in the spring of 1985 to take a position with the Minnesota Department of Education, the board selected New Ulm native Stan Mack to lead the district. The thirty-five-year-old Mack brought nine years of experience as a teacher and director of special services in South St. Paul and as a superintendent of the Eveleth Public Schools. Mack's top priority was to improve the district's public relations and encourage parent participation, though he understood that his immediate challenges would be to implement the reorganization of the elementary schools (from neighborhood to grade-centered) and to address the annual budget deficits. Yet Mack expressed confidence that Northfielders would continue to support its public schools, noting the district's glowing reputation made it a model for other small town school systems throughout Minnesota.

Prairie Creek Community School

Superintendent Stan Mack

Unfortunately, Mack's tenure as superintendent was brief and difficult. Despite declaring improved public relations as his top priority, Mack was less visible than his predecessor and less successful at building relationships with the press, other Northfield organizations, the business community, or the public. Efforts to address a growing deferred maintenance problem, especially in the middle school, were emblematic of Mack's struggle. In the summer of 1985 local Architect Steve Edwins of SMSQ estimated the cost for all improvements needed in the district's physical plant at $25 million. After a year of study and review, Mack reduced the building improvements bond request to $12 million, which was resoundingly defeated — 3,393 NO to 740 YES — in a winter 1987 referendum election. It was by far the district's worst electoral defeat. Finally, in the spring of 1988, a modest $5.5 million facility improvement bond was approved. Three months later Mack submitted his resignation.

Despite this embarrassing referendum defeat, under Mack's leadership the Northfield Public Schools continued to provide students with high quality education. This was confirmed in the 1986–1987 Annual Report,[201] the initial planning, evaluating, reporting (PER) publication required by the state Omnibus Education Act. The report described a new district plan to ensure that each student master basic communication (reading) and mathematics skills: students were evaluated with the California Achievement Test (CAT) in grades 3, 5, 8, and 10, and each student scoring below the 25th national percentile took a diagnostic test and with their teacher developed a plan to strengthen their performance. Results from the 1985–1986 CAT, summarized in charts and graphs, showed that Northfield students consistently scored well above other students in the same grades in Minnesota and nationally.

The CAT results also indicated that Northfield students had a "high mastery" of most classroom objectives.

The decade of the 1980s was the district's most troubled since the Great Depression. Declining enrollments, double digit inflation, and significant cuts in state aid resulted in years of budget deficits and staff and program cuts. Staff morale suffered, and administrative turnover was rapid, especially at the top with superintendent resignations in 1983, 1985, and 1988. It was a decade when the public schools were expected to do more (expand special education and gifted programs and address gender equity with new girls' athletic programs) for more students with less funding. And much was accomplished: new special education programs, expanded athletic programs and cocurricular activities, new school safety and security efforts, and new technologies in the classroom. Yet the Northfield Public Schools, though by many measures as strong and successful as ever, struggled to satisfy the demands and expectations of the federal and state governments and local citizens to educate its children and solve societal social problems. It was an environment that would challenge the next superintendent.

James-Youger Gang reenactors visit Bridgewater elementary students

Chapter Six

Strengthening the "High Performance/Low Cost" School System: Northfield Public Schools in the Twenty-first Century (1989–2018)

The National Context

The Minnesota PER (performance, evaluation, reporting) process in the 1980s was an early version of the outcome-based education (OBE) that by the early 1990s had been adopted by most states and districts in the nation. With this systematic approach of declaring purpose and mission, setting goals and outcome standards, and measuring student learning, state legislators (and taxpayers) sought to make their public schools more accountable. Each year every school district was required to incorporate state educational standards into local goals and outcomes, measure student learning and progress on desired knowledge acquisition and skill development, and report the results to the state and local taxpayers. In 1994 standard-based National Education Goals were established by the U. S. Congress in the "The Goals 2000: Educate America Act." In 1996, President Bill Clinton introduced a competitive grant, the Technology Literacy Challenge Fund (TLCF), to support and encourage states and local districts to ensure that every child in every school utilize technology to achieve high standards by the dawn of the twenty-first century. The standards-based reform movement culminated in the No Child Left Behind Act of 2001, which as of 2018 remained an active nationwide educational mandate for American public schools.

The Kyte Superintendency 1989–2000

In the search for Stan Mack's successor, the board returned to the familiar source for most of the previous superintendents — rural, small town Minnesota. Charles (Charlie) Kyte, a native of the northern Minnesota Iron Range, had served for seven years as superintendent at Eden Valley-Watkins, a rural district of fewer than 4,500 residents southwest of St. Cloud. With a master's degree and PhD from the University of Minnesota, Kyte had previously taught high school science and been principal of Red Rock Central High School. Kyte was a gregarious, energetic educator, experienced and comfortable with the politics of small town education.

Superintendent Charles Kyte

When Charlie Kyte took the district's helm in March 1989, he sensed a "siege mentality" in the school system, the result of turnover in administration and board membership, a decade of roller coaster finances, and cuts in staff and program. Morale among staff and teachers was understandably low. One year later the *Northfield News* reported[202] a remarkable turnaround and credited Kyte's positive energy, visibility, and direct problem-solving approach. Board member Noel Stratmoen attributed Kyte's success at creating a positive atmosphere to his visibility and his ability to communicate effectively with everyone he met, qualities important for any superintendent, but especially expected and appreciated in a community like Northfield. Upon his arrival, Kyte ran "fast and hard" to strengthen the relationship of the public schools with the business community, civic organizations, churches, and the community at large, believing that only with these partnerships could he make needed improvements within the school system. Within his first year as superintendent Kyte had restored the confidence of the teachers, the business community, and the voters in the school district.

The organization of the elementary schools was immediately addressed by the new superintendent. In 1980 the district had abandoned the traditional neighborhood arrangement of grades 1 through 5 in each elementary building, moving to a grade-level system with grades 1 through 3 at Greenvale, 4 and 5 at Sibley, and kindergarten at Longfellow. After careful study, in 1998 the district decided to return to neighborhood schools when a third elementary (Bridgewater) was opened and the efficiencies of the grade-level arrangement diminished. The *Northfield News* and many parents welcomed the return of the neighbor elementary schools, noting that "the commitment to family and friends easily translates to community when the local school a few blocks away is the place where you and your neighbor's kids all go to school."[203] Concerns that neighborhood schools might be unequal or divide the town were addressed by offering all special programs at each school and acknowledging the common leveling and unifying educational experience of the middle and high school. Northfield had returned to its traditional neighborhood elementary schools, where children learned and their "first building blocks of knowledge took place in the cradle of their own neighborhood."

Kyte also supported school choice within the district, actively supporting the programs at the town's private and parochial elementary schools, Prairie Creek and St. Dominic's. Although Kyte initially declined a request to sponsor one of the state's (and nation's) first charter schools, the district later sponsored The Village Charter School, a brief, unsuccessful attempt to establish a public progressive elementary school. However, Northfield got its successful public progressive school in 2002 when the district sponsored Prairie Creek's conversion from a private to a public charter school. By 2016 Northfield was one of only three Minnesota school districts sponsoring one of the state's 175 charter schools, demonstrating ISD 659's commitment to serving all of the children in the Northfield area.

While charter schools were established as alternative schools to encourage educational innovation, Kyte made innovation *within* the school system a high priority. Companeros, a two-way bilingual immersion program in which elementary students learned to speak, read, and write in English and Spanish, started in sections of Greenvale classrooms and was so successful and well received that by 2015 a self-contained Companeros classroom was offered at each grade level in all three elementary schools. The Companeros classrooms were ideally 50 percent native English speakers and 50 percent native Spanish speakers, with a minimum 1/3 and 2/3 composition. The benefits for all participants were supported by research that found all students in a bilingual classroom typically scored higher on middle school standardized tests of academic achievement than students in English-only classrooms and that bilingual instruction was the single most effective method for bringing English learners to academic proficiency. The 1990s Companeros program consequently contributed significantly to reducing the high school drop-out rate of Hispanic students in the first decade of the twenty-first century.

In the decade under the Kyte's leadership, other curricular reforms strengthened the academic program in the Northfield Public Schools. In 1991 a new seven-area Academic Strategic Plan included an expanded accelerated math program, the establishment of the first "technology" classrooms with personal computers, initiatives to make students more globally aware, and research and course development grants for teachers. Kyte was determined to address the needs of all students, both the gifted high performers and the challenged and struggling lower performers. The special education program started small, serving students with autism and other special needs at Longfellow, but it expanded rapidly, placing trained staff and programs into all buildings and all grade levels. The reputation of Northfield's Special Education Program spread statewide, prompting some parents to relocate to Northfield for their special needs children.

Kyte led efforts to strengthen the district's cocurricular program, building on the traditional Northfield participatory emphasis by also recognizing and honoring excellence and competitive success. Activity fees were reduced and new girls' interscholastic programs added. A fledging parent Raiders Booster Club grew and flourished. Kyte hired a corps of young permanent teacher-coaches, including Troy Cohrs (English, girls' soccer, track and field), Doug Davis (physical education, girls' and boys' swimming), and Bubba Sullivan (English, football), who provided effective teaching in the classroom and produced success on the sports field. Two long-standing purposes for American public education, developing good character and good citizens, were realized primarily through the cocurricular program.

By 1990, Kyte's second year, the period of budget deficits and cuts finally ended. In an editorial headlined "Black is back" the *Northfield News* congratulated the superintendent and board for the first balanced budget in seven years, adding: "This bodes well for the district. It should restore the public's confidence in the Board's ability to provide a quality education within the constraints of a $10 million general budget… and shows good faith to those (taxpayers) who supported the 1988 levy and bond referendums."[204] A comparison with similar school districts in the area showed that Northfield's pupil-to-staff ratio of 14.7 was lower than most, and the district had a larger activities budget than many. Kyte noted that this was possible in a town of relatively low taxable property values only because additional revenue had been provided by the recent excess operating levy. Kyte, like superintendents before and after him, needed to regularly remind residents of the challenge of maintaining a quality educational system in a community with an "extraordinary" amount of tax-exempt property and a relatively small business community. Northfield's tax capacity rate (the city's degree of dependence on property taxes) of 64.3 was substantially higher than every other non-metro school district in the state, and most was derived from commercial and residential property taxes. In non-metro communities over 10,000, 42 percent of the revenue from property taxes went to the public schools; in Northfield 53 percent went to the schools. Nearby Red Wing, blessed with a large industrial base and far less tax-exempt property, required only one-third the tax effort to support its schools. This reality, along with Northfielders' inbred fiscal conservatism with public funds, clashed perpetually with the town's deep heartfelt commitment to public education. The result was a community that expected, as Kyte loved to say, "champagne schools on a beer budget," or as Superintendent Terry Tofte wrote in the 2002 newsletter, a "high performance/low cost" educational system.

Superintendent Kyte was remarkably visible, communicating regularly with Northfielders, presenting to civic and business organizations, and writing a weekly column, "Making the Grade," in the *Northfield News*. In the summer of 1990 Kyte's column detailed the significant amount of work and activity at the schools during the summer months, a time when many residents assumed the school system was completely shut down. The district

District makes strides toward fiscal stability

Making the Grade
By Supt. Charles Kyte

operated three important educational programs. Nearly 100 students, ten teachers and ten paraprofessionals participated in the summer special education program, designed to provide additional help for students with special physical and educational needs; several hundred students took music lessons and participated in the summer city band program; and the district's Community Education Program, a cooperative venture with the City of Northfield, operated an extensive summer recreation program of sports activities for children and adults, which included the popular adult softball leagues. Teachers met regularly to revise curriculum and develop new courses: "this quiet behind-the-scenes" planning and preparation work, Kyte noted, was essential for delivering effective classes and programs during the school year. District administrators were especially busy in the summer, closing the books and auditing the July 1–June 30 budget, hiring new staff (fifty staff positions, including a dozen teachers in a typical summer), and registration of students new to the district.

Yet the busiest employees, Kyte noted, were the custodial staff. Custodians were engaged in the enormous task of cleaning and maintaining all of the school buildings. Kyte's regular newspaper columns not only kept the community well informed but also served to boost staff morale, as this summer article concluded: "The summer months are a time for me to regroup and prepare for the next school year. Many staff are working hard to address the educational needs of our students, plan for the new year and the operational needs of our school district. I'm very proud of the work being done this summer by all of the Northfield Schools employees."[205]

The 1990 *Northfield News* Back to School Supplement[206] portrayed a school system on the rise and a second-year superintendent whose energetic, positive problem-solving and relationship-building work was already paying dividends. Kyte assured the community that everything was ready for a successful opening, and he was especially pleased with the improvements made to the district's five school buildings, noting that several buildings were looking the "best they've looked in years." Teachers' in-service seminars reflected their expanding role, with sessions on identifying student's strengths (positive psychology) as well as depression. Enrollment numbers were slightly lower (11 students) in the high school, higher (40) in the elementary grades, and overall 35 pupil units lower than projected, resulting in a possible $100,000 shortfall in state funding. Yet Kyte believed this would be easily addressed and assured the community it was not the kind of financial crisis common in past years.

A new community event, the Northfield School District Youth Activities Fair, coordinated by the Northfield Area Chamber of Commerce, was the final Thursday Night Entertainment on Bridge Square of the summer. The *News* congratulated the chamber and the district for collaborating on a community event to focus students and parents on the impending major transition of school opening but saw a larger more important benefit to the evening: "The activities fair was a clear signal that adults want kids to be a part of their community, part of the lifeblood of Northfield. Kids need to be noticed and seen doing positive things. The fair let them know they are valued and have legitimate standing in this community. And once young people have standing, responsibility and accountability can follow."[207] Kyte wrote in his "Making the Grade" column that "Quality education is a community responsibility."[208] He thanked the community for working hard to provide the funding necessary to support high quality public schools. Kyte acknowledged that the school district needed to be even more collaborative and further strengthen the partnership with students, parents, businesses, and the community so that students and the school system can "benefit from the skill and caring of our entire community." Kyte's simple assertion that "education is a community enterprise" was the central theme, the mantra he repeated often throughout his twelve-year Northfield superintendency.

As Kyte completed his second year, he reported to the board that the district's schools were in good health and performing well. He praised students, parents, and staff for actively and effectively working together to improve the schools. Kyte cited examples of innovative curriculum work, new high school initiatives on affective skills, career planning, and leadership, strengthened activity programs, clustered gifted classrooms, preschool special education, and staff-driven in-service sessions. In September 1992, the *Northfield News* applauded the Northfield Public Schools for "recognizing the individuality and wide variety of learning needs of its students" with various diversity initiatives. That same editorial pointed out that public education was being "stretched" to meet those diverse student needs and to tailor education to those individual needs, a new direction that was appropriate and should yield positive results. But the *News* editors cautioned the community and the schools not to lose touch with the "commonweal — those shared experiences and dependency on each other that weaves all of our lives together,"[209] arguing that at the same time the schools emphasize diversity and individual learning needs, it was more important than ever to "cultivate socialization and an understanding of collective responsibility." Each generation of local educators struggled to strike the appropriate balance between service to the individual and service to the community, to educate individual minds and produce good citizens.

Although Kyte did not label his third year as superintendent the "Year of Diversity," he had discovered the power of identifying broad unifying themes to describe and advance core components of the school program. In 1995 the district adopted a "Year of the Arts" theme and collaborated with the Northfield Arts Guild, the colleges, and other community arts organizations to promote the arts in the lives of all Northfielders, young and old, and Kyte discovered that with themes there was "real power in directing the energies of all our institutions in one direction." The next year the public schools joined with the Healthy Community Initiative, the Community Action Center, and Northfield churches with a "Year of Values" theme.[210] Fending off criticism that he was trying to put religious values into the public schools, Kyte reminded Northfielders that public school teachers had always been teaching values, ethics, and character. Values like equality, self-control, honesty, respect, integrity, caring, and citizenship were emphasized at all grade levels throughout the year. This collaborative effort was yet another manifestation of Kyte's earlier "quality education is a community responsibility" message; as Kyte told the *News*, "As a whole community, emphasizing values becomes the work of everybody."

In the first half of his twelve years as superintendent, Charlie Kyte amassed an impressive list of accomplishments. First, thanks to a sustained period of national and regional economic growth and prosperity, financial stability and balanced budgets were restored in the school district. Kyte's energetic, positive, inclusive leadership boosted staff morale and restored public confidence in the schools. The district curriculum was expanded and strengthened with implementation of a new Academic Strategic Plan that included innovative programs, new initiatives for gifted students and alternative programs for struggling students, and a significantly expanded special education program. The cocurricular program (student activities, organizations, and athletics) was expanded, giving more students opportunity to develop social, leadership, teamwork, and athletic skills. With the schools operating smoothly and students learning, Kyte could finally turn his attention to emerging facility needs.

Since 1990 enrollment had been rising nearly 3 percent per year, causing overcrowded conditions at all levels, especially at Sibley and Greenvale Elementary Schools, where by 1995 more than 450 students attended classes in six temporary classrooms. Furthermore, enrollment was expected to increase by 1,260 (36 percent) in the next decade. Thus, in November 1995 the district held a bond referendum to build a new 600-student elementary school, a 400-student addition to the high school ($17.5 million), and a new middle school ($19 million) with a capacity for 1,100 students. The elementary school (plus the high school addition and a technology upgrade that provided Internet access for all schools) was approved, while the middle school project was defeated. In September 1998 Bridgewater opened as Northfield's fourth elementary school, enabling the district to return to a neighborhood school arrangement: Longfellow continued to house the kindergarten and preschool

Bridgewater Elementary promotional brochure

program, and Greenvale, Sibley, and Bridgewater each hosted multiple classrooms for grades 1 through 5.

Bridgewater opened its doors to over 550 students from the Bridgewater neighborhood (south and southwest sections of the Northfield area) and the district-wide Companeros program. The new building placed twenty-six traditional classrooms in a stimulating architectural space that reflected the school's earth theme. The dedication program explained that every day students would experience the earth theme in the skylight that hovered high above the commons area; in the festive, gold sunburst depicted in the commons floor tile; in the billowing white clouds that adorned the soft curvature of the commons wall; and in the four-acre Rachel Carson Nature Area just east of the school. The facility contained a separate art room (with kiln and gallery space), outstanding music facilities, Internet access, and a hardwood floor gymnasium. The 85,000 square foot brick building, on a fourteen-acre site just south of the high school, cost $8.6 million and had a capacity of 625, ample room to accommodate future enrollment growth. Principal Dianne Kinneberg welcomed the children to "our colorful school" that emphasized nature, the arts, physical education, technology, and traditional learning environments, thanked Northfield citizens for providing the marvelous facility, and committed to making Bridgewater — whose mission was to be a "respectful, successful, safe community of high-achieving learners" — one of the best schools in the world. This described quite nicely the aspirations of Kyte and local educational leaders for the twenty-first century Northfield public schools.

An important part of Kyte's outreach and communication efforts was a quarterly newsletter, *Highlights*, mailed to all Northfield residents to ensure they were well informed about their public schools. Article topics and titles suggest the variety of programs and issues in the district's schools at the end of the twentieth century:

> 1995 District will build new schools; "Environmental Education has a history in the Northfield District"; Graduation Rule implementation; kindergarten program at Longfellow; English as a Second Language (ESL) program; COMPAS writing program; district environmental education; technology update; "Working for Schools Without Bias"; the Alternative Learning Center (ALC); Focusing on Social Justice; Community Education and Recreation: Learning All-year Long.

1996   Band students in the summer; Summer drivers education; construction update on high school addition; Minnesota School Choice (open enrollment); "What is inquiry-based learning"; Northfield Environmental learning center.

1997   Construction update on new elementary school (Bridgewater); Project Resource Center at Greenvale; Introducing School District Student Diversity Community Liaison (Ignacio Briseno); A Day in the Life of the Middle School Media Center; Board approved Village charter school; summer school; new leadership team at High School; excess levy extension vote Nov. 4; All-class reunion planned.

1998   graduation rule update; "walking boundaries for elementary schools"; construction update; computers help students learn the basics; Bridgewater opens; all-class reunion a "Howling success"; return to neighborhood elementary schools; special education program; Fabulous Fridays at elementary schools; School-to-Work program.

1999   Rock and Roll Revival returns; distinguished alumni awards; Proposed excess levy draws near; Minnesota open enrollment.

Into the Twenty-first Century and the Close of the Kyte Superintendency

The Northfield Public School District #659 entered the new century continuing to grapple with the complex issues that defined the contemporary public school. In the first two months of 2000 there were articles in the *Northfield News* on the student activity fee, new uses of technology in the classroom, transportation, the honoring of a long-serving board member, environmental education, new state high school graduation requirements, the outdated and overcrowded middle school, and, of course, the annual budget. Even though the activity fee had been raised significantly (from $35–50 to $50–75) to avoid cuts in programs, student participation also rose to its highest level in five years. Kyte called the increase "gratifying" and confirmation that students valued all of their educational experience, music, arts, academics, and sports. Teachers were finding the Classroom Pages on the high school's new web site useful for posting assignments, class discussions, and communicating with parents.

Noel Stratmoen

While some things were changing, others remained the same. Kyte completed a multi-year transportation contract with the Benjamin Bus Company, solidifying the relationship that continues to the present. Noel Stratmoen was honored by the Minnesota School Board Association for twenty years of service on the Northfield Board of Education. Kyte attributed much of the success of his superintendency to the continuity on the board, noting that six of the seven members served his entire time. But Stratmoen was only getting started, and remarkably he is positioned to celebrate his fortieth anniversary on the board in 2020.

A full page of photographs illustrated the annual fifth-grade science trip to the Wolf Ridge Environmental Center: 258 students, fifty-three parent chaperones, and twelve teachers enjoyed and survived the week-long winter environmental education experience, a common experience for all Northfield fifth graders since the early 1990s. In 1998 high school graduation requirements were increased by the Minnesota Profile of Learning law, and students struggled to find room for electives (languages and music) as they now needed to complete twenty-four subject standards. There were, of course, always financial and facility concerns. The overall financial health of the district remained strong, as Business Director Doug Crane projected a larger fund balance for 2001–2002, possibly as large as $1.9 million. The district had moved a long way from the deficit years in the 1980s. But the facility issue—what to do with the outdated (sections built in 1910, 1934, and 1954) and overcrowded middle school—was still looming large after voters defeated the bond referendum in 1995. Finally, in February 2000 the board agreed to hold another bond referendum to fund a new middle school.

In the winter of 2000 Kyte entered his twelfth year as superintendent with a record of impressive accomplishments. He balanced the budget and built a general fund surplus, established innovative programs (Companeros, LINK, and Reading Recovery at the elementary level, FOCUS and the Area

Learning Center at the high school), built Bridgewater Elementary School, which allowed for return to neighborhood elementary schools, implemented a comprehensive Academic Strategic Plan, strengthened the teaching staff, and reconnected with the business community. Perhaps most importantly, Kyte had humanized the superintendent position; his energetic, positive, communicative, and visible approach lifted staff morale and restored public confidence in the public schools. Kyte and the Northfield ISD 659 were on a roll. Then, the unexpected happened. A banner front page headline in the *Northfield News* announced that Superintendent Kyte had accepted an offer to become the executive director of the Minnesota Association of School Administrators.

The Tofte Superintendency (2000–2004)

Kyte was succeeded in July 2000 by Dr. Terry Tofte, assistant superintendent of schools in Edina, who told the *Northfield News* that the Northfield superintendent position was one of the "best" in the state. The school district had a "great" reputation, he said, and the Northfield community was "second to none."[211] Tofte believed he was inheriting a "great situation" with a well-managed and financially stable district for which he gave credit to Kyte. Tofte, a native of Grand Marais, Minnesota, received his BA in philosophy from Concordia College (Moorhead) and earned a masters degree and PhD in educational administration from the University of Minnesota. After teaching at the Blake School and St. Thomas Academy, Tofte served as principal in Apple Valley, Eagan, and Rosemount and four years as assistant superintendent in Edina, a suburban district southwest of Minneapolis, considered one of the best in the state. Tofte impressed his interviewers as articulate, organized, and thorough, with an educational philosophy that mirrored Northfield's

Superintendent Terry Tofte

emphasis on excellence. Tofte's experience and skills were well suited for the district's needs and goals. At Edina, Tofte had established a mentorship program for new teachers that produced dramatic professional development results and coordinated a robust comprehensive assessment program, collecting data on student achievement, infusion of technology in the classroom, and staff development. The Northfield board's goals for the 2000–2001 year were to review the organizational structure of the elementary schools, attract and develop staff, address the middle school facility needs, and strengthen student support services at all levels. Tofte brought expertise to each goal area. He had extensive administrative experience with school organization, staff development, facility management, and district-wide support services to "make sure no one's needs get lost in the shuffle" or in the language of impending federal legislation, No Child Left Behind.

In addition to selecting a new superintendent, the district hired a new director of Special Education Services. Bob Fischer had recently retired from the Minnesota Department of Children, Families and Learning where he developed the electronic data reporting system that all school districts used to collect state special education funds. "*Highlights*, a Newsletter for Northfield School District Citizens"[212] suggested that having Bob Fischer in charge of special education services was a "little like hiring Martha Stewart to water your plants." When asked why he left a high-profile state position to return to the grassroots level Fisher chuckled: "I have a lot to offer, and I always wanted to finish my career nearer to the people who are most important — the kids. This is certainly not a 'lesser' job — this is where the important work is done." But not only would the children benefit; the district now had Fisher's expertise in the tuition and third-party billing systems that ensured that a district received all the money it was entitled to from outside sources. Like Tofte, Fischer was drawn to Northfield by the strength and reputation of both its school district and community.

A Twenty-first Century School Facility

Soon after Bridgewater Elementary School was opened in 1998, the district actively studied the middle school question, employing consultants to study demographics, make enrollment projections, evaluate the existing middle school facility, and generate cost estimates associated with renovation and new construction. In January 2000 the board authorized a twenty-one member

Northfield Citizen's Facilities Task Force to use the consultant's findings and make recommendations. In September the task force recommended that the district build a new middle school on district property south of Bridgewater Elementary School, and convert the current middle school building to non-school use. After collecting additional community input from public meetings and a resident phone survey, the board authorized a two-question $42,160,000 bond referendum on May 8, 2001. Question 1 was to build a new 208,000-square foot middle school, make improvements to the high school (expanding the technology center and remodeling the media center, science labs, art studios, physical education and vocational ed areas), and set aside money for middle school re-use work. Question 2 was to relocate Memorial Field, a football and soccer facility, to the high school campus. The benefit was four-fold: to provide adequate space and capacity for the growing middle school; to upgrade technology and classroom space in the middle and high school to ensure quality teaching and learning; to provide a safe and efficient middle school and athletic facility (renovating the existing antiquated facilities was cost prohibitive); and meet broader community needs with a 750-seat performance auditorium and a new swimming pool.

In March a four-page referendum information pamphlet[213] was mailed to Northfield residents detailing the cost, tax impact, and benefits of the facilities, a proposed site plan for the new middle school and new Memorial Field, and a sample ballot for the special election. In a letter to district residents Superintendent Tofte was direct and succinct. The Northfield Public Schools were growing, enrollment rising from 3,053 in 1990 to a projected 4,010 by 2006, and the most pronounced growth would be at the secondary level. "More students require more space. We resolved our space needs at the elementary school level when Bridgewater was opened in 1998. The challenge we now face is creating needed instructional space at the middle and high school levels." Tofte reviewed the thorough process of extensive study and community involvement in the building project, and concluded: "The bond referendum includes only those facilities we believe to be absolutely necessary. Our bonding plans have been structured to minimize tax impact on property owners in our school district. Our teachers and staff need these facilities to meet this community's expectations that our education programs be of the highest quality." The new superintendent and the Bond Campaign Committee understood the community's long-standing heritage and commitment to both high quality public education and conservative public spending and assured Northfielders it would continue. The voters were convinced and approved by a decisive margin (62 percent YES) both parts of the referendum.

Planning for the new middle school began immediately, and by summer 2002 work had begun on the $34 million middle school. The thoughtful design of the attractive two-story brick building, Principal Burt Bemmels wrote in his welcome publication, made it a "secure, safe, aesthetically pleasing setting that provides an enriching learning environment for all students."[214] The 208,000-square foot building featured two floors of more than forty-four classrooms for 1,080 sixth, seventh, and eight graders, a two-story atrium cafeteria entrance area, a 750-seat auditorium, music rooms, two gymnasiums, locker rooms and an eight-lane swimming pool. By August 2002 the Construction Update newsletter headline boasted "On time, under budget, and exciting to watch" and detailed the progress on the middle school construction, high school renovations, and the new Memorial Field. By the end of 2002–2003 the industrial tech, art suite, and media center renovations in the high school were completed. In August 2003 the new Memorial Field was dedicated with a patriotic ceremony led by the American Legion color guard and the Minnesota State Band.

On September 26, 2004, the new Northfield Middle School was dedicated, and a grateful school board and district administrators again thanked the community of Northfield for approving the 2001 bond referendum. The construction of Bridgewater Elementary and now the middle school had created a 140-acre campus of three schools (and the district office) and numerous sports facilities in a six-block corridor on Northfield's south side. The migration of the district's secondary schools from its downtown location between Central Park and the Northfield Public Library was complete. The Northfield Public Schools now had the six school buildings — Bridgewater, Greenvale, Longfellow, and Sibley elementary, the middle school, and the high school — that would house and serve Northfield students well into the twenty-first century. The historical 1910 high school facility, after a failed attempt to convert it to a community arts center, was sold to Carleton College and with extensive renovation and expansion reopened as the Weitz Center for Creativity.

Although the 2001 bond referendum and major facility work were the most visible accomplishments of Tofte's four years as superintendent, much was happening throughout the schools. In the pages of the PER Annual Report and two district publications, *Accents* and *Highlights*, Tofte explained that "our bottom line as a district is measured in the achievement of our students" and student

Middle School Dedication Program

achievement was measured with the nationally standardized tests (CAT), state accountability measures (Minnesota Basic Skills Test), and internal tests and class grades. Northfield students continued to compare favorably to the national norms, and the trend for each grade level between 1995 and 1999 in reading and math was positive and upward.[215] High school students were doing well with a new state Graduation Rule that required students to demonstrate competency in basic skills and proficiency in eleven learning areas, Tofte wrote: "We are very proud of our students. The great majority are passing the Basic Skills test on the first try. In Northfield, teachers concentrate on helping students achieve at high levels."

In Tofte's second year the district added staff in special education, an enrichment specialist to develop programs for "exceptionally able" students, and a mentorship program for new teachers. In a public opinion survey of community members, 85 percent rated the quality of education in the district as

excellent (34 percent) or good (51 percent); and 85 percent rated the teachers and instructional staff as excellent (40 percent) or good (45 percent). This was particularly welcome news for the board as it announced the 2001 bond referendum election. Participation levels in activities and sports continued to rise, epitomized by 130 (more than ten percent of the student body) athletes on the track and field team in spring 2002. In 2003 Susan Roosenraad, who offered the school's first Advanced Placement (AP) math course, was named Northfield Teacher of the Year. The high school received a commendation from the State Department of Education for high scores on the math skills test, and Minnesota Commissioner of Education Sheri Yecke praised Northfield for creating a culture of high expectations in which parents encouraged their children to take difficult math courses, for highly qualified and enthusiastic math teachers, and for a clear and cohesive K–12 math curriculum.

In the winter 2003 *Accents*[216] Tofte provided district patrons with a math lesson that demonstrated the school system's efficiency and validated his oft-repeated claim that "Northfield is a high performing, low spending school district." He compared Northfield's budget and funding with St. Louis Park, a similarly sized, highly regarded district in the Twin Cities. St. Louis Park's general fund budget was $40.9 million, while Northfield's was only $26.6 million. The difference was primarily due to revenue generated through local levy referenda: St. Louis Park, with a much larger commercial and industrial tax base than Northfield, generated $1,420 per pupil, Northfield only $87; overall St. Louis Park had $8,512 per pupil to spend, while Northfield had spent $5,921 per pupil. Yet despite the significant difference in spending, Tofte asserted, Northfield offered a "comparable and, in some areas, a superior educational program."

Echoing the words of previous Northfield superintendents, Tofte summed up the district's financial reality: "Over the years, we have learned to live within our means and make the most of every tax dollar we receive." To confirm his "low spending" characterization of the district, Tofte offered two statistics: of the 334 school districts in Minnesota, Northfield ranked 229th in instructional expenditures per pupil, and 232 of the 334 districts received more local levy revenue than Northfield. Fortunately, most Northfield residents understood and believed they had high-performing, low-spending schools, 84 percent agreed that "the community gets its money's worth from the public schools."

In his superintendent's letter in the Spring 2003 *Accents*,[217] Tofte supplied evidence for the "high performing" claim. He repeated the community survey findings that 88 percent of Northfield residents rated the quality of education provided by the Northfield Public Schools favorably. Student performance on recent Minnesota Basic Skills tests ranked Northfield 8th graders in the top 16 percent in math and top 14 percent in reading, while Northfield 10th graders ranked in the top 2 percent in writing. Writing two years after the successful bond referendum, Tofte summarized the enviable position of the district schools: "We enjoy among the highest 'customer satisfaction' ratings in the state, our students are among the highest achievers in Minnesota and our expenditures are modest by comparison with other Minnesota school districts. Our schools deliver a good 'bang for the buck' thanks to a fiscally disciplined Board of Education and administration, an enthusiastic and effective instructional staff, and a supportive and caring community. We appreciate your trust and support but realize that we must earn it every day through our work."

In the fall of 2003, as Tofte began his fourth year as superintendent, the Northfield School District was enjoying a period of relative stability and growth. Much of the renovation work in the high school was complete, the new Memorial Field was hosting soccer and football games, and the construction of the new middle school was nearing a spring 2004 completion. The district was busily responding to the accountability demands of the federal "No Child Left Behind" act and the state's new Basic Skills and graduation standards, complying with assessment requirements while searching for broader multi-faceted means of measuring student performance and school success. The district had expanded its programs to address the needs of all students, especially for special education and gifted students. The teaching corps, traditionally a district asset, was strengthened further. The district seemed to have found in Tofte a leader who could build on Kyte's community building and innovative programs. Unfortunately, in early 2004 Tofte unexpectedly resigned, citing personal family issues that required his attention.

The Richardson Superintendency (2004–2016)

The board found an experienced administrator to lead and further strengthen the fundamentally healthy school district. L. Chris Richardson had served students in large and small communities as a teacher, principal, director of curriculum, and for the previous twenty-three years superintendent of K-12 districts ranging in size from 250 to 22,000 students. For the past seven years Richardson had led the Osseo Area Schools, a large, sprawling (five communities), complex district west of the Twin Cities, but he was looking to finish his career with a more moderate-sized district in a community committed to excellent public schools. For Northfield and Richardson, it appeared to be a very good match.

Superintendent Chris Richardson

Richardson's own experience as a student led him to dedicate his life to education. When he was in kindergarten, his teacher told his parents "not to expect much," that Chris was a poor student and not very bright.[218] This stuck with Richardson throughout his early elementary years. He showed little interest in school until his sixth grade teacher challenged him, told him he was indeed very bright, and pledged to help him be successful in school. With new expectations and the support of a caring teacher, Richardson made a dramatic transformation, found a passion in learning, and excelled in school, ultimately completing a PhD in education. He had experienced the power of a caring teacher, high expectations, and public schooling to transform his life, and he was inspired to dedicate his career to helping others realize their full potential through education.

Like his predecessor Tofte, Richardson was working in a national and state political educational environment that was increasingly critical and distrustful of the public schools. Although most students were learning and most public schools successful, politicians and the public seemed more focused on failing students and failing schools and demanded more accountability with the No Child Left Behind (NCLB) legislation. The federal government had been similarly critical of the public schools in the 1983 *A Nation at Risk* report commissioned by President Reagan. But it only defined the problem and offered broad recommendations, leaving the solutions, assessment, and accountability measures to the states and local boards. The NCLB, however, defined "failing" students and schools using a set of national standards and prescribed a single assessment (a national test) for all students (including special education and ESL students) to measure progress and success. At the same time Minnesota, with a conservative governor and legislature, also adopted a narrow measure for accountability along with a period of reduced state aid funds. Working within this challenging state and national environment, Richardson and the Northfield district struggled with measuring student and school success and sought to increase funding with local excess operating levies.

Richardson began his superintendency with three broad goals. He wanted to address the impending operating deficit, resulting from recent reductions in state aid. This required making program-based budget cuts, based on recommendations from building administrators and the District Educational Program Advisory Council (DEPAC). Second, he wanted to develop a long-range strategic plan for the district. A committee of teachers, parents, students, community members, administrators, and board representatives created a District Improvement Plan that would guide the district for the entire twelve years of his superintendency. Third, in the midst of the national and state criticism of the public schools, Richardson was determined to maintain and strengthen the trust and confidence in Northfield public schools that had been earned in the Kyte and Tofte administrations. The inclusionary nature of the budget cuts and the strategic planning processes — Richardson's first two actions as superintendent — proved very helpful toward meeting the third goal.

In his first Annual Report[219] to the residents of the district, Richardson laid out the challenges facing the district. The first three addressed broad educational issues facing the district. Creating a new district strategic plan was needed to provide a clear focus and direction and to build consensus around a core mission, a set of guiding beliefs, and a set of core strategies. Genuine school improvement efforts must be nurtured, using data and building improvement plans to enhance individual student achievement. New technologies must continue to support learning and school operation.

The fourth challenge was to address the political climate and the impact of No Child Left Behind. Richardson chose his words carefully, suggesting NCLB did not adequately measure the learning of some students (special education and ESL), while asserting the district's commitment to student and school success:

> The Northfield School district is committed to the success of each and every child. We must continually evaluate our efforts and regularly share our successes and failures with the community. As Northfield joins the swelling ranks of districts identified as not making adequate yearly progress, the community must understand that these assessments for some students actually mask their true growth and the positive impact our staff is having on their achievement.
>
> We believe the fate of something very precious rests in our hands — the quality of the lives of the children we serve and the future of our society. We must bravely champion putting children first and constantly ask ourselves, "Is what we're doing providing the best education for all students?"[22]

The new District Strategic Plan was completed in 2005. It established a mission and belief statement and six broad strategies to guide the district through the Richardson era. The public school's twenty-first century mission was emblazoned on the cover of the October 2005 Annual Report: "to deliver educational excellence that empowers all learners to participate in our dynamic world." Four words and phrases assumed special importance. While "educational excellence" continued, as it had throughout the twentieth century, to be the school's ultimate product, the district's raison d'etre, students were now active learners ("empowered participants"), the system was inclusive ("all" equally valued), and education was preparation for an uncertain future in a "dynamic world."

Six beliefs statements defined the Northfield public schools. "We believe," said the strategic plan, that

- *public education* [emphases in the original] is the foundation of our democratic republic
- education is the collective *responsibility* of our students, families, schools, and communities

Northfield Annual Report

Public Schools I.S.D. 659 MINNESOTA

October 2005

OUR MISSION

The mission of the Northfield Public Schools is to deliver educational excellence that empowers all learners to participate in our dynamic world.

Northfield High School One of Ten in the State to Receive a Five Star Rating

2004 - 2005
Annual Report on Curriculum, Instruction and Student Achievement

- everyone can learn and has unique gifts and talents that must be nurtured and valued; *learning* is a life-long, multi-faceted process that involves more than academics
- everyone in our schools has a right to a positive *learning environment* that provides physical, emotional, and intellectual safety, and nurtures mutual respect, responsibility, and rigor
- decisions must be based on the district's mission and beliefs and relevant sources of information in an open *decision-making* process that invites honest dialog
- *all* learners have a right to equitable access to educational opportunities."[221]

The first two beliefs were shared with the nineteenth-century classical educators, and the first three beliefs reflected the legacy of the twentieth-century progressive educators. A positive, safe, and respectful learning environment, increasingly valued after the 1960s, was now seen as a right. Similarly, open decision-making, inclusiveness, and equitable access to educational opportunity all emerged from the 1960s to become foundational beliefs for the twenty-first century public schools in Northfield, Minnesota, and throughout the nation.

After defining the purpose of the Northfield Public Schools and delineating the underlying beliefs and values about public education, the strategic plan listed six primary strategies and established guidelines for how the district's mission and primary purposes (beliefs) would be realized. The district committed itself to:

Quality Education. We will hire and retain highly qualified educators and provide them with ongoing support and training to deliver high quality instruction that meets the unique needs of all learners.

Stewardship. We will consistently demonstrate good stewardship by analyzing information, prioritizing needs and managing our financial, physical, and human resources to support our mission.

Climate. We will create and strengthen an environment that fosters mutual respect, responsibility and rigor, and ensures the right to physical, emotional, and intellectual safety for every person.

Communications/Partnerships. We will create and strengthen bridges of open communication that engage staff, students, families and communities as effective partners in education.

Curricular Outcomes. We will implement a consistent, comprehensive and challenging set of curricular outcomes that reach and engage all learners.

Diversity. We will implement plans and practices that foster full participation by all learners, and that address issues that include, but are not limited to race, gender, culture, religion, sexual orientation, language, disabilities and socio-economic factors.[222]

This set of strategies encapsulated both the continuities and the changes in Northfield Public Schools over its 160-year history. Superintendents from all eras were undoubtedly committed to providing quality education through the hiring and training of highly qualified teachers, though before 1970 the instruction was focused primarily on the subject matter and not the "unique needs" of students.

Similarly, the district boards and administrations, from the 1880s through the present, have all demonstrated effective stewardship. Indeed, responsible fiscal management and the provision of high-performance, low-cost schools has always been a hallmark of the Northfield Public Schools. While the importance of good stewardship has continued, the difficulty and challenge has increased exponentially; fiscal management of the small, simple system of the early years required little of the data-analysis and prioritizing demanded by today's larger, complex, school district operation.

The other four strategies regarding climate, partnerships, curricular outcomes, and diversity revealed the significant transformation of the public schools since the 1960s. School and classroom climate, especially from the student's perspective, received little attention from nineteenth-century educators. The classroom atmosphere was formal, ordered, and serious. Students were expected to be respectful and obedient to the teacher and were regularly subjected to corporal punishment and verbal abuse. A climate that supported good teaching was valued, but little thought was given to the learning environment. With the progressive education movement, the classroom became more child-centered, though most teachers still taught subjects rather than students. Only in the last forty years have educators sought to ensure student's the right to physical, emotional, and intellectual safety. Traditionally communication between the school and families was minimal; parents had total responsibility for their child's home life, teachers for their student's school life. Yet as schools became more student-centered, shifting emphasis from teaching to learning and viewing students' lives holistically, responsibility for schooling was increasingly seen as a genuine partnership among teachers, students, families and communities. Consequently, strengthening those partnerships became a high priority for superintendents like Kyte, Tofte, and Richardson, and it was evident in the proliferation of publications, communications, community committees, and advisory groups.

The shift from a teacher-centered to a student-centered perspective fundamentally changed the curriculum. When schools were most concerned with subjects taught, success was measured by classes taken, seat time, and diplomas issued. When the focus shifted to student learning, attention switched to individual student needs, learning styles, and differing abilities. The result was innovative courses and programs tailored to specific student needs. In Northfield this began slowly in the 1970s and 1980s, but it blossomed under the Kyte, Tofte, and Richardson administrations with new courses and significant expansion of the special education and gifted programs. Assessment was also transformed, with a new focus on measuring outcomes, what students learned, what skills were developed. Student achievement testing, teacher evaluation, and program assessments were expanded.

Perhaps the most far-reaching change for the Northfield Public Schools came with the recognition of the diversity in the schools. There were of course always many differences among the learners in the school classroom, even in relatively homogenous places like Northfield. Yet educators were either blind to the differences or felt they were irrelevant — it was simply the student's responsibility to adjust and learn in the teacher-centered classroom. Since the 1960s, however, administrators and teachers came to understand that those differences, in ability, ethnicity, gender, family background, culture, religion, sexual orientation, language, disability, and socioeconomic level, affected a student's classroom experience and ability to learn. Most importantly, it was now seen as the responsibility of the schools to implement practices and programs that would foster full participation by all learners. It was one of the ironies of the 2002 No Child Left Behind act that the learning and success for all students, including special education and ESL children, was measured with a single standardized test. The Northfield Public Schools recognized and celebrated the diversity of its students and staff and was committed to helping each student reach his or her full potential.

The mission, beliefs, and strategies of the 2005 District Strategic Plan (later called the District Improvement Plan) provided the principles, foundation, and roadmap for the entire Richardson superintendency. In all areas of the district operation — board and district-wide issues, finances and facilities, assessment and accountability, curriculum and instruction, student services, community services, human resources and staff development, and technology — the Northfield Public Schools worked to fulfill its mission "to deliver educational excellence that empowers all learners to participate in our dynamic world." Each year Richardson compiled an annual report, summarizing the issues, programs, and initiatives for each of those operational areas, highlighting the year's accomplishments under the title "Celebrations."[223]

Board and District-wide Issues

The elected seven-member Northfield School Board of Education continued its traditional role of policy-making and oversight of the superintendent and district's budget and program. After approving the new District Strategic Plan in 2005, the board annually reviewed the document and recommitted itself to the district's mission, beliefs, strategies and goals. In the early years of the Richardson superintendency the board also reviewed all of the board policies and provided in-service training for new members. The board established the District Educational Program Advisory Council (DEPAC) to annually identify key goals for district consideration and action; this permanent citizen group kept the board and superintendent well-connected to the community.

The board and district served as the authorizer for two charter schools, the elementary (K–5) Prairie Creek Community School and the secondary (6–12) ArtTech (later called Arcadia). Both schools had a distinctly progressive philosophy that featured project-based learning. Arcadia's mission was to prepare students to transition intellectually, emotionally, and ethically to higher education and future employment through a learning community that encouraged students to express themselves artistically; use technology responsibly, creatively, and with innovation; develop critical thinking and creative problem solving skills; construct knowledge and meaning for themselves understand and strive for wellness of their whole person; recognize and act upon their responsibilities as local citizens within our global context; and achieve proficiency in project-based learning.[224]

The district authorized the charter schools with renewable five-year contracts: Prairie Creek was re-authorized in 2008 and 2013, and Arcadia in 2009 and 2014. Richardson and the board believed that the charter schools offered the district's students and families a valuable educational choice.

Arcadia Charter School

Finances and Facilities

Perhaps the board's most important role was fiduciary, to review and approve the district's annual operating budget and to manage the special levy referendum process. In the Richardson era there were two remarkably similar operating levies. In October 2006 voters were asked to revoke the current $685/pupil operating levy and replace it with a $1,180/pupil levy for the next seven years and to approve a capital project levy of $750,000 per year for seven years to maintain buildings and grounds, support instructional technology, and update textbooks. In October 2011 voters were asked to revoke the current $1,270/pupil operating levy and replace it with a $1,604/pupil levy for the next ten years and again approve a capital project levy of $750,000 per year for ten years to maintain buildings and grounds, support instructional technology, and update textbooks.

The Levy Referendum Guides sent to voters were nearly identical, with only the numbers changed. With each levy the board made the same argument: regular underfunding from the state (state aid comprised nearly 80 percent of the operating budget) forced the district to make substantial budget cuts ($3.3 million in the two years before the 2006 referendum; $4 million in the six years before the 2011 referendum) and required increasing the local contribution. Revenue from the state rose 2 percent while expenditures rose 4 percent (health insurance, energy, and special ed tuition increasing by up to 20 percent), creating a widening gap that could only be closed with the excess operating levy. Voters were assured that the district had spent responsibly, focused funds on children and the classroom, and had less revenue to spend than 62 percent of the state's districts. In both 2006 and 2011 the district made its case effectively, and the voters approved both the operating and capital levies each year. (Chart of Levy Referendum history, 1980–2016)

With the construction of the new middle school in 2004, the district had satisfied all of its major facility needs and was confident it had the classroom capacity and program space necessary for the next decade. Yet Richardson created a ten-year capital facilities plan for building improvements and updates and each year reviewed and completed top priority items. In 2007–2008 all of the gymnasiums and parking lots were improved. The following year was the Sibley addition (which expanded capacity from 350 to 500, similar in size to Greenvale and Bridgewater) and renovation, which including making the playground handicapped accessible. After a facilities security review, each building entrance received new locking arrangements and security cameras.

With the additional funds from the 2006 and 2011 operating and capital levies, the district's facilities were in good shape and well maintained and allowed the district to focus on strengthening the curricular and cocurricular programs. Only in the final year of the Richardson superintendency did study and discussion return to major facility needs, suggesting the need for a new high school and a new building for Greenvale Elementary School.

Assessment and Accountability

After the 1983 *A Nation at Risk* report, federal and state governments demanded increasing accountability from local public school districts and required evidence from formal assessments that students were learning and meeting performance standards. Assessing individual student and school performance and reporting it to the State Department of Education and local taxpayers was the purpose of the 1980s Minnesota PER reports, which after 2000 evolved into the Annual Report on Curriculum, Instruction, and Student Performance. Although Superintendents Kyte, Tofte, and Richardson all resisted using a single standardized test to measure student learning, Northfield students and the district nonetheless fared very well. In 2007–2008, every grade level scored above state averages on the Minnesota Comprehensive Assessments (MCAs); similarly, every grade level scored above national averages on the Measures of Academic Progress (MAP) tests. Northfield high school students outperformed their peers across Minnesota on every section of the American College Test (ACT), something that is quite impressive considering that Minnesota had the highest scores in the nation.

The district also established a continuous improvement process, setting annual goal and outcome objectives for each program, each building, and the district and then assessed those for "adequate yearly progress" (AYP) through the implementation of action plans. The substantial increase in assessment work required the creation of a district assessment office led by a district assessment coordinator. The high school completed a North Central Association National Accreditation Review in 2009–2010, implemented NCA recommendations the following year, and received full accreditation in 2011–2012. Because assessment was an integral component of the continuous improvement process and provided the evidence needed for accountability, it was and has remained an essential component of the successful modern public school system.

Curriculum and Instruction

Under Richardson's leadership the district continued to actively review curriculum and instruction and launch initiatives to improve student learning. The regular curricular review process for all subject areas, courses, and programs established in the 1980s was codified and strengthened with better assessment. New curricular initiatives appeared regularly, though Richardson's fourth year, 2007–2008, was a remarkably fertile time. While reviewing and strengthening established programs like Companeros (which expanded from one to three elementary schools), LINK, and ESL, no fewer than six new programs were launched. Faculty formed "professional learning communities" to improve their teaching, meeting Wednesday afternoons. Response to Intervention (RTI) strategies for struggling students were implemented in the primary grades. A DARE drug education pilot program with the Northfield Police was introduced at Sibley and later expanded to the other elementary schools. A formal "service learning" program was established at the high school. Two programs to support the transition between schools were established: The LINK Crew program connected incoming 9th graders with caring adults, and the Where Everybody Belongs (WEB) program supported incoming middle school 6th graders. With the existing Bridges to Kindergarten program, the district now had transition programs for the elementary, middle, and high school levels.

Superintendent Richardson expanded the "no child left behind" mandate with an inclusive "make sure everyone grows"[225] philosophy that committed the district to helping all students learn, grow, and succeed. The more gifted students benefitted from an expanded set of challenging Advanced Placement (AP) courses, while struggling students received special attention and additional support with programs like Response to Intervention and Read 180 in the primary grades. In 2009 when assessment data showed that 28 percent of 9th graders had failed a course their freshman year, the 9th Grade Academy was established, in which interdisciplinary teacher teams intervened with identified at-risk 9th graders to better prepare them for high school level work. The academy was a clear success, and by 2013 only 7 percent of the freshman class failed a course.

Student Services and Special Education

Northfield's student services, especially the special education program, long considered one of the best outside of the metro area, continued to grow and strengthen during the Richardson years. The superintendent's list of 2008–2009 "Celebrations" noted that the Student Services Handbook was revised and distributed, that additional ESL staff were addressing the needs of ESL students, and the district continued to expand and refine comprehensive autism spectrum programming for students age two to grade 12. The number of students qualifying for early childhood special education was increasing, and in 2013 the district began a cooperative program with the Faribault schools, sharing the special education director position. To address a growing population of students with significant special education needs, the districts implemented a Students with Unique Needs (SUN) program, the Secondary Transition Education Program (STEP), and a Level IV Educational Behavioral Disability (EBD) program.

Student services for special populations were also expanding. Throughout the 1990s and 2000s Northfield's growing Latino population had noticeably high course failure and dropout rates, with only 36 percent graduating in the class of 2004. The district established the Tackling Obstacles and Raising College Hopes (TORCH) program, a collaboration of the school district and community partners to address achievement gap issues by improving the graduation and post-secondary participation rates of Northfield's minority students, low-income students, and youth who would be first-generation college attendees. The program's impact was immediate and dramatic, the graduation rate quickly surpassing the school's laudable overall graduation rate of 91 percent. The graduation rate for the 572 TORCH participants over the next decade was an astounding 97.5 percent. The numbers for the TORCH class of 2015 were equally impressive: 98 percent graduated, 81 percent applied to college, of which 100 percent were accepted. For its remarkable success, Northfield's TORCH program received state and national recognition and awards.

Community Services

Although the district had run an active community education program since the 1970s, in the twenty-first century the public schools further expanded the partnerships with community organizations on curricular initiatives as well as community youth programs. The district and the new Northfield YMCA cosponsored the All Star after school recreational program, the Y providing staff and the district providing the facilities. The after school and summer PLUS and School Readiness programs served more than 300 students in the summer of 2010. When the district reorganized its early education programs, it received a 4 Star Parent Aware rating, signaling to parents a concern for all children and their readiness for school. In 2011 the district developed and implemented a communications plan to help the Northfield community better understand the value of a Northfield Public School education. This regular public relations effort, not connected with bond or levy requests, was an important strategy to maintain public confidence in the public schools. As part of these communications, the district documented the high participation levels of children and adults in the popular Community Education programs: in 2015 there were 79,000 uses of the district facilities and 31,000 registrations in Community Rec and Ed programs.

Charlie Kyte's "quality education is a community enterprise" theme was sustained and expanded by Tofte and Richardson and found full expression in 2013 with the creation of a community collective impact initiative, Northfield Promise. After fifty community groups spent eighteen months of research and conversation about how the community could best serve its children, Northfield Promise was established to "make Northfield the best place in the world to grow up. This means that every single child should have the chance to be happy, healthy, and well-educated."[226] This rather bold and ambitious goal was pursued by connecting and aligning resources, programs, and community members toward "measurable results on 10 benchmarks throughout each child's life." With this Northfield Promise the community committed itself to working "tirelessly to ensure that ALL Northfield children" would:

> Be connected to the community during the early childhood years; Be ready for Kindergarten; Be at grade level in reading and math by the end of 3rd grade; Exhibit physical, social, and emotional well-being in elementary school; Have a connection with a caring adult beyond his/her parents as he/she transitions to middle school; Be at grade level in reading and math by the end of 6th grade; Have interests, goals and a vision for the future by the end of 8th grade; Ex-

hibit physical, social, and emotional well-being in high school; Report feeling connected and engaged in his/her high school and community; Graduate from high school with a plan to reach is his/her potential.[227]

Another remarkable community coalition, the Northfield Healthy Community Initiative (HCI), provided Northfield Promise with vital organizational support, recruited organizational partners, and staffed action teams that worked with each of the ten benchmarks. Indeed, Northfield Promise grew out of and was modeled on HCI's twenty-plus years of groundbreaking, nationally recognized work cultivating a collaborative community that supported, valued, and empowered Northfield youth. A Council of Champions, comprised of leaders and partners from education, business, nonprofits, and the public sector, served as guide and advocate. Council membership reflected the breadth of community involvement and included the superintendent of schools, two school board members, the Northfield United Way executive director, two business owners, the president of Carleton College, a minister representing the Northfield Area Interfaith Association, the Northfield mayor,

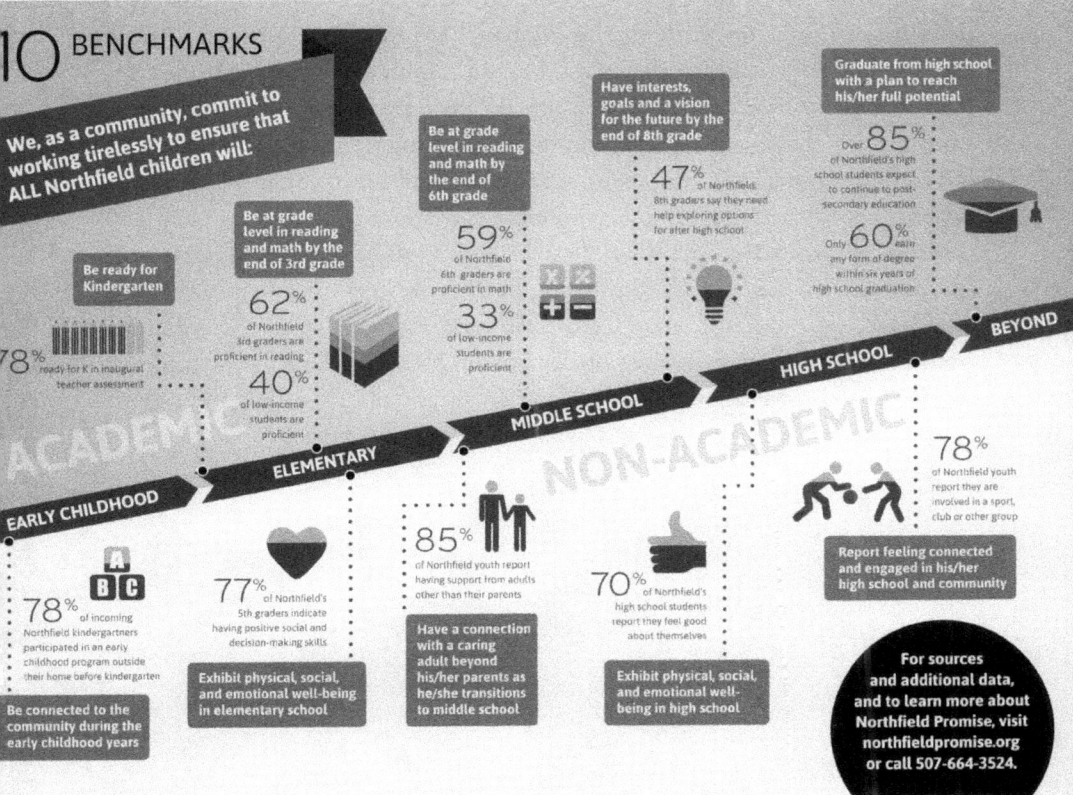

Northfield Promise Benchmarks Map

the Rice County public health and social services directors, and the CEO of Northfield Hospital and Clinics. The Northfield Public Schools benefited immensely from the broad support in their education town, where citizens cared deeply about the quality of life of all its citizens, but especially for its children. The HCI and Northfield Promise demonstrated what an education-centered community could do to supplement and support its public schools.

Human Resources/Staff Development

District superintendents have all understood that the quality of the teachers and staff determined the quality of the public schools. The importance of recruiting, hiring, and developing staff increased significantly as the school district grew in size and complexity; for the twenty-first century public schools, there was perhaps nothing more important. Staff salaries have always been the single largest expenditure in the schools' operating budget. While the district's human resource work in the nineteenth- and much of the twentieth-century fell to the superintendent and building principals, much shifted in the last thirty-five years to the Human Resources Department. During the Richardson superintendency the human resource work has included annual hiring of new teachers and staff, reviewing and revising job descriptions and staff evaluation procedures, negotiating contracts with teaching and non-teaching staff, and revising the Staff Handbook. Staff development has addressed customer service, workplace climate, cultural competency, and student management. The district established a self-funded health insurance program to reduce and stabilize rising health care costs and implemented a staff wellness program. A 2012 reorganization merged the district's human resources and business services operations under a new director of administrative services, Matthew Hillmann.

Technology

Ever since the 1960s new technologies have been changing the classroom and teaching, but with the introduction of the personal computer in the 1980s the technological revolution had begun. Word processing replaced the typewriter, and educational software supplemented the textbook. The creation of the Internet in the 1990s and new digital devices — laptop computers, smart phones, tablets — changed how Americans lived and how American students were schooled. Technology transformed the classroom, changed how teachers taught, and how students learned. The technology changes came swiftly and were pervasive. To manage this technological revolution, the district developed successive three-year plans — in 2005, 2008, 2011, and 2014. Infrastructure and hardware needed constant upgrading, as the classrooms were equipped with digital projectors and smart boards. The district wisely invested early in an expensive fiber optic network, allowing for an easier transition to wireless transmission. Communications, among students, teachers, and parents, went digital with texts, e-mails, social media and web sites. The annual report, newsletter, and other district publications were no longer printed and mailed to residents, but rather attached to e-mails or posted on the district web site.

By 2012, when the district launched its "teaching with tablets" initiative to supply every student in grades 4–12 with a tablet, the term "transformational technology" was used to describe the revolutionary changes in education. With the digital technologies students were learning differently, though not necessarily more or better — receiving immediate feedback, direct access to information, less dependence on the written word. Teachers' roles were also changing, shifting to less lecturing and imparting of information and more to teaching students how to use the technology, how to think critically, and how to learn. Teachers, many less comfortable with technology and less skilled than their students, received enhanced training. Technology became so important to classroom learning and school operations that in 2014 the district established a director of technology position.

When Chris Richardson retired in June 2016, he changed the title of his final annual report summary to the board from "Celebrations" to "Challenges." The listed issues, programs, and initiatives now labeled as challenges were a continuation of the annual celebration lists. Richardson believed that the future of the Northfield Public Schools would, in great part, be defined by how and how well the district and next superintendent addressed existing issues and maintained and improved existing programs and initiatives. Today's celebrations were tomorrow's challenges, hopefully to again become celebrations.

The most immediate tasks for the board were: to review and revise the 12-year-old District Strategic Plan and create a mission, belief, and strategy statement for the future; to review the District Master Facilities Plan and consider a proposal for a bond referendum for new elementary and high school buildings; and to continue to support and reauthorize the district's two healthy charter schools, Prairie Creek and Arcadia.

The remainder of the "Challenges" document detailed the existing programs and initiatives (described previously) to be maintained, implemented, or improved so that the healthy, well-run, "high performance/low cost" Northfield Public School District 659 would flourish far into the future.

The Hillmann Superintendency (2016–)

Superintendent Matthew Hillmann

The district turned to former Superintendent Charlie Kyte, who had developed a flourishing consulting business after retiring from the Minnesota Association of School Administrators (MASA) directorship, to conduct the search for the next superintendent. But when a strong internal candidate, Matthew Hillmann, the district's current director of administrative services, was identified, the board arranged in-depth interviews with teams representing the community, staff, and administrators and then selected Hillman to serve as the next superintendent of the Northfield Public Schools, effective July 1, 2016. Hillmann was a recent recipient of MASA's 2016 Outstanding Central Office Award for "exhibiting a willingness to risk, possessing strong communication skills, being a progressive change agent, and having high expectations for self and others."[228] Richardson's recommendation was unequivocal: "I believe Matt has demonstrated excellent skills and the potential to continue to do great things as a district administrator in Northfield." The board heartily concurred.

Hillmann, a native New Yorker, earned a B.A. in history from St. John's University and a doctorate in education from Minnesota State University, Mankato. He began his education career as a classroom teacher in the Madelia (MN) Public Schools, followed by serving as a principal, director of curriculum and technology, and district assessment coordinator for Belle Plaine (MN) Public Schools. In 2009 Hillmann became Northfield's director of human resources and technology and then director of administrative services. His broad district administrative expertise and experience, especially in technology, human resources, and curriculum assessment, made him ideal for Northfield's twenty-first century superintendency.

Hillmann began his superintendency with four primary goals. First was to sustain the Northfield Public Schools's heritage of excellence, to "keep Northfield Northfield."[229] He understood and appreciated the district's strengths — first-rate staff and excellent classroom teachers; a strong curriculum, especially for college-bound students; an effective assessment program that used data to serve students; and collaborative relationships with a supportive community — and was committed to maintaining them. He realized that Northfield as an education town provided the public schools with special opportunities, benefits, and responsibilities not found in many small rural communities.

Second, Hillmann was committed to continuing the careful financial stewardship of Northfield's high performance/low cost public schools, ensuring residents got value from their tax dollars, satisfying taxpayers's "lobster appetites on a fish stick budget." Third was to improve and expand the diversity initiatives that addressed the achievement gap and ensured all students benefitted from their educational experience. Fourth, was to address the mental health issues many students experience in a high standard/high performance educational environment.

With seven years of experience as second in command in the district, Hillmann made a smooth and immediate transition to the superintendent's position. In the fall of 2016 the board adopted two important district planning documents — a master facilities plan and a new strategic plan. The Master Facilities Plan[230] had two components, a building life cycle management plan and a long-term facilities maintenance plan, which would be reviewed annually with the capital projects budget. The Building Life Cycle Management Plan identified two "next projects:" a $28.4 million elementary project to construct a new Greenvale Park Elementary School, renovate the current Greenvale School for use as the district's Early Childhood Education Center, and make modest renovations at Sibley and Bridgewater Elementary Schools; and a $76.5 million High School project to construct a new Northfield High School on the site of the current building.

The new Strategic Plan[231] was similar to the 2005 plan created early in the Richardson superintendency. Added was a vision statement — "We will prepare every student for lifelong success within a world-class learning environment with a commitment to community partnerships and sustainability" — that continued the emphasis on inclusion, educational excellence, community partnerships, and sustainability. The mission to "deliver educational excellence that empowers all learners to engage in our dynamic world" was unchanged, as were the six Beliefs and six Strategies. The "ongoing priorities" were to recruit and retain diverse staff and provide robust core subject instruction. The four "near-term" priorities were to build and foster relationships and social/emotional health for all, to provide students equitable opportunities and support for all career and college paths, to provide spaces that are modern, innovative, creative, and flexible, and to develop a long-term solution that allowed for "reasonable class size while maintaining financial stability." These priorities, though expressed in twenty-first-century language, were remarkably similar to those of previous generations — provide excellent academic instruction, promote holistic health, prepare students for the future, provide facilities that support learning, and maintain financial stability.

Student Behavior

The expectations, rules, and regulations regarding student behavior evolved throughout the district's history, and were documented in annual Northfield Public School publications: the *Manual of the Public Schools* in the 1890's, the *Raider Guide* in the 1960's, and the Student Citizenship Handbook in the early twenty-first century. The publications reflected the prevailing educational philosophy, societal attitudes, and legal realities of their times. Hillmann wrote parents and students that the K-12 Student Citizenship Handbook[232] provided a clear, consistent, comprehensive policy on student behavior that was necessary to ensure a safe and secure learning environment for all students. While the Handbook detailed the district's guidelines for acceptable student behavior, the school's were more concerned with teaching, practicing, and expecting productive and responsible behavior, to provide an environment to help students become "self-disciplined contributing citizens of school and community." Indeed, the Northfield Public Schools had formal educational programs to address student behavior and support this goal, the Responsive Classroom in the elementary schools and the Positive Behavior Interventions and Supports (PBIS) in the secondary schools. Thus the Ddistrict's contemporary philosophy regarding learning and discipline focused on students developing responsible behaviors and self-discipline, and defined discipline as "a learning experience, not just a punishment."

Since the late 1960's, school behavior guides have delineated student rights and responsibilities as a preface to the discipline guidelines. The Student Citizenship Handbook described student rights and responsibilities in 12 twelve areas — access to records, dress and grooming, equal opportunity, fair treatment, free speech, harassment, learning, nondiscrimination, pledge of allegiance, privacy, student government, and student safety. With that context, the remainder of the Handbook lists 35 thirty-five prohibited behaviors (violations) and recommended consequences. The list included verbal abuse, alcohol or chemical possession or use, arson, assault, inflicting bodily harm, bullying, burglary, cell phone use, scholastic dishonesty, disrespectful or disruptive behavior, careless driving, false reporting, fighting, misuse of fire equipment, possession of fireworks or ammunition, gambling, gang/group activity, harassment and violence, hazing, insubordination, offensive behavior, records falsification, robbery, safety, sexual misconduct, technology and telecommunication misuse, theft, threat, tobacco possession, trespassing, truancy, unexcused absence, vandalism, unauthorized parking, and weapons. While corporal punishment was strictly prohibited, the school retained control over student lockers and can could inspect them any time, without notice, student consent, or a search warrant. Consistent with an educational approach to discipline, the list of possible disciplinary consequences started with student conference and parent conference, but also included the traditional sanctions of detention, fines and restitution, removal from class, in-school suspension, Saturday School (supervised study session on Saturday), out-of-school suspension (maximum 15 fifteen days), exclusion, and expulsion. Expulsion was considered a "last resort," but was possible on the first offence for serious violations including drug distribution, arson, firearms, sexual misconduct, threats, major vandalism, and weapons.

The 2017 Referendum

In the fall of 2017, following the recommendation of the Master Facility Plan, the district asked voters to consider two referendum proposals: $109 million to demolish the 1962 high school facility and build a new high school ($78.5 million) and new elementary school ($30.5 million), and a new, increased ten-year operating levy at the maximum amount authorized by Minnesota law (from $470 to $1,967 per student). The Referendum Guide[233] sent to all district postal patrons explained that "levies are for learning and bonds are for buildings." Hillmann and the board argued that the increased operating levy was necessary to maintain high quality instruction and programs despite the state's long-term underfunding of public schools. The new and updated buildings would provide enhanced security and increased energy efficiency, instructional spaces that support the needs of current and future students, and increased space for early childhood education programs and K-5 Special Education and English Language Learning, and support the recruitment and retainment retention of high quality staff. The passage of the bond referendum was contingent on the approval of the operating levy.

The board understood that the increased levy and building bond would have significant impact on resident and business taxpayers — an estimated annual increase of $532 on a $250,000 home and $1,636 on a $500,000 commercial property. Yet they it believed the levy increase and the new construction was necessary to maintain the school system's excellence and meet the district's future needs. Although there appeared to be broad community support for the increased levy, there was vocal opposition to the bond proposal, expressed by respected business owner (and former School Board member and state legislator) Ray Cox in "Another View" in the *News*. "For the first time in my life I will be casting a no vote for a school board referendum," Cox wrote, because demolishing the 50-year-old high school was, for many reasons, simply not warranted. Demolishing an existing adequate building never makes environmental sense, as "the greenest building was the one you never build." There was real value in renovating and retaining buildings for their useful life (80–110 years for the high school), as Cox's construction company had done for the old downtown Arts Guild and Historical Society buildings; this multi-million dollar asset belongs to the community, and was only half way through its useful life. And finally, the tax burden was unfair to the current taxpayers. It would be wiser to divide the two major building projects and fund one at a time.

The voters apparently agreed with Cox and soundly defeated the bond referendum, 56 percent (NO) to 44 percent (YES). The levy increase, however, was approved by a narrow margin, 51.6% percent voting YES. Hillmann told the *News* he was of course disappointed by the unsuccessful bond referendum, but "really pleased Northfield continues to support student programming at the highest levels."[234] These referendum results were consistent with those of the past. Northfield residents are committed to excellence for their public schools and are willing to tax themselves at the highest level allowed by law. Yet they also are cautious with public expenditures, expect to get value with their expenditures, and were not convinced that the construction of two new buildings were necessary at that time.

The Legacy of the Northfield Public Schools

This history of the Northfield Public Schools tells the story of an educational institution similar to small-town school districts throughout rural Minnesota and the nation. Northfield, like most American communities, was committed to establishing local public schools that would prepare their children for careers, adulthood, and being responsible and productive members of the community. Much of Northfield's history would be generally familiar to those from other small-towns: the story of funding and building school houses, hiring teachers and administrators, creating curriculums and courses of study, and providing activities and services. However, as the preceding narrative has detailed, the public schools' history was unique and specific to Northfield. Four themes emerged from the 160-year history that explain the public school's particular importance and meaning for the Northfield community: 1) the public schools were an integral part of Northfield's community identity and ethos as an education town; 2) four distinctive qualities — academic excellence, priority on the arts, diversity and inclusiveness, and educational choice -- shaped and strengthened the Northfield Public Schools; 3) the public schools were significantly influenced by other Northfield educational institutions, especially the public library, the colleges, and the local newspaper; and 4) the financing the Northfield public schools was especially challenging, as residents sought and expected high performance/low cost schools.

The Northfield Public Schools were shaped by and benefitted from being an integral part of an education town, a "city of schools" and the town's "number one business." The emphasis on education, a core community value from its founding, was further strengthened by the establishment and growth of two liberal arts colleges, which increased the number of highly-educated citizens who valued education and engendered a community civic culture with a collaborative commitment to literacy, scholarship and life-long learning. Northfield was a college town-times-two, and an education town; in such an environment the public schools should be first-rate.

The Northfield Public Schools are and were characterized by four qualities that have been high priorities throughout its history. First, a relentless pursuit for academic excellence, led by talented experienced classroom teachers and effective administrators, especially long-serving Superintendents like Merton Fobes, O. W. Herr, J. H. Wichman, John Longstreet, Charlie Kyte, and Chris Richardson. Second, the arts were considered an important component of the core curriculum, and consequently the art program was protected and even strengthened during the 1930's Great Depression and the 2008–10 Great Recession when other districts were reducing their art programs.

Third, inclusion and diversity were primary district values, beginning with the 19th century democratic frontier common schools, dedicated to serving all children, including immigrants and non-native speakers. The high school demonstrated this commitment to inclusion throughout its history: developing excellent programs for both the college-bound and vocational training, the gifted and the challenged, and for traditional and non-traditional learners. And fourth, while requiring all to complete a common core curriculum, the public schools also offered educational choice. In the late 1800's high school students could choose from three curriculums; in the 20th and 21st centuries students can choose electives to individualize their academic experience. With the district's two charter schools, Prairie Creek and Arcadia, parents and students can choose alternative school settings.

The Northfield Public Schools have been influenced considerably by the town's other educational institutions, especially the two colleges, and less so the public library, and the Northfield Arts Guild. The effect of the two liberal arts colleges on the public schools is difficult to measure but has undoubtedly been profound. Having a substantial portion of the town's parents themselves educators creates a community environment of support for the public schools, and a civic culture in which public education can thrive. Northfielders, as this history has made evident, have come to expect first-rate excellent public schools.

Yet Northfielders are also very cautious about the expenditure of public funds, even for purposes, like education, that they value highly. They expect high-performing public schools at a low cost, often expressed in colorful language: regarding education and the public schools Northfielders seem to have a "lobster appetite on a fish stick budget," or "champagne taste on a beer budget." However, as this history has shown, when Northfielders are convinced of the need and the cost required for excellent high-performing public schools, they have supported the Northfield Public Schools with their interest, their time, and most importantly, with their tax dollars.

Northfield Education Timeline

Prepared by Susan Hvistendahl, 2005–06
The following is an extract of a much longer document that also includes events relating to Carleton and St. Olaf Colleges. The full timeline is available from the Northfield Public School district.

1851 Four years before founding Northfield, John Wesley North writes the charter for the University of Minnesota in the town of St. Anthony Falls, where he and wife Ann Loomis North are living. The bill officially creating the University of Minnesota is ratified by the territorial legislature on February 19, 1851 and signed into law by the governor on February 25. The first teacher, Elijah Merrill, is hired to run the University as a preparatory school and is a guest of the Norths.

1856 The Drake School, said to be the first school in Rice County, is built on land donated by the Drake family. It is located 2 miles south of Northfield, on the northwest corner of the junction of what is now Rice County Road #1 and Minn. Highway #246. After the original school burns around 1880, a new brick building is erected and used until the school is closed in 1938 and students bused to Northfield.

1856 John North opens the first public school in Northfield on November 7, with 25 students, under headmaster Rollins Olin. The price of building the school, located at Union and East 3rd Streets, is $700.

1856 A lyceum is formed by early Northfield inhabitants to provide education on various topics through lectures, debates and library materials. It is organized to "create a taste for literature and a thirst for knowledge." The first meeting on October 1st is held in the new schoolhouse.

1857 The Northfield Lyceum is moved from the schoolhouse to its own building at 109 E. 4th Street. Furthering its educational aims, the Lyceum serves as the town's first library. Today this is Northfield's oldest commercial building.

1861 On the same site as the first Northfield public school (at the corner of Union and Third Streets), another is put up at a cost of $6000, "the envy of neighboring districts for a wide range." Both frame buildings are used until St. Olaf's School buys the buildings in 1874.

1866 Carleton College is founded as Northfield College, a preparatory institution, sparked by Charles M. Goodsell. Northfield's offer of $18,500 and 20 acres of land is accepted by the state Association of Congregational Churches which says of Northfield: "The character of the church and the population as to intelligence, morals and religion is second to none. It is a fine place in which to send children from Christian homes." The formal charter is given in December.

1874 An Independent School District is organized and a large brick building known as Central School is erected for $30,000 (one source, Grabau, says $35,000) on the east side of Union between 3rd and 4th Streets next to a public park. An 1882 history says that the

3-story school has "all the modern school improvements, and standing as it does near the Congregational Church, and not far from the college buildings, it does not suffer in comparison with them, but is a worthy companion for those stately buildings alike devoted to educational purposes." In 1909 it is destroyed by fire.

1874 Led by Rev. Bernt Julius Muus, pastor of Holden Lutheran Church, St. Olaf's School is founded on November 6 when the Articles of Incorporation are signed. Other founders are Harald Thorson, a Northfield businessman who contributes the first $2000 to the school, and area farmers O.K. Finseth, K. P. Haugen and O. Osmundson. The citizens of Northfield raise $5400 to aid the establishment of this Norwegian academy. Lots on Union Street, including two wooden school buildings, are purchased from the Northfield School District for $2500 for school use, with Harald Thorson as negotiator.

1874 An Independent School District is organized and the Central School is completed at a cost of about $35,000 on Union Street on the block shared with Central Park. A substantial three-story, mansard-roofed brick building, it is destroyed by fire on April 29, 1908.

1877 On June 28 Northfield graduates its first high school class of seven members, all girls. (The first boy appears on record in 1879.) In 1877 the total number of high school graduates in Minnesota is 117.

1885 Preparations for Longfellow School, a new west side school, are completed (brick work, stone for the foundation, plastering and seats).

1886 A new four-room school is built to serve Northfield students on the west side of the Cannon River. It is called the West Side or Lincoln School. In 1900 it is replaced with the Longfellow School.

1889 St. Olaf's School becomes St. Olaf College by action of the Board of Trustees on June 20 and Principal Mohn becomes President Mohn. St. Olaf's founder Rev. B.J. Muus completes fifteen years as chairman of the Board of Trustees, thus staying connected to the school until the college department is established.

1891 The preparatory department is severed from Carleton College and begins independent existence as Carleton Academy.

1893 Children vote on a name for the West Side School and, being "enthusiastic admirers of 'The Children's Poet,' decide in favor of Longfellow School by a large majority."

1893 The Board of Education buys the Dilley property for the West Side School Building (Longfellow) for $600.

1893 The new school in the second ward, the Washington School, opens at a cost of $11,157.12. Miss Josephine Apfeld is the principal and is an eighth grade teacher until 1897.

1898 The Laura Baker School, the first boarding school for the mentally retarded west of the Mississippi, moves from Minneapolis (where it was established in Sept., 1897) to 211 Oak Street in Northfield. The school is incorporated in 1919. Baker initiates a progressive program stressing the importance of health care and education in a comfortable home environment. Laura Baker lives to the age of 101, dying in 1960, after 83 years devoted to the care of betterment of the retarded.

1898 The Northfield Public Library is organized by Hiram Scriver and is in the YMCA building until 1910. Edith Pye is the first librarian.

1899 Margaret Evans Huntington, Carleton's Dean of Women, is elected to the Northfield School Board, just after Minnesota begins allowing women to vote in school board elections.

1899 The Washington School is built on Eighth Street near Washington to serve the east side of town.

1900 Frances G. Bishop begins teaching English and geometry in Northfield, teaching until the spring of 1929. She serves as head of the English Department and assistant principal. The *Northfield News* writes, "Probably no teacher in the history of Northfield High School has been so universally loved and admired by her pupils as has Miss Bishop, and none since the founding of the community has served the schools for a longer period. Generations of young people of Northfield have come under her helpful influence, an influence felt in every phase of school life in which she always maintained a genuinely enthusiastic interest."

1904 Mrs. Charlotte Leslie is the principal of the Washington School 1904–05 for grades 6, 7 and 8. Longfellow School has grades 1–4 and Central 1–5 and high school.

1906 Carleton Academy, a preparatory department which began independent existence from the college in 1891, is discontinued as of June.

1908 The original Central High School, built in 1874, is destroyed by fire on April 29. The Northfield News writes that "although there are many fond memories clinging to the old building, sentiment should be brushed aside and the children of today be given the advantages of a new school home."

1910 Lillian Stewart (Carleton Class of 1895) starts teaching at Northfield High School in physics and chemistry, retiring in 1935 after 25 years. She is also active in the community, along with her two sisters Maude and Nina who were also teachers. Lillian Stewart's death is reported in the Northfield News of April 16, 1942.

1910 Andrew Carnegie donates $10,000 to build a new library at the site of the current one.

1910 The new high school is built on the site of the old one at 301 Union Street. Additions are completed in 1936 and 1955. When a new high school is completed in 1966 the school serves as a middle school, finally closing in 2004.

1911 The new high school in Northfield is completed at a cost of $90,000.

1915 M.P. Fobes starts his tenure as superintendent of schools in Northfield. He succeeds Edgar George who spent 15 years in Northfield. Fobes is active in the Northfield community and his service is cut short when, on August 4, 1924, Fobes drowns in Lyman Memorial Lake on the Carleton College campus.

1915 Hattie Subra serves as principal of Longfellow Elementary School from 1915 until 1946.

1917 Flora Wright starts teaching in the Northfield Public Schools where she serves until 1941 as teacher of fifth and sixth grades and as principal in the Washington School. Her death is reported in 1944.

1917 Alberta Ackerman teaches in Northfield public school system from 1917 to 1934. She starts teaching at the normal training school, then teaches at the junior high school from 1920 until retirement. She dies in 1961.

1919 Mary W. Clark (Carleton Class of 1908) joins the faculty of Northfield High School to teach plane and solid geometry and trigonometry and occasionally English. She serves as adviser to the "Periscope" newspaper 1929–1950 and is a beloved teacher for 31 years until her retirement in 1950.

1922 The first issue of the Northfield High School newspaper is published, unnamed, on February 3, 1922. A contest is announced on the front page for name suggestions. On February 17 the newspaper is published with the name "Periscope," suggested by freshman Lois Miller. The staff notes that "We may use our 'Periscope' as the High School eye through which to watch and note the parade of school life as it passes by."

1924 After the drowning death of Merton P. Fobes in Lyman Memorial Lake at Carleton in August, O.W. Herr takes over as superintendent of the Northfield School District and serves until 1935. Fobes had directed the district for nine years. A *Northfield News* caption of Fobes states, "In Superintendent Fobes' untimely death, Northfield schools lose a capable and far-sighted executive, and the whole community a distinguished and well-loved citizen."

1926 The Northfield High School graduating class numbers 84, the biggest class in the first 50 years of high school.

1927 St. Dominic's Rosary School opens on September 2 with 75 students, staffed by the Sisters of Notre Dame.

1933 Estelle Moynihan serves as Principal of Northfield Junior/Senior High School from 1933–36.

1935 J.H. Wichman succeeds O.W. Herr as superintendent of the Northfield School District and serves until 1945.

1936 Florence Nibble becomes principal of the Northfield Junior High School and serves until 1946.

1936 Richard Falck serves as Northfield Senior High principal, serving until 1946.

1937 A new addition to the Northfield High School building is formally dedicated on April 27. The enlargement provides an auditorium, gymnasium, classrooms, offices, home economics rooms, music room, shower and locker rooms. The addition has been in use from September of 1936 and is built and furnished at a cost of nearly $158,000. The President of the University of Minnesota, Dr. Lotus D. Coffman, delivers the dedication address.

1944 A speech in January by Russell Reynolds, Professor of Child Psychology at Carleton, to the Northfield Pre-School Mothers' Club leads to the formation of the Northfield Cooperative Nursery School. It is a non-profit organization, organized by the parents of the pre-school children and governed by a board of directors from this group. Carleton students working as assistants use the school as a laboratory. Opal Vogel Martinson is the first director.

1945 Erling O. Johnson is elected superintendent of the Northfield Schools in the spring, succeeding J.H. Wichman. Johnson is active in community affairs and in bringing about the consolidation of the Northfield School District. He serves for eight years until 1953.

1946 William Carlson serves as Principal of Northfield Junior/Senior High School 1946–1961.

1946 Alice Peterson serves as principal for Longfellow Elementary School, 1946–50, succeeding Hattie Subra who holds the position 1915–46.

1947 The New Longfellow School is built in Northfield.

1948 The Memorial Athletic Field is built by the Northfield school district.

1949 On June 22 ground is broken for a new Indiana limestone school building for Longfellow School, to be adjoined to its predecessor. Plans call for eight classrooms, a library, a two-story physical education room with stage, lunch room and kitchen in the basement, music room with stage, two locker rooms, teachers' room, administrative offices and bathrooms on 1st and 2nd floors.

1953 John H. Longstreet begins his 20-year career as superintendent of Northfield schools. In 1983 he is selected as the Pioneer Educator of the Year by the Southeastern Minnesota Retired Educators Association. He is also known for his work with many Northfield community organizations. He dies in April of 1989.

1955 A final addition is completed at the Old Middle School for classroom space and for use as a bomb shelter and hospital in case of attack.

1955 The new Washington Elementary School addition includes a spacious kindergarten room, 7 classrooms for lower elementary grades, a gym, lunch room, kitchen, principal's office, nurse's office and library.

1961 Arnold Larson serves as Principal of Northfield Junior/Senior High School until 1965.

1963 Demolition begins in June on the old Longfellow School.

1965 Ernest Gustafson serves as Principal of Northfield High School for ten years, until 1975.

1965 Arnold Larson serves as Principal of Northfield Junior High School 1965–68.

1966 The Northfield architectural firm of Edward A. Sovik, St. Olaf Class of 1939, designs the new Northfield High School which opens for fall on Sept. 6. The cornerstone is laid in May. Total cost is estimated at 2.5 million.

1967 Northfield architect Edward Sovik (St. Olaf Class of 1939) is named a Fellow of the American Institute of Architects. Between 1950 and 1992 his Northfield architectural firm designs 28 architectural projects at St. Olaf, two major projects at Carleton, the new Northfield High School and many churches throughout the United States. In 1982 he is only the third recipient of the Minnesota Society, American Institute of Architects gold medal for meritorious service to the public and the profession, the highest honor bestowed by the society.

Late 1960s Northfield's city recreation program is operated mostly by school district teachers, with Faye Miller as the first full-time recreation director.

1968 James Hamblin serves as principal of Longfellow Elementary School 1968–71.

1969 Brad Johnson is Principal of Sibley Elementary School, serving 1969–81.

1969 Wayne Porter serves as Principal of Northfield Junior High School 1969–78, succeeding Arnold Larson.

1971 On June 3rd it is announced that Northfield High School teacher Celeste Magner will be the honorary speaker at commencement this year since these are the last students she taught in 10th grade history before her retirement in 1969. In an article about her, Maggie Lee writes that "She might well have been the most beloved teacher ever to have taught at the school."

1971 Jan Dallenbach succeeds James Hamblin as Principal of Longfellow Elementary School, serving from 1971–82.

1971 James Hamblin becomes Principal of Greenvale Park Elementary School and serves until 1975.

1972 Northfield joins the Community Education movement as the state of Minnesota approves categorical aid to districts offering such programs with no competition for district funds. A Community Board is established and part-time director hired. Governor Harold Levander encourages the concept of "the Lighted School" in 1971–72, where schools are lighted at night for the use of citizens for continuing learning.

1973 Tom McGovern, who holds a degree in recreation, is hired as full-time Director of the Community Education and Recreation program in Northfield. The department includes a half-time education coordinator and a half-time school volunteer coordinator.

1973 Jack W. Geckler succeeds John Longstreet as Superintendent of Northfield Public Schools, serving until 1982.

1975 William Gasho succeeds Ernest Gustafson as Principal of Northfield High School, serving 22 years until 1997.

1975 David Marvin succeeds James Hamblin as Principal of Greenvale Park Elementary School and serves until 1977.

1975 Northfield High School teacher Casey Hero is listed in the new edition of "Outstanding Educators of America." He is hired in 1946 to teach general science and biology, then teaches speech and dramatics and serves as AV director.

1975 Burdell Hero is the first coordinator of the School District Volunteer Program, working with the school district to bring volunteers of all ages, parents, senior citizens, college students, etc., into the schools. This is the oldest specialty program of the Community Education and Recreation Dept.

1977 Harry Hoff succeeds David Marvin as Principal of Greenvale Park Elementary School and serves 1977–81.

1979 Walt Feldbrugge of Fergus Falls, Minnesota, becomes the new director of the Community Education and Recreation program in Northfield.

1979 David Peterson succeeds Wayne Porter as Principal of Northfield Junior High School. In 1982 the name is changed to Northfield Middle School and Peterson continues as principal until 1989.

1981 Judi Brandon succeeds Brad Johnson as Principal of Sibley Elementary School, serving 1981–82.

1981 Brad Johnson succeeds Harry Hoff as Principal of Greenvale Park Elementary School and serves until 1982.

1982 Dwight Lindbloom succeeds Jack W. Geckler as Superintendent of Northfield Public Schools, serving until 1985.

1982 Judi Brandon succeeds Brad Johnson as Principal of Greenvale Park Elementary School and serves 1982–84.

1982 Jan Dallenbach succeeds Judi Brandon as Principal of Sibley Elementary School and serves 1982–90.

1984 Early Childhood Family Education (ECFE) begins in Northfield, first funded with a grant and the second year with state funding. The program is designed to give parenting education and support to all kinds of family in the community. Connie Bragonier Ryberg is the first coordinator of this program and serves 1984–2004.

1984 Adult Basic Education program begins in Northfield, offering classes in basic skills, GED preparation, English as a second language and citizenship classes.

1984 Mary Hertogs becomes Principal of Greenvale/Longfellow Elementary Schools, serving 1984–87.

1985 Stanley Mack succeeds Dwight Lindbloom as Superintendent of the Northfield Public School District, serving until 1988. His challenges are said to be implementation of grade school reorganization and finance.

1985 School Age Care program begins in Northfield.

Mid 1980s After School Unlimited, a school age child care program, starts with eight students and is led by Donna Vanderhoof. Today the school is available before school opens, for kindergarteners, after school and in the summer. Ann Wind is program coodinator for over ten years.

1986 Project ABLE begins in Northfield, a program offering educational, recreational and social opportunities for adults with disabilities.

1987 Audrey Moe is named Community Education and Recreation director in Northfield.

1987 Bonnie Jean Flom serves as Principal of the Greenvale/Longfellow Elementary Schools 1987–89 and then of Greenvale Park Elementary School 1989–90.

1987 Youth Development/Youth Service begins in Northfield, striving to provide activities and support to middle school and high school students outside the school day.

1989 Brad Johnson becomes Principal of Longfellow Elementary School, serving from 1989–92.

1989 Charles Kyte succeeds Stanley Mack as Superintendent of the Northfield Public School District, serving until 2000.

1989 Laura Kay Allen succeeds David Peterson as Principal of the Northfield Middle School and serves until 1992.

1990 Nancy Wittman-Beltz succeeds Bonnie Jean Flom as Principal of Greenvale Park Elementary School and serves 1990–95.

1990 Kurt Nordness succeeds Jan Dallenbach as Principal of Sibley Elementary School, serving 1990–93.

1992 Donald Lapp succeeds Laura Kay Allen as Principal of Northfield Middle School, serving 1992–94.

1992 Mark Brown succeeds Brad Johnson as Principal of Longfellow Elementary School, serving 1992–93.

1993 Pamela McDonnell succeeds Mark Brown as Principal of Longfellow Elementary School, serving 1993–98.

1993 Harold Benson succeeds Kurt Nordness as Principal of Sibley Elementary School and serves 1993–99.

1994 Ron Johnson succeeds Donald Lapp as Principal of Northfield Middle School, serving until 1998.

1995 Rob Metz succeeds Nancy Wittman-Beltz as Principal of Greenvale Park Elementary School and serves 1995–98.

1996 Northfield creates a Parks and Recreation Department with a full-time recreation director, temporarily ending the joint powers agreement between the school district and the city where the city funds all recreation activities and the school district administers the program.

1997 On June 1st the Northfield Montessori School comes into being, a non-profit incorporated entity started by parents when the Twin Cities-based Montessori program announces it is closing in Northfield at the end of March of this year. A loan from Rural Development USDA will help finance the building of a new center to open in the fall of 2005 on North Highway 3, with space for 186 children.

1997 The Village School, Northfield's first charter school, opens in August with 45 students in kindergarten through grade eight. The school is located on the campus of the Laura Baker School and starts with two full-time teachers and three part-time teachers. The Village School is administered and run by parents, teachers and students who develop a learning plan together.

1997 The Cannon Valley Elder Collegium offers its first term of classes to Northfield senior citizens. Founded by Ron and Bettye Ronning and Keith and Beverly Anderson, CVEC provides lifelong learning opportunities with classes held at St. Olaf College, the Northfield Retirement Center, Northfield City Hall and the Northfield Senior Center. Twenty classes are offered during the 1997–98 year with a total of 220 students enrolled.

1997 Bruce Santerre succeeds William Gasho as Principal of Northfield Senior High School. He retires in 2006.

1997 Scott Wallner is named director of the Community Education and Recreation Department in Northfield.

1998 Bridgewater Elementary School is opened in September for a cost of $8.6 million on a 14-acre site south of Northfield. Diane Kinneberg is the Principal.

1998 In February the Cannon Valley Elder Collegium, a community-based program of classes for anyone 50 and older, is featured in a segment on the NBC Nightly News broadcast. A "Today" show segment airs in May, as well as on KSTP-TV the next day. Articles about the CVEC have also appeared in the New York Times, Washington Post, Boston Globe, Houston Chronicle Chronicle on Higher Education and the International Herald-Tribune.

1998 Burt Bemmels succeeds Ron Johnson as Principal of the Northfield Middle School.

1998 Bill Van Loh succeeds Rob Metz as Principal of Greenvale Park Elementary School and serves 1998–2002.

1998 Lynne Karimi succeeds Pamela McDonnell as Principal of Longfellow Elementary School and serves 1998–99.

1999 Amy Hamborg succeeds Lynne Karimi as Principal of Longfellow Elementary School and serves 1999–2004

1999 Scott Sannes succeeds Harold Benson as Principal of Sibley Elementary School.

2000 Hannah Puczo serves as the director of Northfield's Community Education and Recreation program starting in 2000.

2000 Terry G. Tofte succeeds Charles Kyte as Superintendent of the Northfield Public School District, serving until 2004.

2002 Julie Nielsen succeeds Bill Van Loh as Principal of Greenvale Park Elementary School. Nielsen leaves in 2006 to become the new principal at Middleton Elementary School in Woodbury.

2003 The name Community Education and Recreation is restored to Northfield's program when the school district and the city resume their joint powers agreement where the city funds all recreation activities and the school district administers the program.

2003 Northfield School of Arts & Technology is founded, a secondary charter school built on project-based education. The mission statement is: "To provide students with an individualized, innovative, educational program that fosters life-long skills, enhanced through the Arts and aided by technology."

2004 The Northfield Public School District now offers educational services to over 3,800 students in grades K-12. Kindergarten students attend either a half-day program at Longfellow Elementary or a full day program in the other 3 elementary schools. Students in grades 6–8 attend the new (fall, 2004) middle school and grades 9–12 attend the high school.

2004 A handout from the office of Northfield's superintendent of schools, Terry G. Tofte, provides information about a Spanish immersion program for elementary students, alternative education for ages 12–21, and special education instruction for ages birth-21. Through Community Education and Recreation the district offers a variety of services for families with young children including early childhood family education, early childhood screening, pre-school, family literacy program and outreach to families and childcare providers. Also offered are school age child care, youth programs, recreation for all ages, middle school youth center, adult enrichment, adult basic education and programs for adults with disabilities.

2004 In June the old Northfield Middle School formally closes as the United States flag is brought down in a farewell ceremony.

2004 L. Chris Richardson succeeds Terry G. Tofte as Superintendent of the Northfield Public School District. He considers funding of utmost importance in upcoming months.

2004–05 Lisa Carlson succeeds Lynne Karami as principal of Longfellow Elementary School in its final year teaching kindergarteners.

2004 In September the new Northfield Middle School on the south side of the town is dedicated and students and staff enjoy 42 classrooms, nine science rooms, computer labs, a 750-seat auditorium, an eight-lane swimming pool with room for an audience of 250, a fitness room and three gyms. More than 20 acres of school property includes a track and sports fields.

2004 Northfield School District, $650,000 in the red, nears bankruptcy, according to preliminary 2003–04 audit results presented to the Northfield School Board.

2005 In July the Northfield School Board approves sale of the old Middle school to Carleton for approximately $142,000. The building is to be used as a center for the arts for Carleton. The official closing is held October 13.

2006 In April the Northfield School Board considers whether to re-sponsor the K-12 charter school called the Village School, established in 1997, due to academic accountability and safety issues. On May 29 the school board votes 5 to 2 not to renew its charter contract. The Village School holds what may be its last graduation ceremony on June 3.

2006 Northfield High School principal Bruce Santerre retires and is succeeded by Joel Leer, assistant principal at Prior Lake High School, on July 1.

2006 Sister Cheryl Marie Wagner resigns as principal of St. Dominic Elementary School. She is succeeded by Vicky Kalina Marvin on July 1.

2006 Jeff Roland joins the Northfield Public School district as principal of Greenvale Park Elementary.

Endnotes

1. Cremin, Lawrence. *American Education: The Metropolitan Experience 1876–1980.* New York: Harper and Row, 1988, 645.
2. Ibid., 12.
3. "All About Northfield, Minn.", a promotional booklet written by *Northfield News* Editor Joel Heatwole. Northfield: *Northfield News* Printing, 1889. Copies in the Northfield Public Library Pye Room historical collection and the Northfield Historical Society.
4. Clark, Clifford, an essay titled "Minnesota: Image and Identity" in *Minnesota in a Century of Change: The State and Its People Since 1900.* St Paul: Minnesota Historical Society Press, 1989, 1–2.
5. *Rice County Journal,* September 10, 1872.
6. Clifford Clark, "Evolution of a Community," in *Northfield: The History and Architecture of a Community* (Northfield, Minnesota: Northfield Heritage Preservation Commission, 1999), 5.
7. Franklin Curtis-Wedge, *History of Rice County* (Chicago: HC Cooper and Co., 1910 [originally printed 1882]), 458.
8. *Northfield Telegraph,* April 3, 1861, in the Early Northfield History Scrapbook, Northfield Public Library.
9. *Rice County Journal,* December 25, 1872 editorial.
10. Diane Ravitch and Maris Vinovskis (Editors), *Learning From the Past: What History Teaches Us About School Reform.* Baltimore and London: John Hopkins Press 1995.
11. Blegen, Theodore, *Minnesota: A History of the State.* Minneapolis: University of Minnesota Press, 1963, 409
12. Franklin Curtis-Wedge, *History of Rice County,* 624.
13. From the article "When Northfield High Was Young" written by Superintendent O. W. Herr in the 1927 Northfield High School Annual, *The Orange and Black,* 11–12.
14. *Northfield News,* January 19, 1923, page 4. Board records from the first years were found by Superintendent M. P. Fobes, who shared some of the information with the *News* in an article headlined "Northfield School District was Formed on August 12, 1856, Old Records Reveal." The handwritten board minutes were subsequently sent to the Minnesota Historical Society and are in the State Archives collection housed in the Gale Library at the Minnesota History Center in St Paul.
15. The original district charter is in the Minnesota State Archives in the Minnesota Historical Society's Gale Library, Minnesota History Center, St. Paul.
16. Franklin Curtis-Wedge, *History of Rice County,* 625.
17. In time the site would hold Northfield's original high school, which later served as the town's middle school. It is now the home of Carleton College's Weitz Center for Creativity.
18. *Rice County Journal,* January 20, 1875.
19. *Northfield News,* February 8, 1890, 4.
20. *Northfield News,* November 4, 1893), 3.
21. Krug, Edward, *The Shaping of the American High School 1880–1920.* Madison Wi: University of Wisconsin Press, 1964, 3.
22. Op. cit., Herr, 11.
23. Diane Ravitch and Maris Vinovskis (Editors), *Learning From the Past: What History Teaches Us About School Reform.* Baltimore and London: John Hopkins Press 1995, 21.
24. Ibid., 21.
25. "The First Graduation" as described in the July 5, 1877 *Northfield Mail* reprinted in the 1927 issue of the NHS yearbook, *The Orange and Black,* page 13.

26 Op. cit., Krug, 11.
27 Ibid, 12.
28 Op cit., Ravitch and Vinovskis, 19-20.
29 Op. cit., Krug, 171.
30 Op cit., Ravitch and Vinovskis, 26.
31 The *Northfield News*, February 8 1890, 3–6.
32 Ibid., 5.
33 Cuban, Larry, *What Teachers Taught: Constancy and Change in American Classrooms 1890–1980*. New York: Longman, 1984, 18. 30.
34 Ibid., 19.
35 Kliebard, Herbert. *The Struggle for the American Curriculum 1893–1958*. Boston and London: Routledge and Kegan Paul 1986, 5–6.
36 *Manual of the Public Schools: Containing Rules, Regulations, and Laws for the Board of Education and Public Schools*, written and compiled by District Superintendent E. G. Adams, and published in 1895 by *Northfield News* Editor Joel Heatwole. In the historic records files in the District Office.
37 "All About Northfield," printed by the *Northfield News*, 1889, 2. Copy in the Northfield Public Library Pye Room Collection.
38 Op. cit., *Manual of the Public Schools*, 11.
39 Ibid., 12.
40 Ibid., 14.
41 Ibid., 17.
42 Ibid., 20.
43 Ibid., 26.
44 Ibid., 27.
45 Ibid., 28.
46 Ibid., 48-51.
47 Ibid., 52.
48 Ibid., 91.
49 The *Northfield News*, September 10, 1898.
50 The *Northfield News*, November 4, 1899.
51 The *Northfield News*, May 19, 1900, 1.
52 The *Northfield News*, July 28, 1900, 1.
53 The *Northfield News*, September 8, 1900, 1.
54 The *Northfield News*, December 16, 1900, "Northfield as an Educational Center: A Glimpse of What Our City Has Done and is Doing in an Educational Way," 3–5.
55 Ibid., 3.
56 Ibid., 3.
57 Ibid., 4.
58 *The Orange and Black* Fiftieth Anniversary Northfield High School annual yearbook, Northfield Minnesota, May 1927, p. 27. NHS Yearbook collections are in the Pye Room at the Northfield Public Library and the Northfield Historical Society.
59 The *Northfield News*, June 16, 1900 article headlined "New Superintendent: Edgar George, of St. Peter, Will Direct Northfield Schools," 1.
60 The *Northfield News*, December 15, 1906.
61 The *Northfield News*, March 21, 1908.
62 The *Northfield News*, April 4, 1908, "Building is Dangerous."
63 The *Northfield News*, May 2, 1908.
64 The *Northfield News*, May 9, 1908.
65 The *Northfield News*, May 16, 1908.
66 The *Northfield News*, February 27, 1909, "Dr. Hill's Address: Tear Down Old Building."

67 The *Northfield News*, January 8, 1910.
68 The *Northfield News*, February 12, 1910.
69 The *Northfield News*, February 19, 1910.
70 Ibid.
71 Copy of diary pages from Beulah Hulberg Heiberg, attached to a July 18, 1995 letter from her son Dr. Elvin Heiberg to Superintendent Charles Kyte. Dr. Heiberg suggested that his mother's diary entry "might be useful for the upcoming school bond election." Historical file in Superintendent's office, Northfield District 659.
72 The *Northfield News*, February 19, 1910.
73 The *Northfield News*, January 7, 1911, 1.
74 From the Board of Education minutes of July 12, 14, 23, and August 9 of 1910. In the Board Minutes Books, vol. 1, page 5–7. In the District 659 Offices.
75 Biographical information about John Street from an obituary in the November 23, 1950, *Northfield News*.
76 From the Board of Education minutes from June 1912. In the Board Minute Books, vol. 1, page 20. In the District 659 Offices.
77 Ibid., 39.
78 From the Board of Education minutes from January 12, 1920. In the Board Minute Books, vol. 1, page 220. In the District 659 Offices.
79 Ibid., 270.
80 Cremin, Lawrence. *American Education: The Metropolitan Experience 1876–1980*. New York: Harper and Row, 1988, 8.
81 Ibid, 12.
82 Ibid., 644–5.
83 *Northfield News*, August 5, 1911, "Add New Department: Northfield High School to Have a Normal Training Course."
84 Kliebard, Herbert. *The Struggle for the American Curriculum 1893–1958*. Boston and London: Routledge and Kegan Paul 1986, p.28–9.
85 *Northfield News*, March 1912, "President Cyrus Northrop's Visit to the Northfield Schools."
86 Four pages in the Board Minute Book #1, pages contained the testimony of the students involved in the stealing, selling, and buying of state examination questions, and the sanctions imposed by the board.
87 *The Orange and Black*, The 1916 Northfield High School Yearbook. In the Pye Room of the Northfield Public Library, Northfield Minnesota.
88 Ibid., 3.
89 From the Board of Education minutes of July12, 14, 23, and August 9, 1910. In the Board Minute Books, vol. 1, page 5–7. In the District 659 Offices.
90 Clifford Clark, "Evolution of a Community," in *Northfield: The History and Architecture of a Community* (Northfield, Minnesota: Northfield Heritage Preservation Commission, 1999), 12.
91 Golden Jubilee Souvenir, *Northfield News* 1916, 49.
92 From the Board of Education minutes from May 1920. In the Board Minute Books, vol. 1, page 252. In the District 659 Offices.
93 *Northfield News*, August 1912. In the Board Minute Book, vol. 1, page 50. In the District 659 Offices.
94 The Board Minute Book, vol. 1, page 250. In the District Office.
95 The Board Minute Book, vol. 2, page 85. In the District Office.
96 "Educating Administrators," Fred Engelhardt, *Minnesota Journal of Education*, Minnesota Education Association, St. Paul, Minn., April 1930, p. 313.
97 The *Northfield News*, August 8, 1924, "All Northfield Joins in Tribute to Fobes: Associates and Friends Commend Character and Labors of Dead Superintendent," 1, 4.

98 Ibid., 4.
99 *The Orange and Black* Fiftieth Anniversary Northfield High School annual yearbook, Northfield Minnesota, May 1927, p. 26. NHS Yearbook collections in the Pye Room at the Northfield Public Library and the at the Northfield Historical Society.
100 *The Periscope*, February 17, 1922. Copies of the first seven issues from 1922 were provided to the Superintendent's office by Lars Kindum, who has a large private Periscope collection.
101 *The Orange and Black* Fiftieth Anniversary Northfield High School annual yearbook, Northfield, Minnesota, May 1927, 10.
102 Ibid., 10.
103 Ibid., 12.
104 Ibid., 22.
105 Ibid., 30.
106 Ibid., 35.
107 Ibid., 37.
108 Ibid., 39.
109 Ibid., 41.
110 Ibid., 33.
111 Ibid., 42.
112 Ibid., 44.
113 Ibid., 84.
114 The Board Minute Book, vol. 2, page 97. In the District Office.
115 "Then and Now 1905–1930," W. E. Peik, in the *Minnesota Journal of Education*, Minnesota Education Association, St. Paul, Minn., April 1930, p. 307.
116 The *Northfield News*, Nov. 8, 1929, "Invest in Northfield!"
117 The Board Minute Book, vol. 2, 187–88. In the District Office.
118 The Board Minute Book, vol. 2, 209. In the District Office.
119 The Board Minute Book, vol. 2, 221. In the District Office.
120 The *Northfield News*, February 26, 1932, 1.
121 The *Northfield News*, June 10, 1932, 1.
122 Hand written minutes of the September 2, 1932, Special Meeting of the Board of Education. The Board Minute Book, vol. 2, p.273–75. In the District Office.
123 The *Northfield News*, April 28, 1933, 1.
124 The Board Minute Book, vol. 2, 335, March 1935. In the District Office.
125 The Board Minute Book, vol. 2, 335, March 1935. In the District Office.
126 The *Northfield News*, August 2, 1935, 3.
127 Ibid., 3.
128 The *Northfield News*, July 16, 1935, 1935, 2.
129 The *Northfield News*, July 26, 1935, 2.
130 The *Northfield News*, August, 1935, 2.
131 The *Northfield News*, October 18, 1935, 1.
132 The *Northfield News*, October 22, 1935, 2.
133 Ibid., 2.
134 The *Northfield News*, November 5, 1935, 3.
135 The *Northfield News*, September 3, 1942, 1.
136 The Board Minute Book, vol. 3, 65. In the District Office.
137 *Northfield: The History and Architecture of a Community*, 13.
138 The Board Minute Book, vol. 3, 66. In the District Office.
139 The Board Minute Book, vol. 3, 137, March 1939. In the District Office.
140 Ibid., 137.
141 The *Northfield News*, August, 28, 1940, 1.
142 The *Northfield News*, Back to School Section August, 28, 1940.

143   The *Northfield News*, Back to School Section September 3, 1942.
144   The *Northfield News*, Back to School Section September 2, 1944, 2.
145   The Board Minute Book, vol. 4, 4. In the District Office.
146   The *Northfield News*, July 8, 1949, 3.
147   Op. cit., *Northfield: The History and Architecture of a Community*, 15–17.
148   Cremin, Lawrence, *The Transformation of the School*, New York: Vintage Books, 1961, 347.
149   Ibid., 352.
150   *Northfield News*, June 8, 1950, page 1.
151   *The Norhian*, 1950, p. 8. In the Northfield Public Library Pye Room, and the Northfield Historical Society.
152   *Northfield News*, June 15 1950, page 1, 2.
153   *Northfield News*, Back-To-School Edition, August 31, 1950.
154   Ibid., 1.
155   Ibid., 1.
156   "School Building Needs of the Northfield High School Area: A Summary of the School Building Survey of the Northfield High School Area." Publication by the Bureau of Field Studies and Surveys, College of Education, University of Minnesota, July 1952.
157   Ibid., 27.
158   Ibid., 287.
159   Letter of resignation from Erling O. Johnson to the Northfield Board of Education, dated January 26, 1953, in the Board Minutes notebook, p. 242.
160   "Going Forward With Our Schools," a case publication for a May 19, 1953, special bond election, mailed to all residents in the Northfield Public School area. In the District Office historical files.
161   Ibid., last (unnumbered) page of "Going Forward With Our Schools" publication.
162   "Dedication Exercises: Northfield Junior-Senior High School Addition and Washington Elementary School Addition" program, High School Gymnasium, Sunday Afternoon, November 6, 1955. Program was in the historical files, Northfield District Office.
163   School Board Meeting Minutes, ISD # 659 (Northfield), November 13, 1958. In School Board Minutes Books, in the Northfield District Office.
164   "Northfield Facing The Future: A Summary of the Northfield School Survey #3" by the Bureau of Field Studies and Surveys, College of Education, University of Minnesota, November 1960.
165   Ibid., 14.
166   "Continuing Quality Education in the Northfield School System" a full report by the Bureau of Field Studies and Surveys, College of Education, University of Minnesota, December 1968, 70.
167   Early history of the Rosary School from the St. Dominic School web site, at schoolofstdominic.org. November 2016.
168   From an extended caption under a photograph of the new Rosary School addition in the May 21, 1959, *Northfield News*, page 1.
169   *Raiders Guide*, Published by The Student Council of the Northfield Junior-Senior High School, Northfield Minnesota. The *Guide* itself was undated, but administrator/staff names suggest this version was published between 1957 to 1960.
170   Ibid., 4–5.
171   Ibid., "Attendance," 13–18.
172   Ibid., "Co-curricular Activities," pages 31–49.
173   From President Lyndon Johnson's message to Congress, "Towards Full Educational Opportunity," January 12, 1965, in *The School in the United States: A Documentary History*, James Fraser, McGraw-Hill, 2001, 295–6.

174 Information about the new high school from a publication for the Northfield High School Open House, October 30, 1966.
175 Ibid., 2.
176 "Planning Quality Education for the Northfield Public Schools: A Summary of the School Survey Report of Independent School District # 659" by the Bureau of Field Studies and Surveys, College of Education, University of Minnesota, December 1968.
177 "Continuing Quality Education in the Northfield School System," full report, 209.
178 Ibid., 211.
179 Ibid., 212.
180 Ibid., 213.
181 Ibid., 218–19.
182 *A Nation at Risk: The Imperative For Educational Reform, A Report to the Nation and the Secretary of Education*, United States Department of Education, by the National Commission on Excellence in Education. Washington D.C.: U.S. Government Printing Office, 1983, 5.
183 Ibid., 11, 13.
184 Ibid., 23–31.
185 The *Northfield News*, May 14, 1970, front-page article headlined "Two directors to be elected."
186 "Back to School and College" supplement, *Northfield News*, August 20, 1970.
187 This description of the open classroom was taken from a paper titled "Some Ideas To Stimulate Educational Thinking" circulated among teachers who were planning the curriculum for Greenvale, and Cuban's *How Teachers Taught*, 199–200..
188 From the "Summary Report of the Northfield Educational Planning Task Force" Northfield I.S.D. #659, November 13, 1978. In the School District Office historical files.
189 Ibid., 10.
190 Statement "School District Goals for the Northfield Public Schools" adopted 8/15/77." Attached to the PER (Planning-Evaluating-Reporting) 1987–88 Checklist. In an historical file in the District Office.
191 The *Northfield News*, May 1 and 8, 1980, a series of articles titled "Levy Referendum: Questions and Answers."
192 The *Northfield News*, May 1, 1980, 3.
193 The *Northfield News*, May 22, 1980, 1.
194 Ibid., 3
195 The *Northfield News*, November 4, 1982, 3.
196 The *Northfield News*, November 27, 1980, 3.
197 The 1984 "Planning Evaluating Reporting" (PER) report, submitted to the Minnesota State Department of Education and distributed to all district residents. Copy from the District Office historical files.
198 From a brochure titled "Staff Evaluation/Development: A Model for Instructional Improvement" written by assistant superintendent Dwight Lindbloom and program coordinator Mary Lillesve, 1983. In the District historical files.
199 From a "PER Process: Planning-Evaluating-Reporting" paper prepared by the Curriculum Office of the Northfield Public Schools, 1987. In the District Office historical files.
200 The list of "Long Range Goals to be Realized by 1989" was published in the 1985 state mandated PER report sent to the community.
201 Annual Report 1986–87, published by Northfield I.S.D. 659, mailed to each resident in the school district. Copy from the District Office historical files.
202 The *Northfield News*, March 8, 1990, 3A.
203 The *Northfield News*, December 13, 1995, 2.
204 The *Northfield News*, January 11, 1990, 2.
205 The *Northfield News*, August 1990.

206 The *Northfield News*, Back to School Supplement, August 17, 1990.
207 Ibid., 3.
208 The *Northfield News*, August 23, 1990, 3.
209 The *Northfield News*, an Our View editorial, "Diversity in schools," September, 1992.
210 The *Northfield News* article, "District lays out plan for 'Year of Values,'" August, 1996.
211 The *Northfield News* article, "Tofte tabbed as next superintendent," May 17, 2000, 1.
212 *Highlights: A Newsletter for Northfield School District Citizens*, Vol. 6, No. 4, October 2000, 1.
213 "Important Voter Information: School Bond Referendum May 8, 2001," flyer mailed from the Northfield Independent School District (ISD) 659 to every postal patron in the Northfield school district. Flyer in District Office historical files.
214 "Middle School: A Place to Grow," an eight-page booklet describing the new facility and programs for the Northfield Middle School, summer 2004. In the District historical files.
215 *Annual Report on Curriculum, Instruction and Student Performance 1999–2000*. Mailed to all postal patrons in the school district. Copy in District Office historical files.
216 *Education Accents*, Winter 2003, Letter from the Superintendent, p. 2. Copy in District Office historical files.
217 *Education Accents*, Spring 2003, Letter from the Superintendent, p. 2. Copy in District Office historical files.
218 *Education Accents*, Fall 2004, article "Meet your new superintendent. p. 6." Copy in District Office historical files.
219 *Annual Report on Curriculum, Instruction and Student Performance 2003–2004*, Northfield School District I.S.D. 659. Mailed to all postal patrons in the school district. Copy in District Office historical files.
220 Ibid., 2.
221 "The Our Mission, Our Beliefs, and Strategies" statements from the District Strategic Plan, 2005. Copy in District Office historical files.
222 Ibid.
223 "Celebration" documents prepared annually for the School Board of Education from 2007 to 2016 by superintendent Chris Richardson. Copies provided to author by Richardson, June 2016.
224 From the Arcadia Charter School web site, February 2017.
225 From an interview by the author with Chris Richardson and Matt Hillman, June 2016.
226 *Northfield Promise 2015 Annual Report to the Community*, a 4-fold pamphlet mailed to every Northfield area postal customer. Copy in District Office historical files.
227 Ibid.
228 From the district web site, the News Archive, May 2018.
229 From an interview of Matthew Hillmann with the author, April 13, 2018.
230 From the "Executive Summary of the Northfield Public Schools Master Facilities Plan" updated November 2016. Copy in District Office historical files and on the district web site.
231 From the "Northfield Public Schools Strategic Plan" adopted October 24, 2016. Copy in District Office historical files and on the district web site.
232 Northfield Public Schools *Student Citizenship Handbook 2017–2018: A Policy Guide for Student Management in Instructional and Co-curricular Activities*. Print copy from the District Office; online at www.northfield schools.org.
233 *Northfield Public Schools Operating Levy and Bond Referendum Guide*, September 2017. Mailed to each postal patron in IDS #659 and available on the district web site.
234 The *Northfield News*, November 7, 2017, 1.

Index

A

Academic Strategic Plan 154, 158
accreditation 181
Adams, E. G. 8, 19
Advanced Placement (AP) 143, 169, 182
Albers, Alvin 119
Anderson, Elizabeth 8
Annual Report on Curriculum, Instruction, and Student Performance 181
Arcadia 178
Area Learning Center 162
ArtTech. *See* Arcadia

B

Bemmels, Burt 166
Benjamin Bus Company 162
Berg, Helen 113
Berk-Apitz, Anna 11
Berke, Anna 8
Bernard, Anna 61
Bingham, Kitty 10, 64
Black and Orange 117
Blake, Jennie 6
Blotgett, C. W. 19
Boraas, Julius 89, 100
Bridges, [Mr] 4
Bridges to Kindergarten 182

Bridgewater Elementary 159
Broderson, William E. 116
Building Life Cycle Management Plan 190
Burt, David 10

C

California Achievement Test (CAT) 148
Carlson, William F. 99, 113, 117
Castle Rock School 105, 126, 129
Central Park 5, 42, 95
Central School 5, 47
Citizens Referendum Committee 139, 141
Clark, Cliff 140
Clark, Frank L. 64
Clary, Ida 10
Cohrs, Troy 154
Community Education 146, 156, 184
Companeros 153, 160, 162
Comprehensive Test of Basic Skills (CTBS) 144
Cooper, Charles 19
Cox, Ray 193
Crane, Doug 162
curriculum 9, 15, 23, 50, 68, 102, 145, 177, 182
Cutlar, [Miss] 4

D

DARE drug education 182
Davenport, [Miss] 6
Davis, Doug 154
Dennison School 105
Dilley, Ralph 119
District Educational Program Advisory Council (DEPAC) 172, 178
District Improvement Plan 178
Dougherty, C. S. 28
Dougherty, T. J. 19
Drake-Larkin, Matie 11
Dundas School 105, 126, 129

E

Early Childhood Education Center 190
Educational Behavioral Disability (EBD) 183
Educational Planning Task Force 143
Edwins, Steve 148
ESL 160, 182

F

Feiderman, Arthur 11
Felland, O. G. 19
Fick, Sheila 99
Field, Albert M. 57
Fields, Ira S. 3
Finkelson, S. 19
Fischer, Bob 164
Fletcher, William 73
Fobes, Merton 55, 60
Foss, Harlan 119
Fossum, Peter E. 99, 113
Fremont, Albert 78
French, Joseph 11
Frost, D. H. 4

G

Gasho, Bill 143
Geckler, Jack 139
George, Edgar 38
gifted programs 121, 143, 154, 158
Gould, Laurence 113
Greaves, William 28
Greenvale Park Elementary School 135, 190
Grout, Martha 113

H

Hagen, Louise 11
Hall, Alma 37
Hall, Gertrude 11
Harrison, George W. 14
Hatton, Edith 10
Headley, Leal 79
Healthy Community Initiative 158
Heatwole, Joel xii, 17
Heinemann, F. E. 113
Herr, O. W. 62
Hill, Fred 55
Hillmann, Matthew 186, 189
Hinds, P. B. 99, 110
Hulberg, Beulah 45
Human Resources Department 186
Hunt, Vincent 74
Hunt, William A. 19, 29, 47, 55

J

Johnson, Erling O. 92
Johnson, Herman 110

K

Karnes, "Pop" 102
Kelley, D. F. 19
Kinneberg, Dianne 160
Kyte, Charles (Charlie) 152

L

Lashbrook, A. J. 99
Latham, J. 6
Lee, William H. 55
Lincoln School 6. *See* Longfellow School
Lindbloom, Dwight 146
LINK Crew 182
Little McCandless, Aimee 66
Longfellow School 8, 102, 115
Longstreet, John H. 110, 119

M

Mack, Stan 147
Mader, H. H. 99
Manual of the Public Schools ix, 17, 19, 191
Master Facilities Plan 190, 192
McKenzie-McChesney, Anna 11
McNaughton, James 4, 9
McWilliams, Jane 141
Measures of Academic Progress (MAP) tests 181
Memorial Athletic Field 95, 166
Miller, Lois 63
Miller, [Miss] 4
Minnesota Basic Skills Test 167
Minnesota Comprehensive Assessments (MCAs) 181
Mosher, Cora 10

N

No Child Left Behind 151, 173
Northfield Arts Guild 97
Northfield Citizen's Facilities Task Force 165
Northfield Educational Planning Task Force 136
Northfield Healthy Community Initiative 185
Northfield High School 9, 46

Northfield Middle School 166
Northfield Promise 184
Northfield Senior High School 124
North, John W. 3
Norton, A. W. 33

O

Ohm-Bunday, Gertrude 11
Olin, Rollins 1
open classroom 135
Orange and Black 55, 64, 68
Orr, Louise 11
Overby, Oscar 73
Oversea, Ann 100

P

Parks, Adele 6
Parsons, Phil 141
Pattee, W. S. 6
Paulson, George 133
Paulson, Harold 141
Pelseye, [Mrs] 6
PER Annual Report 143, 148, 151, 166, 181
Periscope, The 63
Perman, Orval 119
Phillips, John 50
Prairie Creek Community School 105, 146, 153, 178
Pye, William 47, 79

R

Rachel Carson Nature Area 160
Raider Guide 191
Raiders Booster Club 154
Raiders' Guide 117
Read 180, 182
Reading Recovery 162
Response to Intervention 182
Richardson, L. Chris 171
Riddell, Julia 10
Roe, Herman 100
Rogers, Martha 8
Rosary School 58, 93, 116

S

Sayre, Alice 10, 64

Schilling, William 32, 61
Schmidt, Paul G. 55
Schuler, Barry 99
Scott, Robert 119
Scriver, Hiram 4
Secondary Transition Education Program (STEP) 183
Setter, Donald 113
Sibley Elementary School 115
Skinner, Miron 47
Sletten, J. Oliver 99, 119
special education 123, 154, 164, 168, 183
Staff Handbook 186
Stanford, Alma 19, 66
Stauffacher, A. D. 61
St. Dominic's School 116, 153
Stewart, Lillian 82
Stewart, S. P. 4
Stoughton, Paul 91
Stover, S. 55
Strachan, A. D. 110
Strategic Plan 173, 178, 188, 190
Stratmoen, Noel 141, 152, 162
Street, John 47
student behavior 26, 73, 120, 191
Student Citizenship Handbook, The 191
Student Services Handbook 183
Students with Unique Needs (SUN) 183
Sullivan, Bubba 154
Swanson, Carl 99
Symes, Paul 99

T

Tackling Obstacles and Raising College Hopes (TORCH) 183
technology 151, 154, 160, 178, 187
Tofte, Terry 163

V

Village Charter School 153

W

Walden, J. M. 55
Washington School 8, 111, 138
Way, J. S. 28
Wegner, Kenneth 99
Weicht, Carl 86, 95
West Side School. *See* Longfellow School

Wheaton, Charles 1
Wheaton, Emma 6
Wheaton, Myron 4
Wheeler, Marion 6
Wheeler, M. S. 6
Where Everybody Belongs (WEB) 182
White, Irene 10
White, Meril J. 3
Whiting, Grace 8
Wichman, Jess H. 82
Wilcox, J. F. 4
Williams, M. M. 6
Wilson, Warren 55
Wittemore, Della 8
Wright, Louise 133

Y

Youth Activities Fair 157

About the Author

Historian Bruce William Colwell has researched, authored, and published six local histories: *Everlasting Influences: The Centennial History of the Northfield Carnegie Public Library 1910-2010*; *Learning to Make the World a Better Place: The History of the Prairie Creek Community School, 1983-2015*; *The Enduring Good We Do Today: A History of the Northfield Public Library, 1998-2016*; *This Noble Edifice: A History of Religious and Spiritual Life at Carleton, 1866-2016*; *Carleton 1968: Student Life In A Time Of Turbulence and Transformation*; and *City of Schools: A History of Public Education In Northfield Minnesota*. He also has three projects in progress: histories of the Northfield Arts Guild, the Northfield City Hospital, and a biography of former Carleton College President John William Nason.

Colwell holds a B. A. in history from Lawrence University and a Ph.D. in administration and policy studies from the Northwestern University School of Education and Social Policy.

Prior to becoming a local historian, Colwell worked in higher education, amassing more than thirty years of administrative experience as an associate dean of students at Lawrence University and Northwestern University, and senior associate dean of students at Carleton College. While at Carleton, Colwell wrote the college's first *Residential Life Handbook*, *The Family Guide to Carleton College*, and the *Senior Year Experience Guide 2009*.

Colwell has served as a member and president of the Northfield Public Library Board and the Northfield Historical Society Board. He lives in Northfield.

www.ingramcontent.com/pod-product-compliance
Lightning Source LLC
Chambersburg PA
CBHW050550160426
43199CB00015B/2610